FREE DVD   FREE   FREE DVD

Essential Test Tips DVD from Trivium Test Prep

Dear Customer,

Thank you for purchasing from Cirrus Test Prep! Whether you're looking to join the military, get into college, or advance your career, we're honored to be a part of your journey.

To show our appreciation (and to help you relieve a little of that test-prep stress), we're offering a **FREE *WEST-B Essential Test Tips DVD**** by Cirrus Test Prep. Our DVD includes 35 test preparation strategies that will help keep you calm and collected before and during your big exam. All we ask is that you email us your feedback and describe your experience with our product. Amazing, awful, or just so-so: we want to hear what you have to say!

To receive your **FREE *WEST-B Essential Test Tips DVD*,** please email us at 5star@cirrustestprep.com. Include "Free 5 Star" in the subject line and the following information in your email:

1. The title of the product you purchased.

2. Your rating from 1 – 5 (with 5 being the best).

3. Your feedback about the product, including how our materials helped you meet your goals and ways in which we can improve our products.

4. Your full name and shipping address so we can send your **FREE *WEST-B Essential Test Tips DVD*.**

If you have any questions or concerns please feel free to contact us directly at 5star@cirrustestprep.com.

Thank you, and good luck with your studies!

* Please note that the free DVD is <u>not included</u> with this book. To receive the free DVD, please follow the instructions above.

WEST-B Test Prep Study Guide:

COMPREHENSIVE REVIEW WITH PRACTICE TEST QUESTIONS FOR THE WASHINGTON EDUCATOR SKILLS TEST BASIC READING, WRITING, AND MATHEMATICS EXAMINATION (095/096/097)

J.G. COX

Table of Contents

PART III: MATHEMATICS   91

PART IV: PRACTICE   197

Online Resources

To help you fully prepare for your WEST-B Core Academic Skills exam, Cirrus includes online resources with the purchase of this study guide.

To access these materials, please enter the following URL into your browser: **http://www.cirrustestprep.com/westb-reading-writing-and-mathematics**.

PRACTICE TEST

In addition to the practice test included in this book, we also offer an online exam. Since many exams today are computer-based, getting to practice your test-taking skills on the computer is a great way to prepare.

FLASHCARDS

A convenient supplement to this study guide, Cirrus's e-flashcards enable you to review important terms easily on your computer or smartphone.

CHEAT SHEETS

Review the core skills you need to master with easy-to-read Cheat Sheets. Topics covered include Numbers and Operations, Algebra, Geometry, Statistics and Probability, and Grammar.

FROM STRESS TO SUCCESS

Watch *From Stress to Success*, a brief but insightful YouTube video that offers the tips, tricks, and secrets experts use to score higher on the exam.

REVIEWS

Leave a review, send us helpful feedback, or sign up for Cirrus's promotions—including free books!

Introduction

Congratulations on choosing to take the Washington Educator Skills Test Basic (WEST–B): Reading, Writing, and Mathematics Tests (095/096/097)! By purchasing this book, you've taken the first step toward becoming a teacher, an enriching and satisfying career.

This guide will provide you with a detailed overview of the WEST–B Reading, Writing, and Mathematics Tests, so you know exactly what to expect on test day. It will prepare you for all three of the basic tests: Reading (095), Writing (096), and Mathematics (097). We'll take you through all the concepts covered on these tests and give you the opportunity to test your knowledge with practice questions. Even if it's been a while since you last took a major test, don't worry; we'll make sure you're more than ready!

WHAT IS THE WEST–B?

The WEST–B is an exam used by teacher preparation programs in Washington State to measure applicants' aptitude in reading, writing, and mathematics. It is made up of three subtests in these subjects. The WEST–B is also used for teachers seeking certification in Washington State who are already certified in another state. You may take the subtests individually on separate dates, or you may take them all on the same date. While there are other WEST tests for specific academic subjects you may also be required to take, these core subjects are essential for anyone entering the teaching profession.

WHAT'S ON THE WEST–B?

The WEST–B tests gauge college-level skills in mathematics, reading, and writing in accordance with the Common Core State Standards. Each test—Reading, Writing, and Mathematics—is broken down into different categories based on the skills needed to succeed in a teacher preparation program.

On the Reading Test (095), you will read and answer questions about fiction and nonfiction passages, which will be of varying length. Some will be paired. They may be taken from any reading material an educated adult is likely to encounter, including novels, newspapers, magazines, articles on current events, and visual representations.

The Writing Test (096) tests your ability to analyze purpose, production and types of text, and your language and research skills. You will write two essays and answer multiple-choice questions.

The Mathematics Test (097) focuses on numbers, measurement, algebra and functions, geometry, statistics and probability, and mathematical reasoning. A calculator will appear on screen when you are permitted to use one. A list of mathematical symbols, abbreviations, and formulas will also be made available.

What's on the WEST–B?

Subtest	Concepts	Number of Questions	Time
Reading (095)	Main ideas and supporting details; relationship between ideas; evaluation of reading; analysis of intent, purpose, and perspective; meaning of words and phrases; relevant study skills	60 multiple-choice questions	2 hours
Writing (096)	Role of audience and purpose; development and organization; effective communication; revision strategies; standard writing conventions	50 multiple-choice questions and 2 constructed-response (essay) questions	3 hours
Mathematics (097)	Numbers and operations; measurement; geometry; algebra and functions; probability and statistics; mathematical reasoning	60 multiple-choice questions	2 hours
Total		**152 (and 2 essays)**	**7 hours (5 hours if all tests are taken together)**

How is the WEST–B Scored?

Your scores for the Reading and Mathematics subtests are immediately available upon completion of the test, although the official score reports are not released for another 2 – 6 weeks. Scores from the Writing subtest are released also released 2 – 6 weeks after the exam is taken. You can elect to have your scores emailed to you, or you can download them from your account where they will remain for 2 years after being posted. Your WEST–B scores will automatically be sent to the Office of Superintendent of Public Instruction and the Office of Certification. They are also placed in your certification file. However to have them sent to a college or university, you must make a request when you register for the exam.

Each multiple-choice question is worth one raw point. The total number of questions you answer correctly is added up to obtain your raw score. Your raw score is then scaled. A passing score is 240. To pass the WEST–B, you must pass all of the subtests.

Essay responses are scored by two separate graders (who are unaware of each other's evaluations of your work) based on five criteria: focus and appropriateness, unit and organization, development and rationale, usage and sentence structure, and mechanical conventions. Each essay is graded holistically on a scale of 1 – 4. If the two graders' scores differ by more than a point, a third grader will be assigned to read it. The two scores are then added together to create the total score.

Keep in mind that a small number of multiple-choice questions are experimental and will not count toward your overall score. ETS uses these to test out new questions for future exams. However, as those questions are not indicated on the test, you must respond to every question.

There is no penalty for guessing on the test, so be sure to eliminate answer choices and answer every question. If you still do not know the answer, guess; you may get it right!

How is the WEST–B Administered?

The WEST–B is a computer-based test offered continuously at a range of universities and testing centers both in Washington State and throughout the US. It may be taken in its individual parts or all at once. Check https://home.pearsonvue.com/ for more information. You will need to print your registration ticket from your online account and bring it, along with your identification, to the testing site on test day. No pens, pencils, erasers, or calculators are allowed; on the Mathematics portion of the exam, a calculator will automatically appear on the computer screen for certain questions. You may take the test once every 45 days.

ABOUT CIRRUS TEST PREP

Cirrus Test Prep study guides are designed by current and former educators and are tailored to meet your needs as an incoming educator. Our guides offer all of the resources necessary to help you pass teacher certification tests across the nation.

Cirrus clouds are graceful, wispy clouds characterized by their high altitude. Just like cirrus clouds, Cirrus Test Prep's goal is to help educators "aim high" when it comes to obtaining their teacher certification and entering the classroom.

ABOUT THIS GUIDE

This guide will help you master the most important test topics and also develop critical test-taking skills. We have built features into our books to prepare you for your tests and increase your score. Along with a detailed summary of the test's format, content, and scoring, we offer an in-depth overview of the content knowledge required to pass the test. Our sidebars provide interesting information, highlight key concepts, and review content so that you can solidify your understanding of the exam's concepts. Test your knowledge with sample questions and detailed answer explanations in the text that help you think through the problems on the exam, and with two full-length practice tests that reflect the content and format of the WEST–B. We're pleased you've chosen Cirrus to be a part of your professional journey!

Part I: Reading

Reading Skills

INTRODUCTION

The Reading test assesses overall proficiency in several key reading skills, including building inferences, understanding themes, and describing the organization and craft of writing.

The Reading test contains 56 multiple-choice questions, presented following brief passages of text or other types of media, such as graphs. The number of questions following each passage depends on the length of the passage: four to seven questions follow a 200-word passage or a pair of passages may be followed by four to seven questions; three questions follow a 100-word passage; and single questions follow statements and briefer passages. Question stems may be presented as fill-in-the-blank sentences, straightforward questions, or *LEAST/NEVER/EXCEPT* questions, which ask the test taker to choose the answer that does not fit.

The WEST-B Reading test consists of three main question categories based on the Common Core State Standards. In the sections that follow, several strategies and terms will be briefly discussed, and they will be fully addressed throughout this book.

KEY IDEAS AND DETAILS

Questions in this category focus on the text as a whole; they ask for explanations of the main ideas and how those ideas lead to specific inferences and conclusions. Answers should reflect connections between various sections of the text, discuss the consistency and overall meaning of the author's argument, and identify the piece's theme, summarizing it accurately. To accomplish this, the test taker should incorporate details that support the author's argument and are considered the most important.

Strategies for approaching this type of question include previewing the questions and outlining. Reading through the questions before reading the passage is a way to find a focus. The questions describe what to look for, and wrong answer choices can be eliminated quickly by identifying the main ideas and supporting details. Building an outline of the text assists in accurately identifying these things: jotting down words or phrases that describe the main idea of each paragraph and underlining important details that uphold that idea.

CRAFT, STRUCTURE, AND LANGUAGE SKILLS

This category tests understanding of the craft of writing, including the use of language, point of view, and organization. Questions may require relating the details of a passage to the overall organization and meaning of that passage. Such questions ask for evaluations of specific areas of the text as they relate to the author's purpose and argument, and descriptions of how the author uses specific words, figurative language, or transitions.

For these craft-related questions, the best strategy entails returning to the passage after reading each question and looking for the specific context and location of each question in order to be as accurate as possible. Marking out incorrect answers plus circling the important aspects of the question stem and answer are also helpful strategies.

INTEGRATING KNOWLEDGE AND SKILLS

This final category blends the strategies used with the other two categories. The synthesis of skills employed with previous questions extends in these questions into evaluation and judgment.

Questions may require an assessment of a text, a comparison of multiple texts, or an examination of other kinds of texts, such as visual media. In order to compare two texts, for example, the test taker must understand the purpose and main idea of each text as well as specific details. Determining what to pay attention to is accomplished by reviewing each question before reading its relative passage and returning to the passage as needed. A passage that employs diverse media, such as visuals, requires the same skills used while reading text. Carefully considering each question resolves which skills and knowledge should be integrated to answer it, and deconstructing the question stem best determines what sort of question it is.

The rest of this book will focus on describing in detail the skills, terms, and general content familiarity needed to approach the WEST-B Reading test. Each section contains examples of the sorts of questions the test may ask about each of these topics. These examples are meant to exercise the skills needed for each type of question.

THE MAIN IDEA

The **main idea** of a text describes the author's main topic and general concept; it also generalizes the author's point of view about a subject. It is contained within and throughout the text. The reader can easily find the main idea by considering how the main topic is addressed throughout a passage. In the reading test, the expectation is not only to identify the main idea but also to differentiate it from a text's theme and to summarize the main idea clearly and concisely.

The main idea is closely connected to topic sentences and how they are supported in a text. Questions may deal with finding topic sentences, summarizing a text's ideas, or locating supporting details. The sections and practice examples that follow detail the distinctions between these aspects of text.

IDENTIFYING THE MAIN IDEA

To identify the main idea, first identify the **topic**. The difference between these two things is simple: the **topic** is the overall subject matter of a passage; the **main idea** is what the author wants to say about that topic. The main idea covers the author's direct perspective about a topic, as distinct from the **theme**, which is a generally true idea that the reader might derive from a text. Most of the time, fiction has a theme, whereas nonfiction has a main idea. This is the case because in a nonfiction text, the author speaks more directly to the audience about a topic—his or her perspective is more visible. For example, the following passage conveys the topic as well as what the author wants to communicate about that topic.

> **HELPFUL HINT**
>
> The author's perspective on the subject of the text and how he or she has framed the argument or story hints at the main idea. For example, if the author framed the story with a description, image, or short anecdote, this suggests a particular idea or point of view.

The "shark mania" of recent years can be largely pinned on the sensationalistic media surrounding the animals: from the release of *Jaws* in 1975 to the week of ultra-hyped shark feeding frenzies and "worst shark attacks" countdowns known as Shark Week, popular culture both demonizes and fetishizes sharks until the public cannot get enough. Swimmers and beachgoers may look nervously for the telltale fin skimming the surface, but the reality is that shark bites are extremely rare and they are almost never unprovoked. Sharks attack people at very predictable times and for very predictable reasons. Rough surf, poor visibility, or a swimmer sending visual and physical signals that mimic a shark's normal prey are just a few examples.

Of course, some places are just more dangerous to swim. Shark attack "hot spots," such as the coasts of Florida, South Africa, and New Zealand, try a variety of solutions to protect tourists and surfers. Some beaches employ "shark nets," meant to keep sharks away from the beach, though these are controversial because they frequently trap other forms of marine life as well. Other beaches use spotters in helicopters and boats to alert beach officials when there are sharks in the area. In addition, there is an array of products that claim to offer personal protection from sharks, ranging from wetsuits in different colors to devices that broadcast electrical signals in an attempt to confuse the sharks' sensory organs. At the end of the day, though, beaches like these remain dangerous, and swimmers must assume the risk every time they paddle out from shore.

The author of this passage has a clear topic: sharks and the relationship between humans and sharks. In order to identify the main idea of the passage, the reader must ask what the author wants to say about this topic, what the reader is meant to think or understand. The author makes sure to provide information about several different aspects of the relationship between sharks and humans, and points out that humans must respect sharks as dangerous marine animals, without sensationalizing the risk of attack. This conclusion results from looking at the various pieces of information the author includes as well as the similarities between them. The passage describes sensationalistic media, then talks about how officials and governments try to protect beaches, and ends with the observation that people must take personal responsibility. These details clarify what the author's main idea is. Summarizing that main idea by focusing on the connection between the different details helps the reader draw a conclusion.

HELPFUL HINT

Readers should identify the topic of a text and pay attention to how the details about it relate to one another. A passage may discuss, for example, topic similarities, characteristics, causes, and/or effects.

SAMPLE QUESTIONS

The art of the twentieth and twenty-first centuries demonstrates several aspects of modern societal advancement. A primary example is the advent and ascendancy of technology: New technologies have developed new avenues for art making, and the globalization brought about by the Internet has both diversified the art world and brought it together simultaneously. Even as artists are able to engage in a global conversation about the categories and characteristics of art, creating a more uniform understanding, they can now express themselves in a diversity of ways for a diversity of audiences. The result has been a rapid change in how art is made and consumed.

1)   **This passage is primarily concerned with**

   A.   the importance of art in the twenty-first century.

   B.   the use of art to communicate overarching ideals to diverse communities.

   C.   the importance of technology to art criticism.

   D.   the change in understanding and creation of art in the modern period.

   Answers:

   A.   Incorrect. The focus of the passage is what the art of the twentieth and twenty-first centuries demonstrates.

   B.   Incorrect. Although the passage mentions a diversity of audiences, it discusses the artists expressing themselves, not attempting to communicate overarching ideals.

   C.   Incorrect. The passage discusses how new technologies have "developed new avenues for art making," but nothing about criticism.

   D.   **Correct.** The art of the modern period reflects the new technologies and globalization possible through the Internet.

2)   **Which of the following best describes the main idea of the passage?**

   A.   Modern advances in technology have diversified art making and connected artists to distant places and ideas.

   B.   Diversity in modern art is making it harder for art viewers to understand and talk about that art.

   C.   The use of technology to discuss art allows us to create standards for what art should be.

   D.   Art making before the invention of technology such as the Internet was disorganized and poorly understood.

   Answers:

   A.   **Correct.** According to the text, technology and the Internet have "diversified the art world and brought it together simultaneously."

   B.   Incorrect. The passage explains that the global conversation about art has created a more uniform understanding.

   C.   Incorrect. The passage indicates that artists now engage in a global conversation about art, but this is one detail in the passage. The main idea of the passage concerns the advances in art in the twentieth and twenty-first centuries.

   D.   Incorrect. The invention of technology and the Internet have diversified art; however, that does not mean it was disorganized previously.

TOPIC AND SUMMARY SENTENCES

Identifying the main idea requires understanding the structure of a piece of writing. In a short passage of one or two paragraphs, the topic and summary sentences quickly relate what the paragraphs are about and what conclusions the author wants the reader to draw. These sentences function as bookends to a paragraph or passage, telling readers what to think and keeping the passage tied tightly together.

Generally, the **topic sentence** is the first, or very near the first, sentence in a paragraph. It is a general statement that introduces the topic, clearly and specifically directing the reader to access any previous experience with that topic.

QUICK REVIEW

A **summary** is a very brief restatement of the most important parts of an argument or text. Building a summary begins with the most important idea in a text. A longer summary also includes supporting details. The text of a summary should be much shorter than the original.

The **summary sentence**, on the other hand, frequently—but not always!—comes at the end of a paragraph or passage, because it wraps up all the ideas presented. This sentence provides an understanding of what the author wants to say about the topic and what conclusions to draw about it. While a topic sentence acts as an introduction to a topic, allowing the reader to activate his or her own ideas and experiences, the summary statement asks the reader to accept the author's ideas about that topic. Because of this, a summary sentence helps the reader quickly identify a piece's main idea.

SAMPLE QUESTIONS

Altogether, Egypt is a land of tranquil monotony. The eye commonly travels either over a waste of waters, or over a green plain unbroken by elevations. The hills which inclose (*sic*) the Nile valley have level tops, and sides that are bare of trees, or shrubs, or flowers, or even mosses. The sky is generally cloudless. No fog or mist enwraps the distance in mystery; no rainstorm sweeps across the scene; no rainbow spans the empyrean; no shadows chase each other over the landscape. There is an entire absence of picturesque scenery. A single broad river, unbroken within the limits of Egypt even by a rapid, two flat strips of green plain at its side, two low lines of straight-topped hills beyond them, and a boundless open space where the river divides itself into half a dozen sluggish branches before reaching the sea, constitute Egypt, which is by nature a southern Holland—"weary, stale, flat and unprofitable."

—from *Ancient Egypt* by George Rawlinson

3) **Which of the following best explains the general idea and focus indicated by the topic sentence?**

   A.   Egypt is a boring place without much to do.

   B.   The land of Egypt is undisturbed; the reader will read on to find out what makes it so dull.

   C.   Egypt is a peaceful place; its people live with a sense of predictability.

   D.   The land of Egypt is quiet; the reader wants to know what is missing.

   Answers:

   A.   Incorrect. The word *monotony* does suggest the idea of being bored; however, the focus is the land of Egypt, not what people have to do. In addition, tranquility is part of the general idea.

   B.   Correct. This option indicates both the main idea and what the reader will focus on while reading.

   C.   Incorrect. This option leaves out what the focus will be.

   D.   Incorrect. This option leaves out the general idea of monotony.

4) **Which of the following best states what the author wants the reader to understand after reading the summary sentence?**

   A.   There is not much to get excited about while visiting Egypt.

   B.   Egypt is a poverty-stricken wasteland.

   C.   The land of Egypt is worn out from overuse.

   D.   The land of Egypt lacks anything fresh or inspiring.

   Answers:

   A.   Incorrect. The summary describes the place, not a visit to the place.

   B.   Incorrect. The word *unprofitable* suggests that the land of Egypt is unrewarding, not poverty stricken.

   C.   Incorrect. The reason the land is stale and weary may not be due to overuse. This summary describes; it does not explain the reasons the land is worn.

   D.   Correct. The words *weary*, *stale*, and *unprofitable* suggest a lack of freshness or anything that stimulates enthusiasm.

SUPPORTING DETAILS

Between a topic sentence and a summary sentence, the rest of a paragraph is built with **supporting details**. Supporting details come in many forms; the purpose of the passage dictates the type of details that will support the main idea. A persuasive passage may use facts and data or detail specific reasons for the author's opinion. An informative passage will primarily use facts about the topic to support the main idea. Even a narrative passage will have supporting details—specific things the author says to develop the story and characters.

The most important aspect of supporting details is exactly what the term states: They support the main idea. Examining the various supporting details and how they work with one another will solidify how the author views a topic and what the main idea of the passage is. Supporting details are key to understanding a passage.

IDENTIFYING SUPPORTING DETAILS

How can the reader identify the most important pieces of information in a passage? Supporting details build an argument and contain the concepts upon which the main idea rests. While supporting details will help the reader determine the main idea, it is actually easier to find the most important supporting details by first understanding the main idea; the pieces that make up the main argument then become clear.

Signal words—transitions and conjunctions—explain to the reader how one sentence or idea is connected to another. These words and phrases can be anywhere in a sentence, and it is important to understand what each signal word means. Signal words can add information, provide counterarguments, create organization in a passage, or draw conclusions. Some common signal words include *in particular*, *in addition*, *besides*, *contrastingly*, *therefore*, and *because*.

SAMPLE QUESTIONS

The war is inevitable—and let it come! I repeat it, sir, let it come! It is in vain, sir, to extenuate the matter. Gentlemen may cry, "Peace! Peace!"—but there is no peace. The war is actually begun! The next gale that sweeps from the north will bring to our ears the clash of resounding arms! Our brethren are already in the field! Why stand we here idle? What is it that gentlemen wish? What would they have? Is life so dear, or peace so sweet, as to be purchased at the price of chains and slavery? Forbid it, Almighty God! I know not what course others may take; but as for me, give me liberty or give me death!

—from "Give Me Liberty or Give Me Death" speech
by Patrick Henry

5) **In the fourth sentence of the text, the word *but* signals**

   A.   an example.

   B.   a consequence.

   C.   an exception.

   D.   a counterargument.

Answers:

A. Incorrect. The author includes an example that the war has begun when he says "Our brethren are already in the field!" The word *but* does not signal this example.

B. Incorrect. The phrase "but there is no peace" is a fact, not a consequence.

C. Incorrect. In order to be an exception, the word *but* would have to be preceded by a general point or observation. In this case, *but* is preceded by a demand for peace.

D. Correct. The argument or claim that the country should be at peace precedes the word *but*. *But* counters the demand for peace with the argument that there is no peace; the war has begun.

6) **What argument does the author use to support his main point?**

A. Life in slavery is not the goal of the country.

B. To die bravely is worthwhile.

C. Life without freedom is intolerable.

D. The cost of going to war is too great.

Answers:

A. Incorrect. The main point is that the country has to go to war with England to be free. The author does not support his point with a discussion of the goals of the country.

B. Incorrect. This does not relate to the main point of going to war.

C. Correct. The author indicates that life is not so dear, or peace so sweet, "as to be purchased at the price of chains and slavery."

D. Incorrect. This is inaccurate. The author insists that the cost of not fighting for freedom is too great.

Evaluating Supporting Details

Besides using supporting details to help understand a main idea, the reader must evaluate them for relevance and consistency. An author selects details to help organize a passage and support its main idea. Sometimes, the author's bias results in details left out that don't directly support the main idea or that support an opposite idea. The reader has to be able to notice not only what the author says but also what the author leaves out.

To understand how a supporting detail relates to the main idea, the purpose of the passage should be discerned: what the author is trying to communicate and what the author wants from the reader. Every passage has a specific goal, and each paragraph in a passage is meant to support that goal. For each supporting detail, the position in the text, the signal words, and the specific content work together to alert the reader to the relationship between the supporting ideas and the main idea.

Close reading involves noticing the striking features of a text. For example, does a point made in the text appeal to the reader's sense of justice? Does a description seem rather exaggerated or overstated? Do certain words—such as *agonizing*—seem emotive? Are rhetorical questions being used to lead the reader to a certain conclusion?

Though the author generally includes details that support the text's main idea, the reader must decide how those details relate to one another as well as find any gaps in the support of the author's argument. This is particularly important in a persuasive piece of writing, when an author may allow bias to show through. Discovering the author's bias and how the supporting details reveal that bias is also key to understanding a text.

SAMPLE QUESTIONS

In England in the 'fifties came the Crimean War, with the deep stirring of national feeling which accompanied it, and the passion of gratitude and admiration which was poured forth on Miss Florence Nightingale for her work on behalf of our wounded soldiers. It was universally felt that there was work for women, even in war—the work of cleansing, setting in order, breaking down red tape, and soothing the vast sum of human suffering which every war is bound to cause. Miss Nightingale's work in war was work that never had been done until women came forward to do it, and her message to her countrywomen was educate yourselves, prepare, make ready; never imagine that your task can be done by instinct, without training and preparation. Painstaking study, she insisted, was just as necessary as a preparation for women's work as for men's work; and she bestowed the whole of the monetary gift offered her by the gratitude of the nation to form training-schools for nurses at St. Thomas's and King's College Hospitals.

—from *Women's Suffrage: A Short History of a Great Movement*
by Millicent Garrett Fawcett

7) **Which of the following best states the bias of the passage?**

   A. Society underestimates the capacity of women.

   B. Generally, women are not prepared to make substantial contributions to society.

   C. If women want power, they need to prove themselves.

   D. One strong woman cannot represent all women.

   Answers:

   A. **Correct.** The author is suggesting that the work Florence Nightingale did had not been done before women came forward. Up till that point, what a woman could do had not been recognized.

   B. Incorrect. This fact may have been true at the time this text was written, but only because educational opportunities were not available to women, and women were not encouraged to develop their abilities.

Including this fact reveals the bias that women should be granted opportunities to train and to contribute.

C.   Incorrect. This option does not apply; Florence Nightingale did more than prove herself.

D.   Incorrect. The fact that Florence Nightingale donated the money awarded her to the training of women indicates that other women were preparing themselves to contribute.

8)   **Which of the following best summarizes what the author left out of the passage?**

A.   Women can fight in wars.

B.   Other women should be recognized.

C.   Women need to stop wasting time giving speeches at conventions and start proving themselves.

D.   Without the contributions of women, society suffers.

Answers:

A.   Incorrect. "It was universally felt that there was work for women, even in war" suggests that women had much to offer and didn't need to be sheltered; however, "there was work" does not mean the author thought women should engage in combat.

B.   Incorrect. Since the passage is specifically about Florence Nightingale, nothing in it suggests the author included information about what other women did.

C.   Incorrect. Information about women's suffrage conventions is unrelated to the topic of the paragraph.

D.   Correct. The author emphasizes that "Miss Nightingale's work in war was work that never had been done until women came forward to do it."

FACTS AND OPINIONS

Authors use both facts and opinions as supporting details. While it is usually a simple task to identify the two, authors may mix facts with opinions or state an opinion as if it were a fact. The difference between the two is simple: A **fact** is a piece of information that can be verified as true or false, and it retains the quality of truthfulness or falsity no matter who verifies it. An **opinion** reflects a belief held by the author and may or may not be something each reader agrees with.

HELPFUL HINT

To distinguish between fact and opinion, the reader should rely on what can be proven. Subjectivity is determined by asking if an observation varies according to the situation or the person observing.

SAMPLE QUESTIONS

I remember thinking how comfortable it was, this division of labor which made it unnecessary for me to study fogs, winds, tides, and navigation, in order to visit my friend who lived across an arm of the sea. It was good that men should be specialists, I mused. The peculiar knowledge of the pilot and captain sufficed for many thousands of people who knew no more of the sea and navigation than I knew. On the other hand, instead of having to devote my energy to the learning of a multitude of things, I concentrated it upon a few particular things, such as, for instance, the analysis of Poe's place in American literature—an essay of mine, by the way, in the current *Atlantic*. Coming aboard, as I passed through the cabin, I had noticed with greedy eyes a stout gentleman reading the *Atlantic*, which was open at my very essay. And there it was again, the division of labor, the special knowledge of the pilot and captain which permitted the stout gentleman to read my special knowledge on Poe while they carried him safely from Sausalito to San Francisco.

—from *The Sea-Wolf* by Jack London

9)   **Which of the following best summarizes an opinion stated by the narrator?**

   A.   Poe has a place in American literature.

   B.   People have the time to read magazines like the *Atlantic* because there are other people to take care of other tasks.

   C.   The narrator has no knowledge of the sea and navigation.

   D.   Division of labor is a beneficial practice.

   Answers:

   A.   Incorrect. This is a fact. The *significance* of Poe's place in American literature is an opinion.

   B.   Incorrect. This is a fact. The reader is expected to agree with the point that if someone else had not been managing the boat, the people who wanted to get across the water would have had to do the work of getting themselves across.

   C.   Incorrect. This is a fact. The narrator admits to "this division of labor which made it unnecessary for me to study fogs, winds, tides, and navigation."

   D.   Correct. The narrator provides several facts proving that he and the other passengers benefit from the specialized knowledge and labor of others.

10)   **Which of the following is an opinion expressed by the narrator that is not supported by facts within the passage?**

   A.   People should live life focusing on and learning about only a few things.

   B.   Having general knowledge is good.

   C.   He has time to focus on writing about literature.

   D.   People depend on other people.

Answers:

A.   **Correct.** When the narrator says "instead of having to devote my energy to the learning of a multitude of things, I concentrated it upon a few particular things," he conveys his view that he does not have to learn much. There are no facts to support the view that he has to learn only a few particular things in life.

B.   Incorrect. The narrator does not express this opinion. He is speaking about specialized knowledge.

C.   Incorrect. This is a fact that the narrator shares about his life.

D.   Incorrect. The passage does offer facts to support this; both the narrator and the passenger reading depend on the pilot to navigate the boat safely.

TEXT STRUCTURE

The structure of a text determines how the reader understands the argument and how the various details interact to form the argument. There are many ways to arrange text, and various types of arrangements have distinct characteristics.

The organizing structure of a passage is defined by the order in which the author presents information and the transitions used to connect those pieces. Problem-and-solution and cause-and-effect structures use transitions that show causal relationships: *because, as a result, consequently, therefore.* These two types of structures may also use transitions that show contradiction. A problem-and-solution structure may provide alternative solutions; a cause-and-effect structure may explain alternative causes: *however, alternatively, although.*

> **HELPFUL HINT**
>
> Authors often use repetition to reinforce an idea, including repeated words, phrases, or images.

Specific text structures include not only problem and solution and cause and effect, but also compare and contrast, descriptive, order of importance, and chronological. When analyzing a text, the reader should consider how text structure influences the author's meaning. Most important, the reader needs to be aware of how an author emphasizes an idea by the way he or she presents information. For instance, including a contrasting idea makes a central idea stand out, and including a series of concrete examples creates a force of facts to support an argument.

SAMPLE QUESTIONS

It was the green heart of the canyon, where the walls swerved back from the rigid plan and relieved their harshness of line by making a little sheltered nook and filling it to the brim with sweetness and roundness and softness. Here all things rested. Even the narrow stream ceased its turbulent down-rush long enough to form a quiet pool....On one side, beginning at the very lip of the pool, was a tiny meadow, a cool, resilient surface of green that extended to the base of the frowning wall. Beyond the pool a gentle slope of earth ran up and up to meet the opposing wall. Fine grass covered the slope—grass that was spangled with flowers, with here and there patches of color, orange and purple and golden. Below, the canyon was shut in. There was no view. The walls leaned together abruptly and the canyon ended in a chaos of rocks, moss-covered and hidden by a green screen of vines and creepers and boughs of trees. Up the canyon rose far hills and peaks, the big foothills, pine-covered and remote. And far beyond, like clouds upon the border of the slay, towered minarets of white, where the Sierra's eternal snows flashed austerely the blazes of the sun.

—from "All Gold Canyon" by Jack London

11) **The organizational structure of the passage is**

   A.   order of importance.

   B.   cause and effect.

   C.   problem and solution.

   D.   descriptive.

   Answers:

   A.   Incorrect. A series of reasons is not presented from most to least or least to most important. The passage describes a restful nook in the canyon.

   B.   Incorrect. The passage does not explain the origin of this nook or its effect on anything, although the reader understands from the details what makes the nook so restful.

   C.   Incorrect. The description of the nook presents no problem, although time in the nook could be seen as a solution for many problems.

   D.   Correct. The description of the nook begins with a general impression, moves from one side, to the area beyond the pool, to below the heart of the canyon, and finally to what is above the canyon.

12) **How does the text structure emphasize the central idea of the passage?**

   A.   The logical reasons for needing to rest while hiking make the author's argument compelling.

   B.   By explaining the activities within the canyon, the author convinces the reader that the canyon is safe.

   C.   By describing the areas to the side, below, and above the canyon, the author is able to emphasize the softness at the heart of the canyon.

   D.   The concrete examples included in the passage demonstrate the author's view that beauty is found in nature.

Answers:

A.   Incorrect. The passage does not indicate anything about a hike, although the valley is described as a restful place.

B.   Incorrect. The heart of the canyon is still, without activity; even the water stops rushing and forms a pool.

C.   Correct. The little restful nook is surrounded by the wall of the mountain, a "chaos of rocks," "boughs of trees," "far hills and peaks."

D.   Incorrect. The central idea of the passage is not finding beauty in nature but simply the restfulness of this nook.

DRAWING CONCLUSIONS

Reading text begins with making sense of the explicit meanings of information or a narrative. Understanding occurs as the reader draws conclusions and makes logical inferences. To draw a conclusion, the reader considers the details or facts. He or she then comes to a conclusion—the next logical point in the thought sequence. For example, in a Hemingway story, an old man sits alone in a café. A young waiter says that the café is closing, but the old man continues to drink. The waiter starts closing up, and the old man signals for a refill. Based on these details, the reader might conclude that the old man has not understood the young waiter's desire for him to leave.

An inference is distinguished from a conclusion drawn. An **inference** is an assumption the reader makes based on details in the text as well as his or her own knowledge. It is more of an educated guess that extends the literal meaning. Inferences begin with the given details; however, the reader uses the facts to determine additional facts. What the reader already knows informs what is being suggested by the details of decisions or situations in the text. Returning to the example of the Hemingway story, the reader might infer that the old man is lonely, enjoys being in the café, and is reluctant to leave.

> **DID YOU KNOW?**
>
> When considering a character's motivations, the reader should ask what the character wants to achieve, what the character will get by accomplishing this, and what the character seems to value the most.

When reading fictional text, inferring character motivations is essential. The actions of the characters move the plot forward; a series of events is understood by making sense of why the characters did what they did. Hemingway includes contrasting details as the young waiter and an older waiter discuss the old man. The older waiter sympathizes with the old man; both men have no one at home and experience a sense of emptiness in life, which motivates them to seek the café.

Another aspect of understanding text is connecting it to other texts. Readers may connect the Hemingway story about the old man in the café to other Hemingway stories about individuals struggling to deal with loss and loneliness in a dignified way. They can extend their initial connections to people they know or their personal experiences. When readers read a persuasive text, they often connect the arguments made to counterarguments and opposing evidence of which they are aware. They use these connections to infer meaning.

HELPFUL HINT

Conclusions are drawn by thinking about how the author wants the reader to feel. A group of carefully selected facts can cause the reader to feel a certain way.

SAMPLE QUESTIONS

I believe it is difficult for those who publish their own memoirs to escape the imputation of vanity; nor is this the only disadvantage under which they labor: it is also their misfortune, that what is uncommon is rarely, if ever, believed, and what is obvious we are apt to turn from with disgust, and to charge the writer with impertinence. People generally think those memoirs only worthy to be read or remembered which abound in great or striking events, those, in short, which in a high degree excite either admiration or pity: all others they consign to contempt and oblivion. It is therefore, I confess, not a little hazardous in a private and obscure individual, and a stranger too, thus to solicit the indulgent attention of the public; especially when I own I offer here the history of neither a saint, a hero, nor a tyrant. I believe there are few events in my life, which have not happened to many: it is true the incidents of it are numerous; and, did I consider myself an European, I might say my sufferings were great: but when I compare my lot with that of most of my countrymen, I regard myself as a *particular favorite of Heaven*, and acknowledge the mercies of Providence in every occurrence of my life. If then the following narrative does not appear sufficiently interesting to engage general attention, let my motive be some excuse for its publication. I am not so foolishly vain as to expect from it either immortality or literary reputation. If it affords any satisfaction to my numerous friends, at whose request it has been written, or in the smallest degree promotes the interests of humanity, the ends for which it was undertaken will be fully attained, and every wish of my heart gratified. Let it therefore be remembered, that, in wishing to avoid censure, I do not aspire to praise.

—from *The Interesting Narrative of the Life of Olaudah Equiano, or Gustavus Vassa, The African* by Olaudah Equiano

13) **Which of the following best explains the primary motivation of the narrator?**

A.   He wants his audience to know that he is not telling his story out of vanity.

B.   He is hoping people will praise his courage.

C.   He wants to give credit to God for protecting him.

D.   He is not seeking personal notoriety; he is hoping people will be influenced by his story and the human condition will improve.

Answers:

A.   Incorrect. That motive is how the passage begins, but it is not his primary motive.

B.   Incorrect. He says he does not aspire to praise, and he does not suggest that he was courageous.

C.   Incorrect. He does state that the "mercies of Providence" were always with him; however, that acknowledgement is not his primary motive.

D.   Correct. In the passage "If it…in the smallest degree promotes the interests of humanity, the ends for which it was undertaken will be fully attained, and every wish of my heart gratified," the narrator's use of the word *humanity* could mean he wants to improve the human condition or he wants to increase human benevolence, or brotherly love.

14)   **Given the details of what the narrator says he is *not*, as well as what he claims his story is *not*, it can be inferred that his experience was**

A.   a story that could lead to his success.

B.   an amazing story of survival and struggle that will be unfamiliar to many readers.

C.   an adventure that will thrill the audience.

D.   a narrow escape from suffering.

Answers:

A.   Incorrect. The narrator says that what is obvious in his story is what people "are apt to turn from with disgust, and to charge the writer with impertinence." The narrator is telling a story that his audience couldn't disagree with and might consider rude.

B.   Correct. By saying "what is uncommon is rarely, if ever, believed, and what is obvious we are apt to turn from with disgust," the narrator suggests that his experience wasn't common or ordinary and could cause disgust.

C.   Incorrect. The reader can infer that the experience was horrific; it will inspire disgust, not excitement.

D.   Incorrect. The narrator admits he suffered; he indicates that he narrowly escaped death. This is not an inference.

UNDERSTANDING THE AUTHOR

Many questions on the WEST-B Reading test will ask for an interpretation of an author's intentions and ideas. This requires an examination of the author's perspective and purpose as well as the way the author uses language to communicate these things.

In every passage, an author chooses words, structures, and content with specific purpose and intent. With this in mind, the reader can begin to comprehend why an author opts for particular words and structures and how these ultimately relate to the content.

The Author's Purpose

The author of a passage sets out with a specific goal in mind: to communicate a particular idea to an audience. The **author's purpose** is determined by asking why the author wants the reader to understand the passage's main idea. There are four basic purposes to which an author can write: narrative, expository, technical, and persuasive. Within each of these general purposes, the author may direct the audience to take a clear action or respond in a certain way.

The purpose for which an author writes a passage is also connected to the structure of that text. In a **narrative**, the author seeks to tell a story, often to illustrate a theme or idea the reader needs to consider. In a narrative, the author uses characteristics of storytelling, such as chronological order, characters, and a defined setting, and these characteristics communicate the author's theme or main idea.

In an **expository** passage, on the other hand, the author simply seeks to explain an idea or topic to the reader. The main idea will probably be a factual statement or a direct assertion of a broadly held opinion. Expository writing can come in many forms, but one essential feature is a fair and balanced representation of a topic. The author may explore one detailed aspect or a broad range of characteristics, but he or she mainly seeks to prompt a decision from the reader.

Similarly, in **technical** writing, the author's purpose is to explain specific processes, techniques, or equipment in order for the reader to use that process or equipment to obtain a desired result. Writing like this employs chronological or spatial structures, specialized vocabulary, and imperative or directive language.

HELPFUL HINT
Reading persuasive text requires an awareness of what the author believes about the topic.

In **persuasive** writing, though the reader is free to make decisions about the message and content, the author actively seeks to convince him or her to accept an opinion or belief. Much like expository writing, persuasive writing is presented in many organizational forms, but the author will use specific techniques, or **rhetorical strategies**, to build an argument. Readers can identify these strategies in order to clearly understand what an author wants them to believe, how the author's perspective and purpose may lead to bias, and whether the passage includes any logical fallacies.

Common rhetorical strategies include the appeals to ethos, logos, and pathos. An author uses these to build trust with the reader, explain the logical points of his or her argument, and convince the reader that his or her opinion is the best option.

An **ethos—ethical—appeal** uses balanced, fair language and seeks to build a trusting relationship between the author and the reader. An author might explain his or her credentials, include the reader in an argument, or offer concessions to an opposing argument.

A **logos—logical—appeal** builds on that trust by providing facts and support for the author's opinion, explaining the argument with clear connections and reasoning. At this point, the reader should beware of logical fallacies that connect unconnected ideas and build arguments on incorrect premises. With a logical appeal, an author strives to convince the reader to accept an opinion or belief by demonstrating that not only is it the most logical option but it also satisfies his or her emotional reaction to a topic.

> **TEACHING TIP**
>
> Readers should consider how different audiences will react to a text. For example, how a slave owner's reactions to the narrative of Olaudah Equiano (on page 19) will differ from a slave trader's.

A **pathos—emotional—appeal** does not depend on reasonable connections between ideas; rather, it seeks to remind the reader, through imagery, strong language, and personal connections, that the author's argument aligns with his or her best interests.

Many persuasive passages seek to use all three rhetorical strategies to best appeal to the reader.

Clues will help the reader determine many things about a passage, from the author's purpose to the passage's main idea, but understanding an author's purpose is essential to fully understanding the text.

SAMPLE QUESTIONS

Evident truth. Made so plain by our good Father in Heaven, that all *feel* and *understand* it, even down to brutes and creeping insects. The ant, who has toiled and dragged a crumb to his nest, will furiously defend the fruit of his labor, against whatever robber assails him. So plain, that the most dumb and stupid slave that ever toiled for a master, does constantly *know* that he is wronged. So plain that no one, high or low, ever does mistake it, except in a plainly *selfish* way; for although volume upon volume is written to prove slavery a very good thing, we never hear of the man who wishes to take the good of it, *by being a slave himself*.

Most governments have been based, practically, on the denial of the equal rights of men, as I have, in part, stated them; *ours* began, by *affirming* those rights. *They* said, some men are too *ignorant*, and *vicious*, to share in government. Possibly so, said we; and, by your system, you would always keep them ignorant and vicious. We proposed to give *all* a chance; and we expected the weak to grow stronger, the ignorant, wiser; and all better, and happier together.

We made the experiment; and the fruit is before us. Look at it. Think of it. Look at it, in its aggregate grandeur, of extent of country, and numbers of population, of ship, and steamboat.

—from Abraham Lincoln's speech fragment on slavery

15) **The author's purpose is to**

A.   explain ideas.

B.   narrate a story.

C.   describe a situation.

D.   persuade to accept an idea.

Answers:

A.   Incorrect. The injustice of slavery in America is made clear, but only to convince the audience that slavery cannot exist in America.

B.   Incorrect. The author briefly mentions the narrative of America in terms of affirming the equal rights of all people, but he does not tell a story or relate the events that led to slavery.

C.   Incorrect. The author does not describe the conditions of slaves or the many ways their human rights are denied.

D.   Correct. The author provides logical reasons and evidence that slavery is wrong, that it violates the American belief in equal rights.

16) **To achieve his purpose, the author primarily uses**

A.   concrete analogies.

B.   logical reasoning.

C.   emotional appeals.

D.   images.

Answers:

A.   Incorrect. The author mentions the ant's willingness to defend what is his but does not make an explicit and corresponding conclusion about the slave; instead, he says, "So plain, that the most dumb and stupid slave that ever toiled for a master, does constantly *know* that he is wronged." The implied parallel is between the ant's conviction about being wronged and the slave knowing he is wronged.

B.   Correct. The author uses logic when he points out that people who claim slavery is good never wish "to take the good of it, *by being a slave.*" The author also points out that the principle of our country is to give everyone, including the "ignorant," opportunity; then he challenges his listeners to look at the fruit of this principle, saying, "Look at it, in its aggregate grandeur, of extent of country, and numbers of population, of ship, and steamboat."

C.   Incorrect. The author relies on logic and evidence, and makes no emotional appeals about the suffering of slaves.

D.   Incorrect. The author does offer evidence of his point with an image of the grandeur of America, but his primary appeal is logic.

THE AUDIENCE

The structure, purpose, main idea, and language of a text all converge on one target: the intended audience. An author makes decisions about every aspect of a piece of writing based on that audience, and readers can evaluate the writing through the lens of that audience. By considering the probable reactions of an intended audience, readers can determine many things: whether or not they are part of that intended audience; the author's purpose for using specific techniques or devices; the biases of the author and how they appear in the writing; and how the author uses rhetorical strategies. While readers evaluate each of these things separately, identifying and considering the intended audience adds depth to the understanding of a text and helps highlight details with more clarity.

> **TEACHING TIP**
>
> When reading a persuasive text, students should maintain awareness of what the author believes about the topic.

Several aspects identify the text's intended audience. First, when the main idea of the passage is known, the reader considers who most likely cares about that idea, benefits from it, or needs to know about it. Many authors begin with the main idea and then determine the audience in part based on these concerns.

Then the reader considers language. The author tailors language to appeal to the intended audience, so the reader can narrow down a broad understanding of that audience. The figurative language John Steinbeck uses in his novel *The Grapes of Wrath* reveals the suffering of the migrant Americans who traveled to California to find work during the Great Depression of the 1930s. Steinbeck spoke concretely to the Americans who were discriminating against the migrants.

> **QUICK REVIEW**
>
> A logical argument includes a claim, a reason that supports the claim, and an assumption that the reader makes based on accepted beliefs. All parts of the argument need to make sense to the reader, so authors often consider the beliefs of their audience as they construct their arguments.

Instead of finding work in the "land of milk and honey," migrants faced unbearable poverty and injustice. The metaphor that gives the novel its title is "and in the eyes of the people there is the failure; and in the eyes of the hungry there is a growing wrath. In the souls of the people the grapes of wrath are filling and growing heavy, growing heavy for the vintage." Steinbeck, used the image of ripening grapes, familiar to those surrounded by vineyards, to condemn this harsh treatment, provide an education of the human heart, and inspire compassion in his audience. Readers who weren't directly involved in the exodus of people from Oklahoma to the West, could have little difficulty grasping the meaning of Steinbeck's language in the description: "66 is the path of a people in flight, refugees from dust and shrinking land, from the thunder of tractors and invasion, from the twisting winds that howl up out of Texas, from floods that bring no richness to the land and steal what little richness is there."

SAMPLE QUESTIONS

In the following text, consideration should be made for how an English political leader of 1729 might have reacted.

It is a melancholy object to those, who walk through this great town, or travel in the country, when they see the streets, the roads and cabin-doors crowded with beggars of the female sex, followed by three, four, or six children, all in rags, and importuning every passenger for an alms. These mothers instead of being able to work for their honest livelihood, are forced to employ all their time in strolling to beg sustenance for their helpless infants who, as they grow up, either turn thieves for want of work, or leave their dear native country, to fight for the Pretender in Spain, or sell themselves to the Barbados.

I shall now therefore humbly propose my own thoughts, which I hope will not be liable to the least objection.

I have been assured by a very knowing American of my acquaintance in London, that a young healthy child well nursed, is, at a year old, a most delicious nourishing and wholesome food, whether stewed, roasted, baked, or boiled; and I make no doubt that it will equally serve in a fricassee.

I do therefore humbly offer it to public consideration, that of the hundred and twenty thousand children, already computed, twenty thousand may be reserved for breed, whereof only one fourth part to be males; which is more than we allow to sheep, black cattle, or swine, and my reason is, that these children are seldom the fruits of marriage, a circumstance not much regarded by our savages, therefore, one male will be sufficient to serve four females. That the remaining hundred thousand may, at a year old, be offered in sale to the persons of quality and fortune, through the kingdom, always advising the mother to let them suck plentifully in the last month, so as to render them plump, and fat for a good table. A child will make two dishes at an entertainment for friends, and when the family dines alone, the fore or hind quarter will make a reasonable dish, and seasoned with a little pepper or salt, will be very good boiled on the fourth day, especially in winter.

—from *A Modest Proposal for Preventing the Children of Poor People in Ireland From Being a Burden on Their Parents or Country, and for Making Them Beneficial to the Public* by Jonathan Swift

17) **Which of the following best states the central idea of the passage?**

    A.   Irish mothers are not able to support their children.

    B.   The Irish people lived like savages.

    C.   The people of England are quality people of fortune.

    D.   The kingdom of England has exploited the weaker country of Ireland to the point that the Irish people cannot support their families.

Answers:

A.   Incorrect. This is a fact alluded to in the passage, not a central idea.

B.   Incorrect. Although the author does refer to the Irish as savages, the reader recognizes that the author is being outrageously satirical.

C.   Incorrect. The author does say "That the remaining hundred thousand may, at a year old, be offered in sale to the persons of quality and fortune, through the kingdom," referring to the English. However, this is not the central idea; the opposite is, given that this is satire.

D.   Correct. The author is hoping to use satire to shame England.

18) **The author's use of phrases like "humbly propose," "liable to the least objection," "wholesome food" suggests which of the following purposes?**

A.   to inform people about the attitudes of the English

B.   to use satire to reveal the inhumane treatment of the Irish by the English

C.   to persuade people to survive by any means

D.   to express his admiration of the Irish people

Answers:

A.   Incorrect. The author's subject is the poverty of the Irish, and his audience is the English who are responsible for the suffering of the Irish.

B.   Correct. The intended meaning of a satire sharply contradicts the literal meaning. Swift's proposal is not humble; it is meant to humble the arrogant. He expects the audience to be horrified. The children would make the worst imaginable food.

C.   Incorrect. The author is not serious. His intent is to shock his English audience.

D.   Incorrect. The author is expressing sympathy for the Irish.

TONE AND MOOD

Two important aspects of the communication between author and audience occur subtly. The **tone** of a passage describes the author's attitude toward the topic, distinct from the **mood**, which is the pervasive feeling or atmosphere in a passage that provokes specific emotions in the reader. The distinction between these two aspects lies once again in the audience: the mood influences the reader's emotional state in response to the piece, while the tone establishes a relationship between the audience and the author. Does the author intend to instruct the audience? Is the author more experienced than the audience, or does he or she wish to convey a

> **TEACHING TIP**
>
> To determine the author's tone, students should examine what overall feeling they are experiencing.

friendly or equal relationship? In each of these cases, the author uses a different tone to reflect the desired level of communication.

Primarily **diction**, or word choice, determines mood and tone in a passage. Many readers make the mistake of thinking about the ideas an author puts forth and using those alone to determine particularly tone; a much better practice is to separate specific words from the text and look for patterns in connotation and emotion. By considering categories of words used by the author, the reader can discover both the overall emotional atmosphere of a text and the attitude of the author toward the subject.

HELPFUL HINT

To decide the connotation of a word, the reader examines whether the word conveys a positive or negative association in the mind. Adjectives are often used to influence the feelings of the reader, such as in the phrase "an ambitious attempt to achieve."

Every word has not only a literal meaning but also a **connotative meaning**, relying on the common emotions, associations, and experiences an audience might associate with that word. The following words are all synonyms: *dog, puppy, cur, mutt, canine, pet.* Two of these words—*dog* and *canine*—are neutral words, without strong associations or emotions. Two others—*pet* and *puppy*—have positive associations. The last two—*cur* and *mutt*—have negative associations. A passage that uses one pair of these words versus another pair activates the positive or negative reactions of the audience.

SAMPLE QUESTIONS

Day had broken cold and grey, exceedingly cold and grey, when the man turned aside from the main Yukon trail and climbed the high earth-bank, where a dim and little-travelled trail led eastward through the fat spruce timberland. It was a steep bank, and he paused for breath at the top, excusing the act to himself by looking at his watch. It was nine o'clock. There was no sun nor hint of sun, though there was not a cloud in the sky. It was a clear day, and yet there seemed an intangible *pall* over the face of things, a subtle gloom that made the day dark, and that was due to the absence of sun. This fact did not worry the man. He was used to the lack of sun. It had been days since he had seen the sun, and he knew that a few more days must pass before that cheerful orb, due south, would just peep above the sky-line and dip immediately from view.

—from "To Build a Fire" by Jack London

19)   **Which of the following best describes the mood of the passage?**

   A.   exciting and adventurous

   B.   fierce and determined

   C.   bleak and forbidding

   D.   grim yet hopeful

Answers:

A.   Incorrect. The man is on some adventure as he turns off the main trail, but the context is one of gloom and darkness, not excitement.

B.   Incorrect. The cold, dark day is fierce, and the man may be determined; however, the overall mood of the entire passage is one of grim danger.

C.   Correct. The man is oblivious to the gloom and darkness of the day, which was "exceedingly cold and grey."

D.   Incorrect. The atmosphere is grim, and there is no indication the man is hopeful about anything. He is aware only of his breath and steps forward.

20)   **The connotation of the words *intangible pall* is**

A.   a death-like covering.

B.   a vague sense of familiarity.

C.   an intimation of communal strength.

D.   an understanding of the struggle ahead.

Answers:

A.   Correct. Within the context of the sentence "It was a clear day, and yet there seemed an intangible *pall* over the face of things, a subtle gloom that made the day dark," the words *gloom* and *dark* are suggestive of death; the words *over the face* suggest a covering.

B.   Incorrect. The word *intangible* can mean a vague sense, but there is nothing especially familiar about a clear day that is dark, with no sunlight.

C.   Incorrect. The word *intangible* suggests intimation; however, from the beginning, the author shows the man alone, and reports, "the man turned aside from the main Yukon trail."

D.   Incorrect. A struggle may be indicated by the darkness and gloom, but the man has no understanding of this possibility. The text refers to the darkness, saying, "This fact did not worry the man. He was used to the lack of sun."

MEANING OF WORDS AND PHRASES

CONTEXT CLUES

Vocabulary in context questions ask about the meaning of specific words in the passage. The questions will ask which answer choice is most similar in meaning to the specified word, or which answer choice could be substituted for that word in the passage.

When confronted with unfamiliar words, the passage itself can help clarify their meaning. Often, identifying the tone or main idea of the passage can help eliminate answer choices. For example, if the tone of the passage is generally positive, try eliminating the answer choices with a negative connotation. Or, if the passage is about a particular occupation, rule out words unrelated to that topic.

Passages may also provide specific **context clues** that can help determine the meaning of a word.

One type of context clue is a **definition**, or **description**, **clue**. Sometimes, authors use a difficult word, then include *that is* or *which is* to signal that they are providing a definition. An author also may provide a synonym or restate the idea in more familiar words:

> *Teachers often prefer teaching students with intrinsic motivation; these students have an internal desire to learn.*

The meaning of *intrinsic* is restated as an *internal desire*.

Similarly, authors may include an **example clue**, providing an example phrase that clarifies the meaning of the word:

> *Teachers may view extrinsic rewards as efficacious; however, an individual student may not be interested in what the teacher offers. For example, a student who is diabetic may not feel any incentive to work when offered a sweet treat.*

Efficacious is explained with an example that demonstrates how an extrinsic reward may not be effective.

Another commonly used context clue is the **contrast**, or **antonym**, **clue**. In this case, authors indicate that the unfamiliar word is the opposite of a familiar word:

> *In contrast to intrinsic motivation, extrinsic motivation is contingent on teachers offering rewards that are appealing.*

The phrase "in contrast" tells the reader that *extrinsic* is the opposite of *intrinsic*.

SAMPLE QUESTIONS

21) One challenge of teaching is finding ways to incentivize, or to motivate, learning.

Which of the following is the meaning of *incentivize* as used in the sentence?

A. encourage

B. determine

C. challenge

D. improve

Answers:

A. **Correct.** The word *incentivize* is defined immediately with the synonym *motivate*, or *encourage*.

B. Incorrect. *Determine* is not a synonym for *motivate*. In addition, the phrase "to determine learning" does not make sense in the sentence.

C. Incorrect. *Challenge* is not a synonym for motivate.

D. Incorrect. *Improve* is closely related to motivation, but it is not the best synonym provided.

22) If an extrinsic reward is extremely desirable, a student may become so apprehensive he or she cannot focus. The student may experience such intense pressure to perform that the reward undermines its intent.

Which of the following is the meaning of *apprehensive* as used in the sentence?

A. uncertain

B. distracted

C. anxious

D. forgetful

Answers:

A. Incorrect. Nothing in the sentence suggests the student is uncertain.

B. Incorrect. *Distracted* is related to the clue "focus" but does not address the clue "pressure to perform."

C. **Correct.** The reader can infer that the pressure to perform is making the student anxious.

D. Incorrect. Nothing in the sentence suggests the student is forgetful.

WORD STRUCTURE

In addition to the context of a sentence or passage, an unfamiliar word itself can give the reader clues about its meaning. Each word consists of discrete pieces that determine meaning; the most familiar of these pieces are word roots, prefixes, and suffixes.

Word roots are the bases from which many words take their form and meaning. The most common word roots are Greek and Latin, and a broad knowledge of these roots can greatly improve a reader's ability to determine the meaning of words in context. The root of a word does not always point to the word's exact meaning, but combined with an understanding of the word's place in a sentence and the context of a passage, it will often be enough to answer a question about meaning or relationships.

Table 1.1. Common Word Roots

Root	Meaning	Examples
alter	other	alternate, alter ego
ambi	both	ambidextrous
ami, amic	love	amiable
amphi	both ends, all sides	amphibian
anthrop	man, human, humanity	misanthrope, anthropologist
apert	open	aperture
aqua	water	aqueduct, aquarium
aud	to hear	audience
auto	self	autobiography
bell	war	belligerent, bellicose
bene	good	benevolent
bio	life	biology
ced	yield, go	secede, intercede
cent	one hundred	century
chron	time	chronological
circum	around	circumference
contra, counter	against	contradict
crac, crat	rule, ruler	autocrat, bureaucrat
crypt	hidden	cryptogram, cryptic
curr, curs, cours	to run	precursory
dict	to say	dictator, dictation
dyna	power	dynamic
dys	bad, hard, unlucky	dysfunctional
equ	equal, even	equanimity
fac	to make, to do	factory
form	shape	reform, conform
fort	strength	fortitude
fract	to break	fracture
grad, gress	step	progression
gram	thing written	epigram
graph	writing	graphic
hetero	different	heterogeneous
homo	same	homogenous
hypo	below, beneath	hypothermia
iso	identical	isolate
ject	throw	projection
logy	study of	biology
luc	light	elucidate

Root	Meaning	Examples
mal	bad	malevolent
meta, met	behind, between	metacognition (behind the thinking)
meter, metr	measure	thermometer
micro	small	microbe
mis, miso	hate	misanthrope
mit	to send	transmit
mono	one	monologue
morph	form, shape	morphology
mort	death	mortal
multi	many	multiple
phil	love	philanthropist
port	carry	transportation
pseudo	false	pseudonym
psycho	soul, spirit	psychic
rupt	to break	disruption
scope	viewing instrument	microscope
scrib, scribe	to write	inscription
sect, sec	to cut	section
sequ, secu	follow	consecutive
soph	wisdom, knowledge	philosophy
spect	to look	spectator
struct	to build	restructure
tele	far off	telephone
terr	earth	terrestrial
therm	heat	thermal
vent, vene	to come	convene
vert	turn	vertigo
voc	voice, call	vocalize, evocative

In addition to understanding the base of a word, it is vital to recognize common affixes that change the meaning of words and demonstrate their relationships to other words. **Prefixes** are added to the beginning of words and frequently change their meaning, sometimes to an opposite meaning.

Go on →

Table 1.2. Common Prefixes

Prefix	Meaning	Examples
a, an	without, not	anachronism, anhydrous
ab, abs, a	apart, away from	abscission, abnormal
ad	toward	adhere
agere	act	agent
amphi, ambi	round, both sides	ambivalent
ante	before	antedate, anterior
anti	against	antipathy
archos	leader, first, chief	oligarchy
bene	well, favorable	benevolent, beneficent
bi	two	binary, bivalve
caco	bad	cacophony
circum	around	circumnavigate
corpus	body	corporeal
credo	belief	credible
demos	people	demographic
di	two, double	dimorphism, diatomic
dia	across, through	dialectic
dis	not, apart	disenfranchise
dynasthai	be able	dynamo, dynasty
ego	I, self	egomaniac, egocentric
epi	upon, over	epigram, epiphyte
ex	out	extraneous, extemporaneous
geo	earth	geocentric, geomancy
ideo	idea	ideology, ideation
in	in	induction, indigenous
in, im	not	ignoble, immoral
inter	between	interstellar
lexis	word	lexicography
liber	free, book	liberal
locus	place	locality
macro	large	macrophage
micro	small	micron
mono	one, single	monocle, monovalent
mortis	death	moribund
olig	few	oligarchy
peri	around	peripatetic, perineum
poly	many	polygamy
pre	before	prescient

Prefix	Meaning	Examples
solus	alone	solitary
subter	under, secret	subterfuge
un	not	unsafe
utilis	useful	utilitarian

Suffixes, on the other hand, are added to the end of words, and they generally point out a word's relationship to other words in a sentence. Suffixes might change a part of speech or indicate if a word is plural or related to a plural.

Table 1.3. Common Suffixes

Suffix	Meaning	Examples
able, ible	able, capable	visible
age	act of, state of, result of	wreckage
al	relating to	gradual
algia	pain	myalgia
an, ian	native of, relating to	riparian
ance, ancy	action, process, state	defiance
ary, ery, ory	relating to, quality, place	aviary
cian	processing a specific skill or art	physician
cule, ling	very small	sapling, animalcule
cy	action, function	normalcy
dom	quality, realm	wisdom
ee	one who receives the action	nominee
en	made of, to make	silken
ence, ency	action, state of, quality	urgency
er, or	one who, that which	professor
escent	in the process of	adolescent, senescence
esis, osis	action, process, condition	genesis, neurosis
et, ette	small one, group	baronet, lorgnette
fic	making, causing	specific
ful	full of	frightful
hood	order, condition, quality	adulthood
ice	condition, state, quality	malice
id, ide	connected with, belonging to	bromide
ile	relating to, suited for, capable of	puerile, juvenile
ine	nature of	feminine
ion, sion, tion	act, result, state of	contagion
ish	origin, nature, resembling	impish
ism	system, manner, condition, characteristic	capitalism

Table 1.3. Common Suffixes (continued)

Suffix	Meaning	Examples
ist	one who, that which	artist, flautist
ite	nature of, quality of, mineral product	graphite
ity, ty	state of, quality	captivity
ive	causing, making	exhaustive
ize, ise	make	idolize, bowdlerize
ment	act of, state or, result	containment
nomy	law	autonomy, taxonomy
oid	resembling	asteroid, anthropoid
some	like, apt, tending to	gruesome
strat	cover	strata
tude	state of, condition of	aptitude
um	forms single nouns	spectrum
ure	state of, act, process, rank	rupture, rapture
ward	in the direction of	backward
y	inclined to, tend to	faulty

SAMPLE QUESTIONS

Width and intensity are leading characteristics of his writings—width both of subject-matter and of comprehension, intensity of self-absorption into what the poet contemplates and expresses. He scans and presents an enormous panorama, unrolled before him as from a mountain-top; and yet, whatever most large or most minute or casual thing his eye glances upon, that he enters into with a depth of affection which identifies him with it for a time, be the object what it may. There is a singular interchange also of actuality and of ideal substratum and suggestion. While he sees men, with even abnormal exactness and sympathy, as men, he sees them also "as trees walking," and admits us to perceive that the whole show is in a measure spectral and unsubstantial, and the mask of a larger and profounder reality beneath it, of which it is giving perpetual intimations and auguries.

—from "Prefatory Notice," in the first edition of Walt Whitman's *Leaves of Grass,* by W. M. Rossetti

23) **Which of the following is the best definition of the word** *substratum*?

A.   meaningful crest

B.   distracting idea

C.   reduction

D.   underlying foundation

Answers:

A.   Incorrect. Within the context of the sentence "There is a singular interchange also of actuality and of ideal substratum and suggestion," to say an "ideal meaningful crest" would be inaccurate because the *sub* prefix suggests *under*, a foundation.

B.   Incorrect. Within the context, an "ideal distracting idea" sounds contradictory.

C.   Incorrect. The word *reduction* suggests less than, not under.

D.   Correct. Combining the prefix *sub* (*under*) and the root *strata* (*cover*) with the singular suffix *um*, the word *substratum* means underlying layer or substance. An "ideal underlying foundation" makes sense.

24) **The prefix *un* in a word like *unsubstantial* indicates the meaning of the word is**

A.   not whatever the root word is.

B.   suggestive of an undercurrent of whatever the root word is.

C.   a lower value of the root word.

D.   in opposition to whatever the root word is.

Answers:

A.   Correct. The prefix *un* means not, and the root word *substantial* means real. *Unsubstantial* means not of physical reality.

B.   Incorrect. The prefix *un* does not suggest under.

C.   Incorrect. The prefix *un* does not suggest less than; it is the opposite of the root word.

D.   Incorrect. "In opposition to" suggests working against something, not being the opposite of.

FIGURATIVE LANGUAGE

A figure of speech is an expression that is understood to have a nonliteral meaning. Instead of meaning what is actually said, figurative language suggests meaning by pointing to something else. When Shakespeare says "All the world's a stage, / And all men and women merely players," he is speaking of the world as if it were a stage. Since the world is not literally a stage, the reader has to ask how the world is a stage and what Shakespeare is implying about the world.

Figurative language extends the meaning of words by giving readers a new way to view a subject. Thinking of the world as a stage on which people are performing is a new way of thinking about life. After reading Shakespeare's metaphor, people may reflect on how often they play a role, act a part. Their minds may go in many directions; they may wonder when their behavior is genuine, whether they're too worried about others evaluating their performance, and so on. Figurative language—such as metaphors and similes—generates thought after thought; with just a few words, it engages the reader's imagination and adds emphasis to different aspects of the text's subject.

A **metaphor** describes a *topic* that may be unfamiliar to the reader as though it were something else—a *vehicle*—that is probably familiar to the reader. The familiar vehicle is used to help the reader understand a new or unfamiliar topic. As the reader reflects on the similarities between the topic and the vehicle, he or she forms a new idea about the topic. For example, if a person refers to an issue as "the elephant in the room," the topic is the issue, and "the elephant in the room" is a vehicle communicating how overwhelming the issue is or that the issue is undeniable.

Similarly, in **personification** an object is anthropomorphized in some way or receives a human attribute. In the sentence "The earth swallowed him whole," *earth* is personified because it is described as carrying out a human action. Personification may also represent an abstract quality. For instance, a timid individual may be the "personification of cowardice."

A **simile** directly points to similarities between two things. The author uses a familiar vehicle to express an idea about the topic. For example, in his poem "The Rime of the Ancient Mariner," Samuel Taylor Coleridge describes his ship as "Idle as a painted ship upon a painted ocean." Readers have most likely seen a painting of a ship; Coleridge has used this knowledge to convey that the ship was completely motionless. Like a simile, an **analogy** is a correspondence between two things; it shows a partial similarity.

SAMPLE QUESTIONS

In shape Egypt is like a lily with a crooked stem. A broad blossom terminates it at its upper end; a button of a bud projects from the stalk a little below the blossom, on the left-hand side. The broad blossom is the Delta, extending from Aboosir to Tineh, a direct distance of a hundred and eighty miles, which the projection of the coast—the graceful swell of the petals—enlarges to two hundred and thirty. The bud is the Fayoum, a natural depression in the hills that shut in the Nile valley on the west, which has been rendered cultivable for many thousands of years…. The long stalk of the lily is the Nile valley itself, which is a ravine scooped in the rocky soil for seven hundred miles from the First Cataract to the apex of the Delta, sometimes not more than a mile broad, never more than eight or ten miles. No other country in the world is so strangely shaped, so long compared to its width, so straggling, so hard to govern from a single center.

—from *Ancient Egypt* by George Rawlinson

25) **What kind of figurative language does the author of *Ancient Egypt* use?**

A.   a metaphor

B.   a simile

C.   a comparison

D.   an analogy

Answers:

A.   Incorrect. A metaphor involves speaking of one thing as if it is something else, not just like something else.

B.   **Correct.** To describe Egypt, the author uses a simile. "Egypt is like a lily with a crooked stem." The blossom is the Delta region of Egypt, the bud is the hills on the west, and the long stalk is the Nile valley.

C.   Incorrect. Similes show only how one thing is similar to another. A comparison usually shows both similarities and differences.

D.   Incorrect. An analogy is a correspondence between two things; it shows a partial similarity.

26) **What does the figurative language used in *Ancient Egypt* help the reader understand?**

A.   how outsiders perceive Egypt

B.   the dominance of the Nile River

C.   how difficult it is to live in Egypt

D.   how strange the shape of the country is

Answers:

A.   Incorrect. The problem with this option is the word *outsiders*. Anyone looking at a map can see the similarity between the shape of Egypt and a lily.

B.   Incorrect. The Nile River does run through Egypt, but this does not account for the hills or Delta region.

C.   Incorrect. Egypt being shaped like a lily does not suggest difficulty in living there. Something like a lack of rainfall could create difficulty.

D.   **Correct.** By showing the similarities between a lily and the shape of the country, the author puts a memorable image in the mind of the reader and provides a clear understanding of his point: that there is no center from which to govern the country.

COMPARING PASSAGES

Some of the questions in the WEST-B Reading exam require test takers to compare texts that have similar themes or topics. Questions involve identifying the similarities and differences in main ideas, styles, supporting details, and text structures. Test takers will find it helpful to preview the questions and to note pertinent similarities and differences in texts while reading.

The following example passages discuss Walt Whitman's text *Leaves of Grass*. The first is from the preface of *Leaves of Grass* and is written by Whitman himself. The second is from a critical essay by Ed Folsom and Kenneth M. Price about *Leaves of Grass*.

Readers should keep in mind the following questions:

▸ What central idea about Whitman's response to slavery is being expressed in the passages?

▸ How does Folsom and Price's explanation of Whitman's response to the issue of slavery in America differ from Whitman's own statement of his intention?

SAMPLE QUESTIONS

One

No great literature, nor any like style of behavior or oratory or social intercourse or household arrangements or public institutions, can long elude the jealous and passionate instinct of American standards. Whether or not the sign appears from the mouths of the people, it throbs a live interrogation in every freeman's and freewoman's heart after that which passes by.

Are its disposals without ignominious distinctions? Is it for the ever-growing communes of brothers and lovers, large, well united, proud beyond the old models, generous beyond all models?

I know that what answers for me, an American, must answer for any individual or nation that serves for a part of my materials. Does this answer? Or is it without reference to universal needs?

Does this acknowledge liberty with audible and absolute acknowledgment, and set slavery at naught, for life and death? Will it help breed one good-shaped man, and a woman to be his perfect and independent mate?

—from preface to *Leaves of Grass* by Walt Whitman

Two

A pivotal and empowering change came over Whitman at this time of poetic transformation. His politics—and especially his racial attitudes—underwent a profound alteration. As we have noted, Whitman the journalist spoke to the interests of the day and from a particular class perspective when he advanced the interests of white workingmen while seeming, at times, unconcerned about the plight of blacks. Perhaps the New Orleans experience had prompted a change in attitude, a change that was intensified by an increasing number of friendships with radical thinkers and writers who led Whitman to rethink his attitudes toward the issue of race. Whatever the cause, in Whitman's future-oriented poetry blacks become central to his new literary project and central to his understanding of democracy....His first notebook lines in the manner of *Leaves of Grass* focus directly on the fundamental issue dividing the United States. His notebook breaks into free verse for the first time in lines that seek to bind opposed categories, to link black and white, to join master and slave:

I am the poet of the body
And I am the poet of the soul
I go with the slaves of the earth equally with the masters
And I will stand between the masters and the slaves,
Entering into both so that both shall understand me alike.

The audacity of that final line remains striking. While most people were lining up on one side or another, Whitman placed himself in that space—...*between* master and slave. His extreme political despair led him to replace what he now named the "scum" of corrupt American politics in the 1850s with his own persona—a shaman, a culture-healer, an all-encompassing "I."

—from "Walt Whitman: Racial Politics and the Origins of *Leaves of Grass*" by Ed Folsom and Kenneth M. Price, http://www.whitmanarchive.org/biography/walt_whitman/index.html#racial

27) What main idea do both sources make about Walt Whitman's perspective?

  A.   Slavery is anti-American.

  B.   Democracy is a force of brotherhood.

  C.   Walt Whitman is the voice of American individuality.

  D.   American politics is corrupt.

Answers:

  A.   Correct. The main idea of both passages reveals that Whitman's perspective about the issue of slavery is that slavery is anti-American because it is undemocratic. Whitman saw the liberty of America as a unifying force, a force of brotherhood that could not permit slavery to continue.

  B.   Incorrect. Whitman does view democracy this way; however, he is speaking specifically about slavery being undemocratic.

  C.   Incorrect. This option is true but far too broad an interpretation of the passages. A main idea is more specific statement.

  D.   Incorrect. This option is mentioned in only one passage.

28) What is the main difference between the passages?

  A.   In the first passage, the writer is concerned about slavery, but in the second passage the writers reveal the American confusion about slavery.

  B.   The first passage is a biography of Whitman; the second passage discusses Whitman's poetry.

  C.   The second passage reveals Whitman's consistent opposition to slavery; the first passage details Whitman's pain in relation to slavery.

  D.   In the first passage, Whitman states his perspective on slavery, but the second passage is about Whitman's change of perspective on slavery.

Answers:

A.   Incorrect. In the first passage, Whitman explains his viewpoint. In the second passage, the authors critique Whitman's changing views on slavery. Initially, as a journalist, Whitman was sympathetic to the white working class, not the blacks. The authors go on to explain that, in time, Whitman's poetic response to the issue of slavery in America displayed his sympathy for the slave that originated in his soul and his ability to form a union with what he observed. He could see the spiritual significance of different aspects of life and nature, including slavery.

B.   Incorrect. The first passage is written by Whitman; he is expressing his own perspective.

C.   Incorrect. The second passage clearly states that Whitman's view of slavery changed. The first passage is not about pain.

D.   Correct. Whitman's perspective is abstract. The second passage helps to make Whitman's thinking clear.

Part II: Writing

Language and Research Skills

PARTS OF SPEECH

The **parts of speech** are the building blocks of sentences, paragraphs, and entire texts. Grammarians have typically defined eight parts of speech—nouns, pronouns, verbs, adverbs, adjectives, conjunctions, prepositions, and interjections—all of which play unique roles in the context of a sentence. Thus, a fundamental understanding of the parts of speech is necessary in order to form an understanding of basic sentence construction.

> **DID YOU KNOW?**
>
> Although some words fall easily into one category or another, many words can function as different parts of speech based on their usage within a sentence.

NOUNS AND PRONOUNS

Nouns are the words used to give names to people, places, things, and ideas. Most often, nouns fill the position of subject or object within a sentence. The category of nouns has several subcategories: common nouns (*chair, car, house*), proper nouns (*Julie, David*), abstract nouns (*love, intelligence, sadness*), concrete nouns (*window, bread, person*), compound nouns (*brother-in-law, rollercoaster*), non-countable nouns (*money, water*), countable nouns (*dollars, cubes*), and verbal nouns (*writing, diving*). There is much crossover between these subcategories (for example, *chair* is common, concrete, and countable).

Sometimes, a word that is typically used as a noun will be used to modify another noun. The word then would be labeled as an adjective because of its usage within the sentence. In the following example, *cabin* is a noun in the first sentence and an adjective in the second:

The family visited the <u>cabin</u> by the lake.

> Our <u>cabin</u> stove overheated during vacation.

Pronouns replace nouns in a sentence or paragraph, allowing a writer to achieve a smooth flow throughout a text by avoiding unnecessary repetition. The unique aspect of the pronoun as a part of speech is that the list of pronouns is finite: while there are innumerable nouns in the English language, the list of pronouns is rather limited in contrast. The noun that a pronoun replaces is called its **antecedent**.

Pronouns fall into several distinct categories. **Personal pronouns** act as subjects or objects in a sentence:

> <u>She</u> received a letter; I gave the letter to <u>her</u>.

Possessive pronouns indicate possession:

> The apartment is <u>hers</u>, but the furniture is <u>mine</u>.

Reflexive (intensive) **pronouns** intensify a noun or reflect back upon a noun:

> I <u>myself</u> made the dessert. I made the dessert <u>myself</u>.

Personal, possessive, and reflexive pronouns must all agree with the noun that they replace both in gender (male, female, or neutral), number (singular or plural), and person. **Person** refers to the point of view of the sentence. First person is the point of view of the speaker (I, me), second person is the person being addressed (you), and third person refers to a person outside the sentence (he, she, they).

HELPFUL HINT

The subject performs the action of a sentence, while the object has the action performed on it.

Table 2.1. Personal, Possessive, and Reflexive Pronouns

Case	First Person		Second Person		Third Person	
	singular	plural	singular	plural	singular	plural
Subject	I	we	you	you (all)	he, she, it	they
Object	me	us	you	you (all)	him, her, it	them
Possessive	mine	ours	yours	yours	his, hers	theirs
Reflexive	myself	ourselves	yourself	yourselves	himself, herself, itself	themselves

Relative pronouns begin dependent clauses. Like other pronouns, they may appear in subject or object case, depending on the clause. Take, for example, the sentence below:

> Charlie, <u>who</u> made the clocks, works in the basement.

Here, the relative pronoun *who* is substituting for Charlie; that word indicates that Charlie makes the clocks, and so *who* is in the subject case because it is performing the action (*makes the clocks*).

In cases where a person is the object of a relative clause, the writer would use the relative pronoun *whom*. For example, read the sentence below:

My father, <u>whom</u> I care for, is sick.

Even though *my father* is the subject of the sentence, in the relative clause the relative pronoun *whom* is the object of the preposition *for*. Therefore that pronoun appears in the object case.

When a relative clause refers to a non-human, *that* or *which* is used. (*I live in Texas, which is a large state.*) The relative pronoun *whose* indicates possession. (*I don't know whose car that is.*)

Table 2.2. Relative Pronouns

Pronoun Type	Subject	Object
Person	who	whom
Thing	which, that	
Possessive	whose	

Interrogative pronouns begin questions (*Who worked last evening?*). They request information about people, places, things, ideas, location, time, means, and purposes.

Table 2.3. Interrogative Pronouns

Interrogative Pronoun	Asks About	Example
who	person	<u>Who</u> lives there?
whom	person	To <u>whom</u> shall I send the letter?
what	thing	<u>What</u> is your favorite color?
where	place	<u>Where</u> do you go to school?
when	time	<u>When</u> will we meet for dinner?
which	selection	<u>Which</u> movie would you like to see?
why	reason	<u>Why</u> are you going to be late?
how	manner	<u>How</u> did the ancient Egyptians build the pyramids?

Demonstrative pronouns point out or draw attention to something or someone. They can also indicate proximity or distance.

⟶

Go on

Table 2.4. Demonstrative Pronouns

Number	Subject/ Proximity	Example	Object/ Distance	Example
Singular	this (subject)	This is my apartment—please come in!	that (object)	I gave that to him yesterday.
	this (proximity)	This is the computer you will use right here, not the one in the other office.	that (distance)	That is the Statue of Liberty across the harbor.
Plural	these (subject)	These are flawless diamonds.	those (object)	Give those to me later.
	these (proximity)	These right here are the books we want, not the ones over there.	those (distance)	Those mountains across the plains are called the Rockies.

Indefinite pronouns simply replace nouns to avoid unnecessary repetition:

Several came to the party to see both.

Indefinite pronouns can be either singular or plural (and some can act as both depending on the context). If the indefinite pronoun is the subject of the sentence, it is important to know whether that pronoun is singular or plural so that the verb can agree with the pronoun in number.

Table 2.5. Common Indefinite Pronouns

Sigular		Plural	Singular or Plural
each	everybody	both	some
either	nobody	few	any
neither	somebody	several	none
one	anybody	many	all
everyone	everything		most
no one	nothing		more
someone	something		*These pronouns take their singularity or plurality from the object of the prepositions that follow: Some of the pies were eaten.*
anyone	anything		
	another		*Some of the pie was eaten.*

VERBS

Verbs express action (*run, jump, play*) or state of being (*is, seems*). The former are called action verbs, and the latter are linking verbs. Linking verbs join the subject of the sentence to the subject complement, which follows the verb and provides more information about the subject. See the sentence below:

> The dog is cute.

The dog is the subject, *is* is the linking verb, and *cute* is the subject complement.

Verbs can stand alone or they can be accompanied by **helping verbs**, which are used to indicate tense. Verb tense indicates the time of the action. The action may have occurred in the past, present, or future. The action may also have been simple (occurring once) or continuous (ongoing). The perfect and perfect continuous tenses describe when actions occur in relation to other actions.

Table 2.6. Verb Tenses

Tense	Past	Present	Future
Simple	I <u>answered</u> the question.	I <u>answer</u> your questions in class.	I <u>will answer</u> your question.
Continuous	I <u>was answering</u> your question when you interrupted me.	I <u>am answering</u> your question; please listen.	I <u>will be answering</u> your question after the lecture.
Perfect	I <u>had answered</u> all questions before class ended.	I <u>have answered</u> the questions already.	I <u>will have answered</u> every question before the class is over.
Perfect Continuous	I <u>had been answering</u> questions when the students started leaving.	I <u>have been answering</u> questions for 30 minutes and am getting tired.	I <u>will have been answering</u> students' questions for 20 years by the time I retire.

Helping Verbs: is/am/are/was/were, be/being/been, has/had/have, do/does/did, should, would, could, will

Changing the spelling of the verb and/or adding helping verbs is known as **conjugation**. In addition to being conjugated for tense, verbs are conjugated to indicate *person* (first, second, and third person) and *number* (whether they are singular or plural). The conjugation of the verb must agree with the subject of the sentence. A verb that has not be conjugated is called an infinitive and begins with *to* (*to swim, to be*).

> **HELPFUL HINT**
>
> A noun that receives the direct object is the indirect object.
>
> The pitcher will throw <u>Antoine</u> the ball.

Go on →

Table 2.7. Verb Conjugation (Present Tense)

Person	Singular	Plural
First Person	I answer	we answer
Second Person	you answer	you (all) answer
Third Person	he/she/it answers	they answer

Verbs may be regular, meaning they follow normal conjugation patterns, or irregular, meaning they do not follow a regular pattern.

Table 2.8. Regular and Irregular Verbs

	Simple Present	Present Participle	Simple Past	Past Participle
Regular	help	helping	helped	(have) helped
	jump	jumping	jumped	(have) jumped
Irregular	am	been	was	(have) been
	swim	swimming	swam	(have) swum
	sit	sitting	sat	(have) sat
	set	setting	set	(have) set
	lie	lying	lay	(have) lain
	lay	laying	laid	(have) laid
	rise	rising	rose	(have) risen
	raise	raising	raised	(have) raised

Verbs can be written in the active or passive voice. In the **active voice**, the subject of the sentence performs the main action of the sentence. In the sentence below, Alexis is performing the action:

Alexis played tennis.

In the passive voice, the subject of the sentence is receiving the action of the main verb. In the sentence below, the subject is *tennis*, which receives the action *played*:

Tennis was played.

Note that, in the passive voice, there is no indication of who performed the action. For this reason, passive voice is used when the subject is unknown or unimportant. For example, in science, it is common to use the passive voice:

The experiment was performed three times.

At most other times, it is considered more appropriate to use the active voice because it is more dynamic and gives more information.

Finally, verbs can be classified by whether they take a **direct object**, which is a noun that receives the action of the verb. Transitive verbs require a direct object. In the sentence below, the transitive verb *throw* has a direct object (ball):

The pitcher will throw the ball.

Intransitive verbs do not require a direct object. Verbs like *run*, *jump*, and *go* make sense without any object:

He will run.

She jumped.

Many sets of similar verbs include one transitive and one intransitive verb, which can cause confusion. These troublesome verbs include combinations such as *lie* or *lay*, *rise* or *raise*, and *sit* or *set*.

Table 2.9. Intransitive and Transitive Verbs

Intransitive Verbs	Transitive Verbs	
lie – to recline	lay – to put	lay something
rise – to go or get up	raise – to lift	raise something
sit – to be seated	set – to put	set something
Hint: These intransitive verbs have *i* as the second letter. *Intransitive* begins with *i*.	Hint: The word *transitive* begins with a *t*, and it *TAKES* an object.	

ADJECTIVES AND ADVERBS

Adjectives modify or describe nouns and pronouns. In English, adjectives are usually placed before the word being modified, although they can also appear after a linking verb such as *is* or *smells*.

The beautiful blue jade necklace will go perfectly with my dress.

I think that lasagna smells delicious.

When multiple adjectives are used, they should be listed in the following order:

1. Determiners: articles (*a*, *an*, and *the*), possessive adjectives (e.g., *my*, *her*), and descriptors of quantity (e.g., *three*, *several*)
2. Opinions: modifiers that imply a value (e.g., *beautiful*, *perfect*, *ugly*)
3. Size: descriptions of size (e.g., *small*, *massive*)
4. Age: descriptions of age (e.g., *young*, *five-year-old*)
5. Shape: descriptions of appearance or character (e.g., *smooth*, *loud*)

> **HELPFUL HINT**
>
> Adverbs typically answer the questions Where? When? Why? How? How often? To what extent? Under what conditions?

6. Color: descriptions of color (e.g., *blue, dark*)
7. Origin: modifiers that describe where something came from (e.g., *American, homemade*)
8. Material: modifiers that describe what something is made from (e.g., *cotton, metallic*)
9. Purpose: adjectives that function as part of the noun to describe its purpose (e.g., *sewing machine, rocking chair*)

Adverbs, which are often formed by adding the suffix *–ly*, modify any word or set of words that isn't a noun or pronoun. They can modify verbs, adjectives, other adverbs, phrases, or clauses.

> He <u>quickly</u> ran to the house next door. (*Quickly* modifies the verb *ran*.)
>
> Her <u>very</u> effective speech earned her a promotion. (*Very* modifies the adjective *effective*.)
>
> <u>Finally</u>, the table was set and dinner was ready. (*Finally* modifies the clause *the table was set and dinner was ready*.)

CONJUNCTIONS

Conjunctions join words into phrases, clauses, and sentences by use of three mechanisms. There are three main types of conjunctions. **Coordinating conjunctions** join together two independent clauses (i.e., two complete thoughts). These include *and, but, or, for, nor, yet, so* (FANBOYS). Note that some of these can also be used to join items in a series.

> I'll order lunch, <u>but</u> you need to go pick it up.
>
> Make sure to get sandwiches, chips, <u>and</u> sodas.

Correlative conjunctions (whether/or, either/or, neither/nor, both/and, not only/but also) work together to join items:

> <u>Both</u> the teacher <u>and</u> the students needed a break after the lecture.

Subordinating conjunctions join dependent clauses (thoughts that cannot stand alone as sentences) to the related independent clause. They usually describe some sort of relationship between the two parts of the sentence, such as cause/effect or order. They can appear at the beginning or in the middle of a sentence:

> We treat ourselves during football season to several orders <u>because</u> we love pizza.
>
> <u>Because</u> we love pizza, we treat ourselves during football season to several orders.

Table 2.10 Subordinating Conjunctions

Subordinating Conjunctions	
Time	after, as, as long as, as soon as, before, since, until, when, whenever, while
Manner	as, as if, as though
Cause	because
Condition	although, as long as, even if, even though, if, provided that, though, unless, while
Purpose	in order that, so that, that
Comparison	as, than

When using correlative conjunctions, be sure that the structure of the word, phrase, or clause that follows the first part of the conjunction mirrors the structure of the word, phrase, or clause that follows the second part.

> I will neither mow the grass nor pull the weeds today. (correct)
>
> I will neither mow the grass nor undertake the pulling of the weeds today. (incorrect)

PREPOSITIONS

Prepositions set up relationships in time (*after* the party) or space (*under* the cushions) within a sentence. A preposition will always function as part of a prepositional phrase, which includes the preposition along with the object of the preposition. If a word that usually acts as a preposition is standing alone in a sentence, the word is likely functioning as an adverb:

> She hid underneath.

Table 2.11 Common Prepositions

Prepositions	**Compound Prepositions**
along, among, around, at, before, behind, below, beneath, beside, besides, between, beyond, by, despite, down, during, except, for, from, in, into, near, of, off, on, onto, out, outside, over, past, since, through, till, to, toward, under, underneath, until, up, upon, with, within, without	according to, as of, as well as, aside from, because of, by means of, in addition to, in front of, in place of, in respect to, in spite of, instead of, on account of, out of, prior to, with regard to

INTERJECTIONS

Interjections have no grammatical attachment to the sentence itself other than to add expressions of emotion. These parts of speech may be punctuated with commas or exclamation points and may fall anywhere within the sentence itself:

<u>Ouch</u>! He stepped on my toe.

She shopped at the stores after Christmas and, <u>hooray</u>, found many items on sale.

I have seen his love for his father in many expressions of concern—<u>Wow</u>!

SAMPLE QUESTIONS

1) **List all of the adjectives used in the following sentence:**

    Her camera fell into the turbulent water, so her frantic friend quickly grabbed the damp item.

    A. turbulent, frantic, damp

    B. turbulent, frantic, quickly, damp

    C. her, turbulent, frantic, damp

    D. her, the, turbulent, frantic, damp

    Answers:

    A. Incorrect. This list is incomplete; it does not include the articles or possessive adjectives.

    B. Incorrect. This list is incomplete and inaccurate; *quickly* is an adverb.

    C. Incorrect. This list is incomplete; it does not include the articles.

    D. Correct. *Turbulent, frantic,* and *damp* are adjectives; *her* is modifying first *camera* and then *friend*; and *the* is always a limiting adjective—the definite article.

2) **List all of the pronouns used in the following sentence:**

    Several of the administrators who had spoken clearly on the budget increase gave both of the opposing committee members a list of their ideas.

    A. several, of, their

    B. several, who, both

    C. several, who, both, their

    D. several, both

    Answers:

    A. Incorrect. The word *of* is a preposition; the word *their* is being used as a possessive adjective.

B.   **Correct.** *Several* is an indefinite plural pronoun; *who* is a relative pronoun introducing the adjectival clause *who had spoken clearly on the budget increase*; *both* is an indefinite plural pronoun.

C.   Incorrect. The word *their* is being used as a possessive adjective.

D.   Incorrect. The list is missing the word *who* which is a relative pronoun introducing the adjectival clause *who had spoken clearly on the budget increase*.

3)   **Which of the following words is functioning as a coordinating conjunction in the sentence below?**

The political parties do not know if the most popular candidates will survive until the election, but neither the voters nor the candidates will give up their push for popularity.

A.   if

B.   until

C   but

D.   neither

Answers:

A.   Incorrect. *If* is a subordinating conjunction.

B.   Incorrect. *Until* is a preposition.

C.   **Correct.** *But* is a coordinating conjunction joining two clauses.

D.   Incorrect. *Neither* is half of the correlative conjunction pair neither/nor.

CONSTRUCTING SENTENCES

Syntax is the study of how words are combined to create sentences. In English, words are used to build phrases and clauses, which, in turn, are combined to create sentences. By varying the order and length of phrases and clauses, writers can create sentences that are diverse and interesting.

Phrases and clauses are made up of either a subject, a predicate, or both. The **subject** is what the sentence is about. It will be a noun that is usually performing the main action of the sentence, and it may be accompanied by modifiers. The **predicate** describes what the subject is doing or being. It contains the verb(s) and any modifiers or objects that accompany it.

PHRASES

A **phrase** is a group of words that communicates a partial idea and lacks either a subject or a predicate. Several phrases may be strung together, one after another, to add detail and interest to a sentence.

> The animals crossed <u>the large bridge to eat the fish on the wharf</u>.

Phrases are categorized based on the main word in the phrase. A **prepositional phrase** begins with a preposition and ends with an object of the preposition; a **verb phrase** is composed of the main verb along with its helping verbs; and a **noun phrase** consists of a noun and its modifiers.

> prepositional phrase: The dog is hiding <u>under the porch</u>.
>
> verb phrase: The chef <u>would have created</u> another soufflé, but the staff protested.
>
> noun phrase: The big, red barn rests beside <u>the vacant chicken house</u>.

An **appositive phrase** is a particular type of noun phrase that renames the word or group of words that precedes it. Appositive phrases usually follow the noun they describe and are set apart by commas.

> My dad, <u>a clock maker</u>, loved antiques.

Verbal phrases begin with a word that would normally act as a verb but is instead filling another role within the sentence. These phrases can act as nouns, adjectives, or adverbs. **Gerund phrases** begin with gerunds, which are verbs that end in *–ing* and act as nouns. The word *gerund* has an *n* in it, a helpful reminder that the gerund acts as a noun. Therefore, the gerund phrase might act as the subject, the direct object, or the object of the preposition just as another noun would.

> gerund phrase: <u>Writing numerous Christmas cards</u> occupies her aunt's time each year.

A **participial phrase** is a verbal phrase that acts as an adjective. These phrases start with either present participles (which end in *–ing*) or past participles (which usually end in *–ed*). Participial phrases can be extracted from the sentence, and the sentence will still make sense because the participial phrase is playing only a modifying role:

> <u>Enjoying the stars that filled the sky</u>, Dave lingered outside for quite a while.

Finally, an **infinitive phrase** is a verbal phrase that may act as a noun, an adjective, or an adverb. Infinitive phrases begin with the word *to*, followed by a simple form of a verb (to eat, to jump, to skip, to laugh, to sing).

> <u>To visit Europe</u> had always been her dream.

Clauses

Clauses contain both a subject and a predicate. They can be either independent or dependent. An **independent** (or main) **clause** can stand alone as its own sentence:

The dog ate her homework.

Dependent (or subordinate) **clauses** cannot stand alone as their own sentences. They start with a subordinating conjunction, relative pronoun, or relative adjective, which will make them sound incomplete:

<u>Because</u> the dog ate her homework

Table 2.12. Words That Begin Dependent Clauses

Subordinating Conjunctions	Relative Pronouns and Adjectives
after, before, once, since, until, when, whenever, while, as, because, in order that, so, so that, that, if, even if, provided that, unless, although, even though, though, whereas, where, wherever, than, whether	who, whoever, whom, whomever, whose, which, that, when, where, why, how

TYPES OF SENTENCES

Sentences can be classified based on the number and type of clauses they contain. A **simple sentence** will have only one independent clause and no dependent clauses. The sentence may contain phrases, complements, and modifiers, but it will comprise only one independent clause, one complete idea.

The cat under the back porch jumped against the glass yesterday.

A **compound sentence** has two or more independent clauses and no dependent clauses:

The cat under the back porch jumped against the glass yesterday, and he scared my grandma.

A **complex sentence** has only one independent clause and one or more dependent clauses:

The cat under the back porch, who loves tuna, jumped against the glass yesterday.

A **compound-complex sentence** has two or more independent clauses and one or more dependent clause:

The cat under the back porch, who loves tuna, jumped against the glass yesterday; he left a mark on the window.

Go on

Table 2.13. Sentence Structure and Clauses

Sentence Structure	Independent Clauses	Dependent Clauses
Simple	1	0
Compound	2 +	0
Complex	1	1 +
Compound-complex	2 +	1 +

Writers can diversify their use of phrases and clauses in order to introduce variety into their writing. Variety in **sentence structure** not only makes writing more interesting but also allows writers to emphasize that which deserves emphasis. In a paragraph of complex sentences, a short, simple sentence can be a powerful way to draw attention to a major point.

SAMPLE QUESTIONS

4)   Identify the prepositional phrase in the following sentence:

Wrapping packages for the soldiers, the kind woman tightly rolled the t-shirts to see how much space remained for the homemade cookies.

A.   Wrapping packages for the soldiers

B.   the kind woman

C.   rolled the t-shirts

D.   for the homemade cookies

Answers:

A.   Incorrect. This is a participial phrase that begins with the participle *wrapping*.

B.   Incorrect. This is a noun phrase that contains the noun *woman* and modifiers.

C.   Incorrect. This is a verb phrase that contains the verb and its object.

D.   Correct. This phrase begins with the preposition *for*.

5)   Which of the following sentences is complex?

A.   The grandchildren and their cousins enjoyed their day at the beach.

B.   Most of the grass has lost its deep color despite the fall lasting into December.

C.   The committee members cheered when the amendment passed.

D.   The recipes calls for many ingredients that are hard to find or too expensive.

Answers:

A.   Incorrect. This sentence is simple with only one independent clause.

B.   Incorrect. This sentence is simple with one independent clause but several phrases.

C.   Correct. This sentence is complex. It has an indpendent clause (The committee members cheered) and a dependent clause (when the amendment passed).

D.   Incorrect. This sentence is simple with only one independent clause.

PUNCTUATION

Many of the choices writers must make relate to **punctuation**. While creative writers have the liberty to play with punctuation to achieve their desired ends, academic and technical writers must adhere to stricter conventions. The main punctuation marks are periods, question marks, exclamation marks, colons, semicolons, commas, quotation marks, and apostrophes.

> **DID YOU KNOW?**
>
> Many people are taught that a comma represents a pause for breath. While this trick is useful for helping young readers, it is not a helpful guide for comma usage when writing.

There are three terminal punctuation marks that can be used to end sentences. The **period** is the most common and is used to end declarative (statement) and imperative (command) sentences. The **question mark** is used to end interrogative sentences, and exclamation marks are used to indicate that the writer or speaker is exhibiting intense emotion or energy.

> Sarah and I are attending a concert.
>
> How many people are attending the concert?
>
> What a great show that was!

The **colon** and the **semicolon**, though often confused, have a unique set of rules surrounding their respective uses. While both punctuation marks are used to join clauses, the construction of the clauses and the relationship between them varies.

The **semicolon** is used to show a general relationship between two independent clauses (IC; IC):

> The disgruntled customer tapped angrily on the <u>counter; she</u> had to wait nearly ten minutes to speak to the manager.

Coordinating conjunctions (FANBOYS) cannot be used with semi-colons. However, conjunctive adverbs can be used following a semi-colon:

> She may not have to take the course this <u>year; however,</u> she will eventually have to sign up for that specific course.

The **colon**, somewhat less limited than the semicolon in its usage, is used to introduce a list, definition, or clarification. While the clause preceding the colon must be an independent clause, the clause that follows does not have to be one:

> The buffet offers three choices that include: ham, turkey, or roast. (incorrect)
>
> The buffet offers three choices: ham, turkey, or roast. (correct)
>
> The buffet offers three choices that include the following: ham, turkey, or roast. (correct)

Note that neither the semicolon nor the colon should be used to set off an introductory phrase from the rest of the sentence.

> After the trip to the raceway; we realized that we should have brought ear plugs. (incorrect)
>
> After the trip to the raceway: we realized that we should have brought ear plugs. (incorrect)
>
> After the trip to the raceway, we realized that we should have brought ear plugs. (correct)

The **comma** is a complicated piece of punctuation that can serve many different purposes within a sentence. Many times comma placement is an issue of style, not mechanics, meaning there is not necessarily one correct way to write the sentence. There are, however, a few important hard-and-fast comma rules to be followed.

1. Commas should be used to separate two independent clauses along with a coordinating conjunction.

   > George ordered the steak, but Bruce preferred the ham.

2. Commas should be used to separate coordinate adjectives (two different adjectives that describe the same noun).

   > The shiny, regal horse ran majestically through the wide, open field.

3. Commas should be used to separate items in a series. The comma before the conjunction is called the Oxford or serial comma, and is optional.

   > The list of groceries included cream, coffee, donuts, and tea.

4. Commas should be used to separate introductory words, phrases, and clauses from the rest of the sentence.

   > Slowly, Nathan became aware of his surroundings after the concussion.

Within an hour, the authorities will descend on the home.

After Alice swam the channel, nothing intimidated her.

5. Commas should be used to set off non-essential information and appositives.

Estelle, our newly elected chairperson, will be in attendance.

Ida, my neighbor, watched the children for me last week.

6. Commas should be used to set off titles of famous individuals.

Charles, Prince of Wales, visited Canada several times in the last ten years.

7. Commas should be used to set off the day and month of a date within a text.

My birthday makes me feel quite old because I was born on February 16, 1958, in Minnesota.

8. Commas should be used to set up numbers in a text of more than four digits.

We expect 25,000 visitors to the new museum.

Quotation marks are used for many purposes. First, quotation marks are used to enclose direct quotations within a sentence. Terminal punctuation that is part of the quotation should go inside the marks, and terminal punctuation that is part of the larger sentence goes outside:

She asked him menacingly, "Where is my peanut butter?"

What is the original meaning of the phrase "king of the hill"?

In American English, commas are used to set quotations apart from the following text and are placed inside the marks:

"Although I find him tolerable," Arianna wrote, "I would never want him as a roommate."

Additionally, quotation marks enclose titles of short, or relatively short, literary works such as short stories, chapters, and poems. (The titles of longer works, like novels and anthologies, are italicized.) Writers also use quotation marks to set off words used in special sense or for a non-literary purpose:

The shady dealings of his Ponzi scheme earned him the ironic name "Honest Abe."

Apostrophes, sometimes referred to as single quotation marks, show possession; replace missing letters, numerals, and signs; and form plurals of letters, numerals, and signs in certain instances.

1. To signify possession by a singular noun not ending in *s*, add *'s*.

boy → *boy's*

2. To signify possession by a singular noun ending in *s*, add *'s*.

   class → class's

3. To signify possession by an indefinite pronoun not ending in *s*, add *'s*.

   someone → someone's

4. To signify possession by a plural noun not ending in *s*, add *'s*.

   children → children's

5. To signify possession by a plural noun ending in *s*, add only the apostrophe.

   boys → boys'

6. To signify possession by singular, compound words and phrases, add *'s* to the last word in the phrase.

   everybody else → everybody else's

7. To signify joint possession, add *'s* only to the last noun.

   John and Mary's house

8. To signify individual possession, add *'s* to each noun.

   John's and Mary's houses

9. To signify missing letters in a contraction, place the apostrophe where the letters are missing.

   do not → don't

10. To signify missing numerals, place the apostrophe where the numerals are missing.

    1989 → '89

11. There are differing schools of thought regarding the pluralization of numerals and dates, but be consistent within the document with whichever method you choose.

    1990's/1990s; A's/As

Other marks of punctuation include:

▶ **en dash** (–) to indicate a range of dates

▶ **em dash** (—) to indicate an abrupt break in a sentence and emphasize the words within the em dashes

▶ **parentheses** ( ) to enclose insignificant information

▶ **brackets** [ ] to enclose added words to a quotation and to add insignificant information within parentheses

▶ **slash** (/) to separate lines of poetry within a text or to indicate interchangeable terminology

▶ **ellipses** (…) to indicate information removed from a quotation, to indicate a missing line of poetry, or to create a reflective pause

SAMPLE QUESTIONS

6) Which of the following is the correct version of the underlined portion of the sentence below?

Fred's brother wanted the following items for <u>Christmas a</u> red car a condo and a puppy.

A.   Christmas a

B.   Christmas, a

C.   Christmas. A

D.   Christmas: a

Answers:

A.   Incorrect. The sentence needs punctuation to introduce the list.

B.   Incorrect. A comma should not be used to introduce a list.

C.   Incorrect. Adding a period creates a sentence fragment (A red car, a condo, and a puppy).

D.   **Correct.** A colon can be used to introduce a list.

7) Which of the following sentences contains a comma usage error?

A.   On her way home she stopped to pick up groceries, pay her electric bill, and buy some flowers.

B.   I used to drink coffee every morning but my office took away the coffee machine.

C.   Elizabeth will order the cake for the party after she orders the hats.

D.   My cousin, who lives in Indiana, is coming to visit this weekend.

Answers:

A.   Incorrect. The commas are used correctly in this series.

B.   **Correct.** This compound sentence requires a comma before the conjunction *but*.

C.   Incorrect. This complex sentence does not require a comma.

D.   Incorrect. The appositive phrase *who lives in Indiana* is appropriately set apart by commas.

AVOIDING COMMON USAGE ERRORS

ERRORS IN AGREEMENT

Some of the most common grammatical errors are those involving agreement between subjects and verbs, and between nouns and pronouns. While it is impossible to cover all possible errors, the lists below include the most common agreement rules to look for on the test.

SUBJECT/VERB AGREEMENT

1. Single subjects agree with single verbs; plural subjects agree with plural verbs.

    The <u>girl walks</u> her dog.

    The <u>girls walk</u> their dogs.

2. Compound subjects joined by *and* typically take a plural verb unless considered one item.

    <u>Correctness and precision are required</u> for all good writing.

    <u>Macaroni and cheese makes</u> a great snack for children.

3. Compound subjects joined by *or* or *nor* agree with the nearer or nearest subject.

    Neither <u>I nor my friends are</u> looking forward to our final exams.

    Neither <u>my friends nor I am</u> looking forward to our final exams.

4. For sentences with inverted word order, the verb will agree with the subject that follows it.

    Where <u>are Bob and his friends going</u>? Where <u>is Bob going</u>?

5. All single, indefinite pronouns agree with single verbs.

    <u>Neither</u> of the students <u>is</u> happy about the play.

    <u>Each</u> of the many cars <u>is</u> on the grass.

    Every <u>one</u> of the administrators <u>speaks</u> highly of Trevor.

6. All plural, indefinite pronouns agree with plural verbs.

    <u>Several</u> of the students <u>are</u> happy about the play.

    <u>Both</u> of the cars <u>are</u> on the grass.

    <u>Many</u> of the administrators <u>speak</u> highly of Trevor.

7. Collective nouns agree with singular verbs when the collective acts as one unit. Collective nouns agree with plural verbs when the collective acts as individuals within the group.

    The <u>band plans</u> a party after the final football game.

    The <u>band play</u> their instruments even if it rains.

    The <u>jury announces</u> its decision after sequestration.

    The <u>jury make</u> phone calls during their break time.

8. The linking verbs agree with the subject and the predicate.

    My <u>favorite is</u> strawberries and apples.

    My <u>favorites are</u> strawberries and apples.

9. Nouns that are plural in form but singular in meaning will agree with singular verbs.

Measles is a painful disease.

Sixty dollars is too much to pay for that book.

10. Singular verbs come after titles, business corporations, and words used as terms.

"Three Little Kittens" is a favorite nursery rhyme for many children.

General Motors is a major employer for the city.

> **HELPFUL HINT**
>
> Ignore words between the subject and the verb to help make conjugation clearer:
>
> The new library ~~with its many books and rooms~~ fills a long-felt need.

PRONOUN/ANTECEDENT AGREEMENT

1. Antecedents joined by *and* typically require a plural pronoun.

   The children and their dogs enjoyed their day at the beach.

2. For compound antecedents joined by *or*, the pronoun agrees with the nearer or nearest antecedent.

   Either the resident mice or the manager's cat gets itself a meal of good leftovers.

3. When indefinite pronouns function in a sentence, the pronoun must agree with the number of the pronoun.

   Neither student finished his or her assignment.

   Both of the students finished their assignments.

4. When collective nouns function as antecedents, the pronoun choice will be singular or plural depending on the function of the collective.

   The audience was cheering as it rose to its feet in unison.

   Our family are spending their vacations in Maine, Hawaii, and Rome.

5. When *each* and *every* precede the antecedent, the pronoun agreement will be singular.

   Each and every man, woman, and child brings unique qualities to his or her family.

   Every creative writer, technical writer, and research writer is attending his or her assigned lecture.

ERRORS IN SENTENCE CONSTRUCTION

Errors in parallelism occur when items in a series are not put in the same form. For example, if a list contains two nouns and a verb, the sentence should be rewritten so that all three items are the same part of speech. Parallelism should be maintained in words, phrases, and clauses:

> The walls were painted green and gold.
>
> Her home is up the hill and beyond the trees.

> If we shop on Friday and if we have enough time, we will then
> visit the aquarium.

Sentence errors fall into three categories: fragments, comma splices (comma fault), and fused sentences (run-on). A **fragment** occurs when a group of words does not have both a subject and verb as needed to construct a complete sentence or thought. Many times a writer will mirror conversation and write down only a dependent clause, for example, which will have a subject and verb but will not have a complete thought grammatically.

> Why are you not going to the mall? Because I do not like
> shopping. (incorrect)
>
> Because I do not like shopping, I will not plan to go to the mall.
> (correct)

A **comma splice** (comma fault) occurs when two independent clauses are joined together with only a comma to "splice" them together. To fix a comma splice, a coordinating conjunction should be added, or the comma can be replaced by a semicolon:

> My family eats turkey at Thanksgiving, we eat ham at
> Christmas. (incorrect)
>
> My family eats turkey at Thanksgiving, and we eat ham at
> Christmas. (correct)
>
> My family eats turkey at Thanksgiving; we eat ham at
> Christmas. (correct)

Fused (run-on) sentences occur when two independent clauses are joined with no punctuation whatsoever. Like comma splices, they can be fixed with a comma and conjunction or with a semicolon:

> My sister lives nearby she never comes to visit. (incorrect)
>
> My sister lives nearby, but she never comes to visit. (correct)
>
> My sister lives nearby; she never comes to visit. (correct)

COMMONLY CONFUSED WORDS

a, an: *A* is used before words beginning with consonants or consonant sounds; *an* is used before words beginning with vowels or vowel sounds.

affect, effect: *Affect* is most often a verb; *effect* is usually a noun. (*The experience affected me significantly* OR *The experience had a significant effect on me.*)

among, amongst, between: *Among* is used for a group of more than two people; *amongst* is archaic and not commonly used in modern writing; *between* is reserved to distinguish two people, places, things, or groups.

amount, number: *Amount* is used for non-countable sums; *number* is used with countable nouns. (*She had a large amount of money in her purse, nearly fifty dollars.*)

cite, site: *Cite* is a verb used in documentation to credit an author of a quotation, paraphrase, or summary; *site* is a location.

elicit, illicit: *Elicit* means to draw out a response from an audience or a listener; *illicit* refers to illegal activity.

every day, everyday: *Every day* is an indefinite adjective modifying a noun—*each day* could be used interchangeably with *every day*; *everyday* is a one-word adjective to imply frequent occurrence. (*Our visit to the Minnesota State Fair is an everyday activity during August.*)

fewer, less: *Fewer* is used with a countable noun; *less* is used with a non-countable noun. (*Fewer parents are experiencing stress since the new teacher was hired; parents are experiencing less stress since the new teacher was hired.*)

firstly, secondly: These words are archaic; today, *first* and *second* are more commonly used.

good, well: *Good* is always the adjective; *well* is always the adverb except in cases of health. (*She felt well after the surgery.*)

implied, inferred: *Implied* is something a speaker does; *inferred* is something the listener does after assessing the speaker's message. (*The speaker implied something mysterious, but I inferred the wrong thing.*)

irregardless, regardless: *Irregardless* is non-standard usage and should be avoided; *regardless* is the proper usage of the transitional statement.

its, it's: *Its* is a possessive case pronoun; *it's* is a contraction for *it is*.

moral, morale: *Moral* is a summative lesson from a story or life event; *morale* is the emotional attitude of a person or group of people.

principal, principle: *Principal* is the leader of a school in the noun usage; *principal* means *main* in the adjectival usage; *principle* is a noun meaning *idea* or *tenet*. (*The principal of the school spoke on the principal meaning of the main principles of the school.*)

quote, quotation: *Quote* is a verb and should be used as a verb; *quotation* is the noun and should be used as a noun.

reason why: *Reason why* is a redundant expression—use one or the other. (*The reason we left is a secret. Why we left is a secret.*)

should of, should have: *Should of* is improper usage, likely resulting from misunderstood speech—*of* is not a helping verb and can therefore cannot complete the verb phrase; *should have* is the proper usage. (*He should have driven.*)

than, then: *Than* sets up a comparison of some kind; *then* indicates a reference to a point in time. (*When I said that I liked the hat better than the gloves, my sister laughed; then she bought both for me.*)

their, there, they're: *Their* is the possessive case of the pronoun *they*. *There* is the demonstrative pronoun indicating location, or place. *They're* is a contraction of the words *they are*, the third-person plural subject pronoun and third-person plural, present-tense conjugation of the verb *to be*. These words are very commonly confused in written English.

to lie (to recline), to lay (to place): *To lie* is the intransitive verb meaning *to recline*, so the verb does not take an object; *to lay* is the transitive verb meaning *to place something*. (*I lie out in the sun; I lay my towel on the beach.*)

to try and: *To try and* is sometimes used erroneously in place of *to try to*. (*She should try to succeed daily.*)

unique: *Unique* is an ultimate superlative. The word *unique* should not be modified technically. (*The experience was ~~very~~ unique.*)

who, whom: *Who* is the subject relative pronoun. (*My son, who is a good student, studies hard.*) Here, the son is carrying out the action of studying, so the pronoun is a subject pronoun (*who*). *Whom* is the object relative pronoun. (*My son, whom the other students admire, studies hard.*) Here, *son* is the object of the other students' admiration, so the pronoun standing in for him, *whom*, is an object pronoun.

your, you're: *Your* is the possessive case of the pronoun *you*. *You're* is a contraction of the words *you are*, the second-person subject pronoun and the second-person singular, present-tense conjugation of the verb *to be*. These words are commonly confused in written English.

SAMPLE QUESTIONS

8)   **Which sentence does NOT contain an error?**

　　A.   My sister and my best friend lives in Chicago.

　　B.   My parents or my brother is going to pick me up from the airport.

　　C.   Neither of the students refuse to take the exam.

　　D.   The team were playing a great game until the rain started.

Answers:

　　A.   Incorrect. Because the sentence reads <u>My sister</u> and <u>my</u> best friend, the subject is plural and needs a plural verb (*live*).

　　B.   Correct. The verb agrees with the closest subject—in this case, the singular *brother*.

C.   Incorrect. *Neither* is a singular, indefinite pronoun, so the agreement is singular. *Neither refuses*

D.   Incorrect. In the context of a game, the *team* is functioning as a singular, so it should take a singular verb. *The team was*

9)   **Which sentence does NOT contain an error?**

A.   The grandchildren and their cousins enjoyed their day at the beach.

B.   Most of the grass has lost their deep color.

C.   The jury was cheering as their commitment came to a close.

D.   Every boy and girl must learn to behave themselves in school.

Answers:

A.   **Correct.** *Grandchildren and cousins/their*

B.   Incorrect. *Most of the grass has lost its deep color.*

C.   Incorrect. *The jury was cheering as its commitment came to a close.*

D.   Incorrect. *Every boy and girl must learn to behave himself or herself in school.*

10)   **Which of the following sentences contains a comma splice?**

A.   Since she went to the store.

B.   The football game ended in a tie, the underdog caught up in the fourth quarter.

C.   If we get rid of the bookcase, we'll have enough room for a couch.

D.   When the players dropped their gloves, a fight broke out on the ice hockey rink floor.

Answers:

A.   Incorrect. The group of words in A is not a complete thought and would be classified as a fragment.

B.   **Correct.** The sentence in B joins two complete thoughts with only a comma and would therefore be classified as a comma splice.

C.   Incorrect. This sentence correctly joins a dependent and independent clause using a comma.

D.   Incorrect. The sentence in D is punctuated properly and constructed correctly.

EVALUATING SOURCES

Research is a process of gathering sources containing documented facts that answer specific questions and provide information about an issue. In the twenty-first century, locating sources is easy; however, finding and determining quality sources involves careful evaluation.

It is best to begin by evaluating the credibility of a source's author. Consideration should be given to the author's motivation—the purpose or reason he or she had for writing the text. Next, research involves identifying the author's background and expertise. Although educational credentials are significant, firsthand experience offers equally reliable information.

Questions a researcher should be able to answer about a source include:

- ▶ Is it current or written fairly recently?
- ▶ If it is secondary, is it based on both primary as well as other secondary sources?
- ▶ Is the author an expert in the area of study? Does he or she include or cite relevant information from other authorities on the topic? Are the conclusions based on scientific evidence? How well does the scientifically gathered evidence explain the topic?
- ▶ Is the purpose of the source clear? Is there any bias?
- ▶ What does the author assume is true?
- ▶ Does the author present several viewpoints on issues?
- ▶ Does the content agree with what other reliable sources on the topic indicate?

Evaluating a website entails determining who the site's intended audience is and if the site has an agenda, such as selling something or promoting a belief system. If the site is educational, researchers should verify whether it was created by authoritative authors and authors that have identified themselves. Grammatically correct content on the site is a helpful indicator. Plus, the site's address should work and be relatively current. (Typing "javascript:alert(document.lastModified)" in the address bar provides a site's most recent modification date.)

SAMPLE QUESTIONS

11) **What legitimizes the claims made in a source?**

A.   Similar information and conclusions are apparent in other sources.

B.   The background of the writer is clear.

C.   The publisher of the source is a respected organization.

D.   A journalist or an admired writer has written the source.

Answers:

A.   Correct. The content is in agreement with what other reliable sources on the topic indicate.

B.   Incorrect. The writer's background may be clear, but that background is not the subject of the source.

C.   Incorrect. A respected organization is unrelated to scholarly research, an author's qualifications, or the use of verifiable data.

D.   Incorrect. The writer may be a journalist or admired, but that does not mean the writer is knowledgeable about the subject of the text or has collected data that supports the ideas of the source.

12) **A quality source**

A.   is free of the clutter of citations, quotations, footnotes, and a works-cited page.

B.   is peer-reviewed by scholars who have credentials in a wide variety of areas, not just the subject of the source article.

C.   has remained in publication for decades.

D.   includes accurate, well-documented information.

Answers:

A.   Incorrect. A quality source has citations, quotations, footnotes, and a works-cited page.

B.   Incorrect. A peer-reviewed source has been assessed by scholars who have credentials in the same area as the author of the source.

C.   Incorrect. A quality source may be a recent publication.

D.   **Correct.** The author of a quality source is an expert in the source's area of study and will have included or cited relevant information from other authorities on the topic.

TYPES OF SOURCES

Which sources a researcher uses depends on his or her purpose. If the purpose is to analyze, interpret, or critique an historical event, a creative work, or a natural phenomenon, the researcher will use a **primary**, or **original**, **source**. Examples of primary sources include:

▶ letters and e-mails

▶ autobiographies, diaries, and memoirs

▶ firsthand or eyewitness accounts or descriptions of events

▶ interviews, questionnaires, and surveys

▶ speeches and lectures

▶ photographs, drawings, and paintings

▶ news stories written at the time of the event

The written analysis or interpretation of a primary source is considered a **secondary source**. These sources are written by people who do not have firsthand experience of the topic being described. Instead, authors of secondary sources examine primary sources in order to draw conclusions or make generalizations about people, events, and ideas. Examples of secondary sources include:

- ▸ literary criticism and interpretation essays
- ▸ biographies
- ▸ historical criticism
- ▸ political analyses
- ▸ essays on ethics and social policies

To research a problem or question that has not been researched before, an analysis of the relevant primary documents is recommended. In addition, researchers can conduct their own observations, interviews, surveys, or experiments.

If the purpose is to report on, explain, or summarize what is known about a topic, the researcher will use texts written by other researchers or secondary sources. Of note, most primary research studies begin with a review of literature, which summarizes what secondary sources are saying about a topic.

Research on topics of interest usually begins with a critical analysis of existing research; researchers draw conclusions from secondary sources that deal with their specific topic. Initially, thought should be given to searching databases. Annotated bibliographies are helpful in locating the most relevant sources for a topic. Web pages created by associations, government agencies, and institutions have a wealth of source material. Although print sources continue to be helpful, most researchers use the Internet to locate digital versions of print sources. Reports by research agencies are often available, particularly in areas concerning the environment. If scholarly sources are required—that is, texts written by those who are highly educated in a particular field—instead of a web search, Google Scholar and databases like JSTOR, EBSCO, and GALE can be more helpful. Public libraries are the best places to avoid the cost of subscription-based databases like JSTOR.

SAMPLE QUESTIONS

13) **A secondary source**

   A.   summarizes or evaluates an original source or research study.

   B.   is written by a person who conducted an original study or wrote an original text.

   C.   must be peer reviewed.

   D.   is published by the government or a private publisher.

Answers:

   A.   **Correct.** A secondary source is a written analysis or interpretation of a primary source. Examples include literary and historical criticism.

   B.   Incorrect. This option describes a primary source.

   C.   Incorrect. This is a possibility, but it does not define what a secondary source is.

D.   Incorrect. These are possibilities, but they don't explain what a secondary source is.

14) What kind of source is a political speech?

A.   a secondary source

B.   an authoritative source

C.   a confusing source

D.   a primary source

Answers:

A.   Incorrect. A secondary source is a written analysis or interpretation of a primary source. Examples include literary and historical criticism.

B.   Incorrect. The speaker may not be authoritative, or even knowledgeable.

C.   Incorrect. This is possible but hopefully not true.

D.   Correct. Primary sources are firsthand accounts of a topic. They are created by authors who have direct experience with the subject and are usually created at the time the authors are involved with the subject. A political speech is written or given by a person who is directly involved with the issues presented in the speech.

RESEARCH STRATEGIES

Research begins with curiosity about a specific topic, then moves from curiosity to a research question. Doing preliminary reading on the topic refines that question and gains the researcher an overview. A search of *available sources related to the question* is also wise. For example:

▶ **Research topic**: Emily Dickinson and feminism

▶ **Question**: What feminist ideas did Emily Dickinson express?

▶ **Preliminary sources**: Literary criticism on Emily Dickinson, especially feminist interpretations of Dickinson's poetry

Next, the researcher will need to decide which primary sources and critical essays to use. After skim-reading these sources, a preliminary *organizational plan* should be determined. Some considerations include: What basic background information does the reader (also considered the audience) need in order to understand the topic? What is the basis of the ideas to be presented? In other words, what topics need to be explained first so other topics can be understood by the reader? What is the most logical way to present the information that has been located? The reader prefers one topic to lead to the next. Organizational plans detail the characteristics, causes, effects, sequences of events, similarities, and contrasts.

A sample organizational plan for the Emily Dickinson research example could involve presenting in the first section a historical account of the nineteenth-century women's rights movement and a definition of the concept of feminism during Dickinson's life. The next sections could delve into the main feminist ideas Dickinson expressed in her poetry.

Once an organizational plan is outlined, the researcher should start taking *notes* from the sources gathered. Most important, each note must include identifying information about the source, including publication details and page numbers. In addition, the section of the outline that corresponds with the source information noted must be designated above each note. This way, the notes are categorized according to the outline, or organizational plan.

Notes come in four different forms. A **direct quotation** is three or more consecutive words copied precisely from a source. It must be designated by quotation marks or by block indentation if the quotation is longer than four lines of prose or three lines of poetry. A quotation can be a definition or a well-worded or authoritative statement that will amplify a main point. A **paraphrase** is a reworded version of any sentence in a source. Typically, a sentence with complex or sophisticated wording needs to be paraphrased. The main thoughts are pulled apart and the language is simplified, but the original meaning is retained. A **summary** is a shortened version of a section of a source, containing only the main points or events of the original. Any type of descriptive, detailed, or narrative text, such as news stories, fictional stories, or chronicles of events needs to be summed up. An **idea and list**—the most common form of notes—consists of the key idea of a section of text followed by a bulleted list of related details. Again, all notes should be marked with corresponding outline sections, so it will be easy to put the notes in the order of the outline and use the information to compose the paper.

The following are sample notes for research on feminist ideas expressed by Emily Dickinson:

Cooper, Susan Fenimore. "Female Suffrage: A Letter to the Christian Women of America." *Harper's New Weekly Magazine* XLI (June–November 1870): 594 – 600.

Outline Section I

Three Reasons Women Remain in a Subordinate Position:

1. They are physically weaker and depend on men for protection.

2. They are intellectually inferior.

   ► This claim is considered debatable.

   ► Why women have not educated themselves is of concern.

3. Christianity teaches that men are the head of the household.

   ► But protects her more than other systems

Figure 2.2a. A Primary Source

Dickinson, Emily. "My Life had stood – a Loaded Gun." Stanzas 1 – 3.

Outline Section I

My Life had stood—a Loaded Gun—
In Corners—till a Day
The Owner passed—identified—
And carried Me away—

And now We roam in Sovereign Woods—
And now We hunt the Doe—
And every time I speak for Him—
The Mountains straight reply—
And do I smile, such cordial light
Upon the Valley glow—
It is as a Vesuvian face
Had let its pleasure through—

Figure 2.2b. A Primary Source

Rich, Adrienne. "Vesuvius at Home: The Power of Emily Dickinson."
Reprinted in *Literary Theories in Praxis*. Edited by Shirley F. Staton. Phila-
delphia: University of Pennsylvania Press, 1987. pp. 258–59.

Outline Section I

Speaking of Emily Dickinson's poem "My Life had stood – a Loaded
Gun," Adrienne Rich explains, "But I think that for us, at this time, it
is a central poem in understanding Emily Dickinson, and ourselves,
and the condition of the woman artist, particularly in the nineteenth
century. It seems likely that the nineteenth-century woman poet,
especially, felt the medium of poetry as dangerous….Poetry is too
much rooted in the unconscious; it presses too close against the
barriers of repression; and the nineteenth-century woman had much
to repress."

Paraphrase of the above quotation:

Nineteenth-century women had to repress many of their thoughts. In
other words, they pushed these thoughts into their unconscious minds
and weren't aware of them. Since the unconscious mind is the source of
poetic expression, writing poetry was dangerous for a nineteenth-
century woman; in doing so, she gave expression to these repressed
thoughts and feelings.

Figure 2.3. A Secondary Source, Literary Criticism

SAMPLE QUESTIONS

15) **Which of the following is an example of a secondary source for an article on local highways?**

   A.   an online opinion column promoting tax incentives for those who carpool

   B.   photographs of traffic accidents

   C.   data from the city's transportation department

   D.   an autobiography of a city official who led efforts to improve local infrastructure

Answers:

   A.   **Correct.** Only this option describes a secondary source, since it offers analysis of a topic, not firsthand experience of it.

   B.   Incorrect. Photographs are a primary source.

   C.   Incorrect. The analysis or interpretation of data could be considered a secondary source, but the data itself is a primary source.

   D.   Incorrect. An autobiography is a primary source.

16) **What is a good reason for a writer of a research paper to include a short section of text copied word for word from a source?**

   A.   The text is a secondary source.

   B.   The vocabulary is sophisticated.

   C.   The text is well worded.

   D.   The information relates to several areas of the research.

Answers:

   A.   Incorrect. The type of source does not affect whether a direct quote should be included in a research paper.

   B.   Incorrect. Sophisticated vocabulary is not a good enough reason to quote text; the text should be still be paraphrased.

   C.   **Correct.** Quoting a statement with wording that is emphatic or memorable can be an especially effective way to amplify an argument in a research paper.

   D.   Incorrect. Ideally all the information in a research paper is relevant, so this is not a reason to include direct quotations.

CITATIONS

In general, any ideas or details that are not original to the writer must be documented. Specifically, this includes any information quoted, paraphrased, or summarized from sources.

Information taken from sources is documented with **in-text citations**, **internal documentation**, or **parenthetical references**. These terms are used interchangeably to mean that the source information—usually the author's last name or the first main words of the title plus the page, line, or section number—is put in parentheses right after the paraphrase, quotation, or summary. If the source of the information is introduced in the text with the author's name, the writer puts just the page, line, or section number in the parentheses.

3

Writing the Essay

Regardless of the format or topic, a high-scoring essay can be written by following several simple rules. First, identify the type of essay to be written: if the essay doesn't correctly address the prompt, it will always receive a low score. Second, determine what the main point and organizational structure of the essay will be. It is much easier to write using a clear outline than to haphazardly organize along the way. Third, make sure that the essay uses sound evidence while maintaining a style that's appropriate to the test. A good essay doesn't have to be complicated; it just needs to have a clear, well-reasoned position. Finally, all of this must be accomplished within a limited time frame. Fortunately, the essay graders will understand that a first draft written under test conditions does not need to be as polished as a final essay in a classroom assignment.

TYPES OF ESSAYS

It is important to note that essays do not follow a single format. Rather, the format is determined by the intended purpose of each essay. For example, an essay may attempt to inform or persuade the reader, or perhaps describe or narrate a scene. It is important to use the appropriate type of essay for a given task.

PERSUASIVE

A **persuasive essay** is meant to convince the reader of the author's point of view on a particular issue. Typically, such an essay will also include a call to action. Thus, a persuasive essay should cause the reader to feel and act in a particular way.

A persuasive essay can be written on any topic on which people can have a difference of opinion. For example, an essay may argue that social media is harmful to teenagers or that a noise ordinance should be adopted in a community. These both seek to sway the reader's opinion to that of the author's. In contrast, essays describing the social media habits of teenagers or telling the story of a neighborhood's attempt to pass local noise ordinances are not persuasive because they do not present a specific opinion.

In writing a persuasive essay, it is vital to take a clear stance on an issue. The reader should be left with no doubt as to which side of an issue the writer supports. In addition, a persuasive essay must include facts and logical reasoning to show that the ideas put forth by the author are superior to other ideas on the topic. This type of essay should be written with a specific audience in mind to tailor the arguments and language to the intended readers.

When writing persuasive essays in an exam setting, keep in mind that the actual stance taken in the essay is not important. The graders don't care about the specific opinion expressed in the essay; they only care that the opinion is well written and supported by logically relevant evidence.

PERSUASIVE ESSAY EXAMPLE

PROMPT: Technology has launched us into a new era and, with it, a new way of living with and relating to one another. It has opened doors and allowed us to accomplish things that would have been impossible in the past: we are able to keep up closely with a large number of people in an easy and comfortable way. As it continues to develop, social media technology will, time and again, offer us new and better ways of staying in touch with one another and, because of it, will make our lives and our relationships fuller and more meaningful.

Discuss the extent to which you agree or disagree with this opinion. Support your position with specific reasoning and examples from your experience, observations, and reading.

One would be foolish to argue that technology has not had a real and pervasive impact on our daily lives. Many of us rely daily on cell phones, tablets, and computers that allow us to reach family, friends, and business associates with little to no trouble. However, this ease of access does not necessarily mean our relationships are improving: the impersonal and anonymous nature of social media and other communication technologies make it even more difficult for us to make meaningful, lasting connections with the people around us.

Social media is, by nature, impersonal. Though we are able to build personal profiles that reflect whom we want the world to see, these profiles do little to improve our connection and communication with others. In fact, it is these very tools that are distancing us from our fellow humans. Birthday notifications, for example, remind social media users every day of the "friends" who are celebrating that day. While this tool seems, in theory, to be a great way to keep up with others, it actually desensitizes us. In truth, when I receive birthday notifications via social media, I end up either ignoring them altogether or sending an impersonal "Happy Birthday" just to be able to say I did. In fact, I never send birthday notes via social media to friends and family whose birthdays I actually care about because I do so in a more personal way—via a phone call or in person. Furthermore, I don't need an app to remember those birthdays. Though it may seem more useful or convenient to be able to stay in touch through social media, the relationships that rely on it are, in my experience, rarely very meaningful. By allowing us to stay in touch with larger numbers of people, social media also makes our connections shallower.

In addition to being impersonal, social media and other communication technologies can also be anonymous, creating a world of users that are disconnected from the things they post and read and, ultimately, from each other. Cyberbullying has been a significant concern of the twenty-first century, with numerous incidents leading to depressing outcomes, like teenage suicide. Through the lens of social media, bullies are able to disregard the humanity of the person on the other end and say things that they might never say in real life. A similar effect is clear during important political events: people post, with aggressive fervor, in favor of their own beliefs and respond, with equally aggressive insults, to anyone they disagree with. While this may, on the surface, seem to encourage open dialogue, social media and other communication technologies fail to have any effect on the quality of the conversation itself. Rather than learning to interact with one another respectfully, a tactic that may actually lead to increased understanding and greater acceptance of others, social media users learn that what they say has little to no consequence in real life.

The sense of community created by social media is deceptive. The ease with which people can "connect" often makes those connections meaningless. The friend who "Likes" a photo you post isn't putting any real energy into that friendship—he just clicked once and moved on. Similarly, people can use the anonymity of the internet to just as easily create enemies. One angry comment (that would never be said face-to-face) can launch a hundred nasty replies. These types of relationships don't make our lives fuller or more meaningful. They make our lives empty and shallow.

EXPOSITORY

An **expository essay** is one in which the author tells the reader something in a straightforward manner. This essay type is meant to explain, inform, or clarify a topic for which the reader may have no prior knowledge. It is also a chance for the writer to display his or her own understanding of a topic. Subjects for an expository essay might include many different sides, but an expository essay doesn't dive into these controversies. Instead, it simply explains a topic with as much neutrality as possible.

To compose a successful expository essay, the author must present facts from verifiable sources and arrange the information in a logical sequence. Language should be clear and precise, and relevant context should be provided since the reader may not be familiar with the topic. It is important that the essay remains objective and does not include the author's opinion.

DID YOU KNOW?

The word *expository* is related to the word *expose*, which means to show.

EXPOSITORY ESSAY EXAMPLE

PROMPT: Following the Second World War, the United States and the Soviet Union emerged as the dominant world powers, ushering in the Cold War and a "bipolar world." Only a few years before, however, European powers like England and France controlled colonial empires around the world, dominating world affairs; in fact, the Soviet Union itself was only a few decades old.

Using your knowledge of world history, explain how the two superpowers were able to rapidly dominate world affairs following World War II.

The United States and the Soviet Union—victorious allies in the Second World War—were not able to maintain a strong relationship for long. Despite losses in the millions, the Soviet Union still had an enormous and powerful military and, in violation of the agreements made at Yalta, Stalin later occupied several Eastern European countries, preventing free elections. The US-led West formed NATO as a result; in response, the USSR organized the Warsaw Pact. This rapid rise in the prominence of the United States and the USSR was a result of both countries' advanced industrial capabilities, large resource reserves, and expanded global military presence.

In the United States, the New Deal and mobilization for the war had strengthened the national economy. At the end of the war, the United States had proven its weapons capacity by using the nuclear bomb: this technology, on the heels of its military domination of Europe and the Pacific, made it an undisputed global superpower.

At the same time, the Soviet Union dominated land throughout Europe, Central, and East Asia. The Soviet Union's Five Year Plans of the 1920s had sped up industrialization, and their wealth included vast mineral, petroleum, timber, and other natural resources. They also developed nuclear weapons and a military with a global reach.

Furthermore, both countries extended their global reach diplomatically and militarily to spread their respective ideologies—communism and democratic capitalism—in order to ensure global security. By promulgating the Marshall Plan and supporting the establishment of the Bretton Woods institutions (the World Bank and the International Monetary Fund), the United States found ways to promote global capitalism. At the same time, the Soviet Union supported Marxist independence movements worldwide in colonies and resistance movements in former colonies; many Cold War battles were fought as proxy wars between the superpowers in Africa, Asia, and Latin America. Each country also had a global presence with bases, officers, diplomats, and military personnel in nearly every country in the world.

Since the European empires had collapsed in the wake of the Second World War, the Soviet Union and the United States dominated the global stage in a way no other country could match. Each used their natural and industrial resources, alongside a growing military and diplomatic presence, to quickly fill the void left by the fall of European powers.

WRITING A THESIS STATEMENT

The thesis, or **thesis statement**, is central to the structure and meaning of an essay: it presents the writer's argument or position on an issue. In other words, it tells readers specifically what the author is going to say in the essay. A strong, direct thesis statement is key to the organization of any essay. It introduces both the central idea of the essay and the main points that will be used to support that idea. Thus, the thesis will mirror the organization of the essay as a whole: each paragraph can elaborate on each supporting point.

In writing a thesis statement, it is important to respond to the prompt provided. The author must identify keywords in the prompt and think about what the prompt is asking. For example, the prompt may be asking for a clear stance to be taken a particular issue, or it may require a detailed explanation of a topic. Once a clear understanding of the task is reached, the author must develop a central idea along with supporting points from relevant sources, including any provided documents and personal knowledge or experience. The central idea and supporting points can then be concisely packaged into a one or two sentence statement. Generally, a thesis statement is no more than two sentences.

> **HELPFUL HINT**
>
> Find an op-ed article in the newspaper. Read it carefully and try to identify the thesis and supporting points.

THESIS STATEMENT EXAMPLES

PROMPT: Many high schools have begun to adopt 1:1 technology programs, meaning that each school provides every student with a computing device, such as a laptop or tablet. Educators who support these initiatives say that the technology allows for more dynamic collaboration and that students need to learn technology skills to compete in the job market. On the other hand, opponents cite increased distraction and the dangers of cyberbullying or unsupervised internet use as reasons not to provide students with such devices.

In your essay, take a position on this question. You may write about either one of the two points of view given, or you may present a different point of view on this question. Use specific reasons and examples to support your position.

Possible thesis statements:

1) Providing technology to every student is good for education because it allows students to learn important skills such as typing, web design, and video editing, and it also gives students more opportunities to work cooperatively with their classmates and teachers.

2) I disagree with the idea that schools should provide technology to students because most students will simply be distracted by the free access to games and websites when they should be studying or doing homework.

3) By providing each student with a laptop or tablet, schools can help students apply technology to work more effectively with other students,

communicate with teachers and classmates, and conduct research for class projects.

STRUCTURING THE ESSAY

There are a lot of different ways to organize an essay. In the limited timeframe of an exam, however, it is best to stick to a basic five-paragraph essay that includes an introduction, body, and conclusion. This structure can be used to discuss nearly any topic and will be easy for graders to follow.

INTRODUCTIONS

The purpose of an **introduction** is to set the stage for the essay. This is accomplished by capturing the reader's interest, introducing and providing context for the topic, and stating the central idea and main points of the essay. Usually the introductory paragraph ends with a thesis statement, which clearly sets forth the position or point the essay will argue.

INTRODUCTION EXAMPLE

Technology has changed massively in recent years, but today's generation barely notices—high school students are already experienced with the internet, computers, apps, cameras, cell phones, and more. It's inevitable that these technologies will be begin to make their way into classrooms. Opponents of 1:1 technology programs might argue that students will be distracted or misuse the technology, but that is exactly why schools must teach them to use it. Students need to know how to navigate technology safely and effectively, and schools have a responsibility to ensure they learn these skills. By providing each student with a laptop or tablet, schools can help students learn how to apply technology to work more effectively with other students, communicate with teachers and classmates, and conduct research for class projects.

Explanation: This introduction *introduces* the topic in the first sentence. It then provides context by discussing why technology in the classroom is an important—and controversial—topic. The paragraph closes with a thesis statement that takes a firm stance and introduces the supporting ideas that the essay will be organized around.

THE BODY PARAGRAPHS

The body of the essay should consist of two to four paragraphs, each of which is focused on a single supporting idea. The body of an essay can be organized in a number of ways:

▶ Body paragraphs can explain each supporting detail given in the thesis statement.

- ▶ Body paragraphs can describe a problem then discuss the pros and cons of a solution in separate paragraphs.
- ▶ Body paragraphs can tell a story, with the story broken into two to four logical parts.
- ▶ Body paragraphs can compare and contrast the merits of two arguments, possibly drawing a conclusion about which is better at the end.

Each paragraph should be structurally consistent, beginning with a topic sentence to introduce the main idea, followed by supporting ideas and examples. No extra ideas unrelated to the paragraph's focus should appear. Transition words and phrases can be used to connect body paragraphs and to improve the flow and readability of the essay.

QUICK REVIEW

Which essay structure would be better suited to a persuasive essay? What about an expository essay?

BODY PARAGRAPH EXAMPLE

Technology can be a powerful tool for collaboration. When all of the students in a classroom have access to reliable laptops or tablets, they are able to more effectively share information and work together on projects. Students can communicate quickly via email, share files through a cloud service, and use a shared calendar for scheduling. They also have the opportunity to teach each other new skills since each student may bring to the group unique knowledge about particular apps or programs. When the availability of technology is limited or inconsistent, these opportunities are lost.

Explanation: This body paragraph discusses a supporting detail given the thesis (*schools can help students apply technology to work more effectively with other students*). It introduces the topic, then provides concrete examples of how technology makes it easier to work with other students. The final sentence reemphasizes the paragraph's main idea.

CONCLUSIONS

To end an essay smoothly, the author must compose a conclusion that reminds the reader of the importance of the topic and then restates the essay's thesis and supporting details. The writer should revisit the ideas in the introduction and thesis statement, but these ideas should not be simply repeated word-for-word. Rather, a well-written conclusion will reinforce the argument using wording that differs from the thesis statement but conveys the same idea. The conclusion should leave the reader with a strong impression of the essay's main idea and provide the essay with a sense of closure.

CONCLUSION EXAMPLE

As technology continues to change and become more incorporated into everyday life, students will need to adapt to it. Schools already teach young people a myriad of academic and life skills, so it makes sense that they would teach students how to use technology appropriately, too. When technology is incorporated into schoolwork, students will learn to collaborate, communicate, and research more effectively. Providing students with their own devices is one part of this important task, and schools that do so should be supported.

> **Explanation**: This conclusion reminds the reader why the topic is important and then restates the thesis and supporting ideas. It ends with a strong, clear statement of the writer's stance on the issue.

SUPPORTING EVIDENCE

An essay's arguments are made up of claims, which in turn are backed by supporting evidence. This evidence can be drawn from a number of sources. Some essay prompts will include texts from which to draw supporting evidence. Other essays will require the writer to use his or her own background knowledge of the issue. For some essay prompts, it may be appropriate to use personal anecdotes and experiences. Regardless of the source of the evidence, it is important that it be conveyed in a clear, specific, and accurate manner.

PROVIDING SPECIFIC EXAMPLES

In body paragraphs, general statements should be followed with specific examples that will help to convince the reader that the argument has merit. These specific examples do not bring new ideas to the paragraph; rather, they explain or defend the general ideas that have already been stated. A poorly written essay will be full of general claims supported by little to no evidence or specific examples. Conversely, successful essays will use multiple specific examples to back up general claims.

EXAMPLES OF GENERAL AND SPECIFIC STATEMENTS

The following are some examples of general statements, followed by examples of specific statements that provide more detailed support of an idea.

> **General**: Students may get distracted online or access harmful websites.

> **Specific**: Some students spend too much time using chat features or social media, or they get caught up in online games. Others spend time reading websites that have nothing to do with an assignment.

> **Specific**: Teens often think they are hidden behind their computer screens. However, providing personal information online can lead to danger in the real world.

> **General**: Schools can teach students how to use technology appropriately and expose them to new tools.

Specific: Schools can help students learn how to use technology to work on class projects, communicate with classmates and teachers, and carry out research for classwork.

Specific: Providing students with laptops or tablets will allow them to get lots of practice using technology and programs at home, and only school districts can ensure that these tools are distributed widely, especially to students who may not have access to them otherwise.

INCORPORATING SOURCES

Providing evidence from outside sources is an excellent way to provide support for the claims in an essay. Some essay prompts will include texts that may be cited in the essay, or writers may want to cite sources from memory. In either case, this supporting evidence should be incorporated smoothly into the essay. Context should be provided for the quote, and the quote should always be followed by a discussion of its importance or relevance to the essay.

> **HELPFUL HINT**
>
> In an essay, a quote never speaks for itself; the writer must always explain where it came from and why it is important.

When using outside sources, it is vital to credit the author or source within the text. Usually a full citation isn't needed—it can simply be sufficient to note the author's name in the text. And, as always, the writer must make sure to place direct quotations in quotation marks.

> **INCORPORATING SOURCES EXAMPLE**
>
> In addition to helping students work better with each other, technology can also help students communicate more effectively with teachers. A recent study from the University of Montana showed that over 75 percent of students have at some point been too intimidated to speak up in class, even if they thought they had something valuable to contribute (Higgins, 2015). But what if technology could provide a way to make speaking up easier? Private online messaging, comment boards for questions, and online tutorials are all made possible by introducing technology to the classroom. A well-trained teacher will be able to use these resources to encourage more effective classroom communication. In my personal experience, I have seen numerous students respond effectively when given the chance to communicate in the privacy of an online interaction.
>
> **Explanation**: This first-person paragraph incorporates two sources: a scientific study and a personal anecdote from the author.

WRITING WELL

Although the content of an essay is of primary importance, the writing itself will also factor into the essay's final score. Writing well means that the language and tone are appropriate for the purpose and audience of the essay, the flow of ideas and the relationships among them are logical and clear, and the sentences are varied enough to keep the reader interested.

TRANSITIONS

Transitions are words, phrases, and ideas that help connect ideas throughout a text both between sentences and between paragraphs. Transitions can be used to imply a range of relationships, including cause and effect, sequence, contradictions, and continuance of an idea. Consistent and creative use of transitions will help the essay flow logically from one idea to the next and will make the essay easy for the reader to follow.

> **HELPFUL HINT**
>
> Common transitions include *then, next, in other words, as well, in addition to, another, because, first, finally, in conclusion, however, in fact, therefore,* and *on the other hand.*

Transitions between paragraphs can also be polished by starting paragraphs with references to ideas mentioned in previous paragraphs or by ending them with a transition to the next topic. Such guideposts will guide the reader from one paragraph to the next.

EXAMPLES OF TRANSITIONS

Teens often think they are hidden behind their computer screens. <u>However,</u> providing personal information online can lead to danger in the real world.

<u>In addition to</u> helping students work better with each other, technology can also help students communicate more effectively with teachers.

They <u>also</u> have the opportunity to teach each other new skills.

SYNTAX

A variety of well-written sentences will help maintain the reader's interest in the essay. To create this theme, a writer can use sentences that differ in length and that begin with varying words, rather than repeating the same word at the start of each new sentence. It is also important for the writer to use a mix of different sentence structures, including simple, complex, compound, and compound-complex sentences.

SYNTAX EXAMPLE

Technology can be a powerful tool for collaboration. When all of the students in a classroom have access to reliable laptops or tablets, they are able to more effectively share information and work together on projects. Students can communicate quickly via email, share files through a cloud service, and use a shared calendar for scheduling. They also have the opportunity to teach each other new skills since each student may bring to the group unique knowledge about particular apps or programs. When the availability of technology is limited or inconsistent, these opportunities are lost.

> **Explanation**: This paragraph starts with a short, simple sentence and follows with a longer, more complex sentence. The next sentence is also long, but it is a simple sentence with a single clause. The second-to-last sentence is complicated with multiple clauses, but it is immediately followed with a short, easy-to-read statement that ends the paragraph.

WORD CHOICE AND TONE

The words a writer chooses influence the reader's assessment of the essay. When writing essays, it is always necessary to choose words that are appropriate to the task.

For instance, a formal essay on an academic topic may benefit from complex sentences and an expansive vocabulary. However, a first-person essay on a personal topic may use a more casual vocabulary and organization. In general, when writing for exam graders, it is best to use clear, direct vocabulary and avoid using vague, general words such as good, bad, very, or a lot. Showing variety in word choice can also help improve an essay's score. However, it is better to use more familiar vocabulary than to try to impress the exam grader with unfamiliar words or words that do not fit the context of the essay.

WORD CHOICE EXAMPLES

Technology has changed massively in recent years, but today's generation barely notices—high school students are already experienced with the internet, computers, apps, cameras, cell phones, and more. It is inevitable that these technologies will be begin to make their way into classrooms. Opponents of 1:1 technology programs might argue that students will be distracted or misuse the technology, but that is exactly why schools must teach them to use it. Students need to know how to navigate technology safely and effectively, and schools have a responsibility to ensure they learn these skills. By providing each student with a laptop or tablet, schools can help students apply technology to work more effectively with other students, communicate with teachers and classmates, and conduct research for class projects.

Technology is everywhere in modern life. We've all walked into a coffee shop full of laptops or have seen people walking with their phones in front of their faces. I know I've often looked up from my tablet to realize I've missed a whole conversation. With technology everywhere, it seems obvious that we would start using it in classrooms. Opponents of 1:1 technology programs say that technology will be too distracting or will be abused by students, but it seems like that's an even more important reason for students to learn how to use it. Schools are where students learn all kinds of life skills, and technology is just another skill to learn. By giving students laptops or tablets, schools can help students work better with each other, work better with teachers, and learn to do better research.

Explanation: The two paragraphs above discuss the same topic. The first has a word choice and tone for an academic essay; the second is written in a more relaxed, personal style.

MANAGING TIME

When working on an essay under time constraints, it is important to manage time wisely. Simply launching into the introduction will likely result in a hurried, unorganized essay and a low score. Instead, the writer should take a few minutes to plan.

HELPFUL HINT

Underline key words in the prompt so you can refer to them while writing the essay. This can help keep you and your essay focused.

As a first step, the writer should thoroughly read the prompt and any accompanying texts, and then determine the type of essay that is required. Next, the writer must decide on a thesis and what kind of supporting evidence to use. Once the thesis is clear, it is a good idea for the writer to create a brief outline of the essay. This whole process should only take a few minutes, leaving the bulk of the time for writing. However, it is always a good idea to leave a few minutes at the end to proofread and revise as necessary.

EXAMPLE ESSAYS

PROMPT: The rise in popularity of e-cigarettes has reduced the overall smoking rate according to the Centers for Disease Control and Prevention. Many hail the new technology for helping smokers quit traditional tobacco cigarettes. However, others raise concerns about the appeal of e-cigarettes to young people and advocate FDA regulation of e-cigarettes to prevent negative side effects of their use on a new generation of smokers.

In your essay, take a position on this question. You may write about either one of the two points of view given, or you may present a different point of view on this question. Use specific reasons and examples to support your position.

EXAMPLE ESSAY ONE

For decades, youth smoking was a major concern for both parents and public health advocates. With education campaigns informing youth of the dangers of smoking and legal action taken against tobacco producers for their advertising tactics, the number of youth smoking traditional cigarettes has never been lower. But new technology is threatening to overturn that progress as electronic cigarettes (e-cigarettes) have skyrocketed in popularity among both adults and youth. E-cigarettes should be regulated by the FDA to prevent youth from smoking since the long-term effects of e-cig use are unknown, youth are still becoming addicted to nicotine, and e-cigs could be a gateway to traditional smoking.

Smoking has long been a way for young people to feel cool or sophisticated. Popular culture, including film and television, glamorized smoking and led generations of Americans to pick up the habit. Although traditional smoking is no longer considered cool, the use of e-cigarettes, or vaping, threatens to take the same position in popular culture. Companies which produce traditional cigarettes have long been banned from advertising their products on television, but because e-cigarettes are not regulated by the FDA, there are no restrictions on their advertisement. This allows e-cig companies to reach youth through a wide range of media. Furthermore, the gadget-like design of e-cigs and the variety of candy-like flavors make them especially appealing to youth—a tactic that seems designed to hook a new generation on smoking.

This is particularly concerning as the long-term effects of vaping are not yet known for either adults or youth. The technology is too new to have been studied adequately. The FDA must study a drug for years before it can become available to the general public. Yet a device that delivers a highly-addictive substance remains unregulated. It is true that e-cigarettes are healthier for smokers than traditional cigarettes, but we cannot yet know the impact on youth who would have otherwise not smoked but for the easy access to these drug-delivery devices.

In addition, we do know that nicotine is a highly-addictive drug and that once this habit is established, it is very difficult to quit. If nothing else, this is a wasteful way for young people to spend their money. But even more concerning is the danger that nicotine use could alter the brain chemistry of young people and potentially make them prone to other addictions. Even if vaping does not become a gateway to hard drug use, it does make the leap to traditional smoking much more likely, and we know how harmful cigarettes have been.

The FDA has a responsibility to protect the public's health, and it is clear that regulation is needed to stop the momentum of the e-cigarette industry from getting youth addicted to their products. Although long-term health effects of vaping are unknown at this time, we must be cautious and err on the side of safety. At the very least, youth can be spared from an expensive, addictive habit; at best, an entire generation can live longer, healthier lives.

Explanation: This response provides good context for the discussion of the topic and takes a clear stance on the issue raised in the prompt. Strong examples and sound reasoning support the thesis. The essay is cohesive, and strong transitions connect ideas. Vocabulary and tone are appropriate, and the conclusion leaves the reader with a sense of the importance of the issue. Overall, this response would receive a high score.

EXAMPLE ESSAY TWO

Everyone knows smoking is bad for you. So, it's good that lots of people are quitting, and I think e-cigarettes, or vapes as they are also called, are helping people quit. Even though I don't use them, I know some people who use vapes, and they seem pretty healthy. It may be true that e-cigarettes have harmful side effects, but it will be too far into the future before we know. The FDA should be studying this so that we do know if vapes are safe to use, especially for kids. No one wants kids to get hooked on drugs or to be unhealthy.

If they do start smoking, it is better for the kids to use e-cigarettes. They are less harmful because they don't use real tobacco or produce the terrible smelling smoke that normal cigarettes do. Some of my friends vape, and I don't even mind being in the same room. They actually smell pretty sweet. I don't think it's good to vape too much, but once in a while is fine, and I hope people make good choices about smoking.

> **Explanation**: This response does not sufficiently address the prompt. The writer seems to disagree with the position of FDA regulation of e-cigarettes but does not develop this into a clear thesis. The writer's position is further confused by stating that the FDA should be studying the matter. The response is short and lacks adequate supporting detail. Although some personal examples are used, they are weak and a divergence from the main point. Although free of most errors, the language is simplistic, personal pronouns are overused, and the tone is not appropriate for academic writing. Overall, this response would receive a low score.

Part III: Mathematics

4

Numbers and Operations

This chapter provides a review of the basic yet critical components of mathematics such as manipulating fractions, comparing numbers, and using units. These concepts will provide the foundation for more complex mathematical operations in later chapters.

Types of Numbers

Numbers are placed in categories based on their properties.

- A **natural number** is greater than 0 and has no decimal or fraction attached. These are also sometimes called counting numbers {1, 2, 3, 4, ...}.

- **Whole numbers** are natural numbers and the number 0 {0, 1, 2, 3, 4, ...}.

- **Integers** include positive and negative natural numbers and 0 {..., –4, –3, –2, –1, 0, 1, 2, 3, 4, ...}.

- A **rational number** can be represented as a fraction. Any decimal part must terminate or resolve into a repeating pattern. Examples include -12, $-\frac{4}{5}$, 0.36, $7.\overline{7}$, $26\frac{1}{2}$, etc.

- An **irrational number** cannot be represented as a fraction. An irrational decimal number never ends and never resolves into a repeating pattern. Examples include $-\sqrt{7}$, π, and $0.34567989135...$

- A **real number** is a number that can be represented by a point on a number line. Real numbers include all the rational and irrational numbers.

- An **imaginary number** includes the imaginary unit i, where $i = \sqrt{-1}$ Because $i^2 = -1$, imaginary numbers produce a negative value when squared. Examples of imaginary numbers include $-4i$, $0.75i$, $i\sqrt{2}$ and $\frac{8}{3}i$.

▸ A **complex number** is in the form $a + bi$, where a and b are real numbers. Examples of complex numbers include $3 + 2i$, $-4 + i$, $\sqrt{3} - i\sqrt[3]{5}$ and $\frac{5}{8} - \frac{7i}{8}$. All imaginary numbers are also complex.

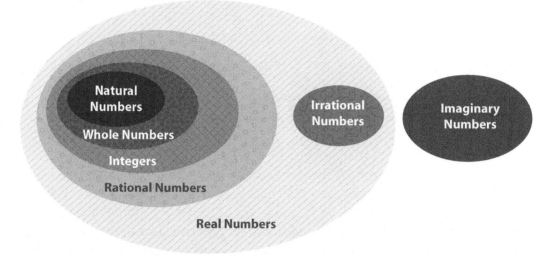

Figure 4.1. Types of Numbers

The **factors** of a natural number are all the numbers that can multiply together to make the number. For example, the factors of 24 are 1, 2, 3, 4, 6, 8, 12, and 24. Every natural number is either prime or composite. A **prime number** is a number that is only divisible by itself and 1. (The number 1 is not considered prime.) Examples of prime numbers are 2, 3, 7, and 29. The number 2 is the only even prime number. A **composite number** has more than two factors. For example, 6 is composite because its factors are 1, 6, 2, and 3. Every composite number can be written as a unique product of prime numbers, called the **prime factorization** of the number. For example, the prime factorization of 90 is $90 = 2 \times 3^2 \times 5$. All integers are either even or odd. An even number is divisible by 2; an odd number is not.

> **HELPFUL HINT**
>
> If a real number is a natural number (e.g., 50), then it is also a whole number, an integer, and a rational number.

PROPERTIES OF NUMBER SYSTEMS

A system is **closed** under an operation if performing that operation on two elements of the system results in another element of that system. For example, the integers are closed under the operations of addition, subtraction, and multiplication but not division. Adding, subtracting, or multiplying two integers results in another integer. However, dividing two integers could result in a rational number that is not an integer $\left(-2 \div 3 = \frac{-2}{3}\right)$.

▸ The rational numbers are closed under all four operations (except for division by 0).

▸ The real numbers are closed under all four operations.

▸ The complex numbers are closed under all four operations.

▸ The irrational numbers are NOT closed under ANY of the four operations.

The **commutative property** holds for an operation if order does not matter when performing the operation. For example, multiplication is commutative for integers: $(-2)(3) = (3)(-2)$.

The **associative property** holds for an operation if elements can be regrouped without changing the result. For example, addition is associative for real numbers: $-3 + (-5 + 4) = (-3 + -5) + 4$

The **distributive property** of multiplication over addition allows a product of sums to be written as a sum of products: $a(b + c) = ab + ac$. The value a is distributed over the sum $(b + c)$. The acronym FOIL (First, Outer, Inner, Last) is a useful way to remember the distributive property.

When an operation is performed with an **identity element** and another element a, the result is a. The identity element for multiplication on real numbers is $1(a \times 1 = a)$, and for addition is $0(a + 0 = a)$.

An operation of a system has an **inverse element** if applying that operation with the inverse element results in the identity element. For example, the inverse element of a for addition is $-a$ because $a + (-a) = 0$. The inverse element of a for multiplication is $\frac{1}{a}$ because $a \times \frac{1}{a} = 1$.

SAMPLE QUESTIONS

1) Classify the following numbers as natural, whole, integer, rational, or irrational. (The numbers may have more than one classification.)

   A. 72

   B. $-\frac{2}{3}$

   C. $\sqrt{5}$

   Answers:

   A. The number is **natural**, **whole**, an **integer**, and **rational** (72 can be written as the fraction $\frac{72}{1}$).

   B. The fraction is **rational**.

   C. The number is **irrational**. (It cannot be written as a fraction, and written as a decimal is approximately 2.2360679... Notice this decimal does not terminate nor does it have a repeating pattern.)

2)   **Determine the real and imaginary parts of the following complex numbers.**

   A.   20

   B. $10 - i$

   C. $15i$

Answers:

A complex number is in the form of $a + bi$, where a is the real part and b is the imaginary part.

   A. $20 = 20 + 0i$
         The real part is 20, and there is no imaginary part. (The imaginary part is 0.)

   B. $10 - i = 10 - 1i$
         The real part is 10, and −1 is the imaginary part.

   C. $15i = 0 + 15i$
         The real part is 0, and the imaginary part is 15.

3)   **Answer True or False for each statement:**

   A.   The natural numbers are closed under subtraction.

   B.   The sum of two irrational numbers is irrational.

   C.   The sum of a rational number and an irrational number is irrational.

Answers:

   A.   **False.** Subtracting the natural number 7 from 2 results in $2 - 7 = -5$, which is an integer, but not a natural number.

   B.   **False.** For example, $(5 - 2\sqrt{3}) + (2 + 2\sqrt{3}) = 7$. The sum of two irrational numbers in this example is a whole number, which is not irrational. The sum of a rational number and an irrational number is sometimes rational and sometimes irrational.

   C.   **True.** Because irrational numbers have decimal parts that are unending and with no pattern, adding a repeating or terminating decimal will still result in an unending decimal without a pattern.

4)   **Answer True or False for each statement:**

   A.   The associative property applies for multiplication in the real numbers.

   B.   The commutative property applies to all real numbers and all operations.

Answers:

   A.   **True.** For all real numbers, $a \times (b \times c) = (a \times b) \times c$. Order of multiplication does not change the result.

   B.   **False.** The commutative property does not work for subtraction or division on real numbers. For example, $12 - 5 = 7$, but $5 - 12 = -7$ and $10 \div 2 = 5$, but $2 \div 10 = \frac{1}{5}$.

SCIENTIFIC NOTATION

Scientific notation is a method of representing very large and small numbers in the form $a \times 10^n$, where a is a value between 1 and 10, and n is a nonzero integer.

For example, the number 927,000,000 is written in scientific notation as 9.27×10^8. Multiplying 9.27 by 10 eight times gives 927,000,000. When performing operations with scientific notation, the final answer should be in the form $a \times 10^n$.

65000000.
7 6 5 4 3 2 1

6.5×10^7

.0000987
-1-2-3-4-5

9.87×10^{-5}

Figure 4.2. Scientific Notation

When adding and subtracting numbers in scientific notation, the power of 10 must be the same for all numbers. This results in like terms in which the a terms are added or subtracted and the 10^n remains unchanged. When multiplying numbers in scientific notation, multiply the a factors, and then multiply that answer by 10 to the sum of the exponents. For division, divide the a factors and subtract the exponents.

SAMPLE QUESTIONS

5)   Simplify: $(3.8 \times 10^3) + (4.7 \times 10^2)$

Answer:

$(3.8 \times 10^3) + (4.7 \times 10^2)$	
$3.8 \times 10^3 = 3.8 \times 10 \times 10^2 = 38 \times 10^2$	To add, the exponents of 10 must be the same. Change the first number so the power of 10 is 2.
$38 \times 10^2 + 4.7 \times 10^2 = 42.7 \times 10^2$	Add the a terms together.
$= \mathbf{4.27 \times 10^3}$	Write the number in proper scientific notation.

6)   Simplify: $(8.1 \times 10^{-5})(1.4 \times 10^7)$

Answer:

$(8.1 \times 10^{-5})(1.4 \times 10^7)$	
$= 11.34 \times 10^2$	Multiply the a factors and add the exponents on the base of 10.

$$= 1.134 \times 10^3$$

> Write the number in proper scientific notation by placing the decimal so that the first number is between 1 and 10 and adjusting the exponent accordingly.

POSITIVE AND NEGATIVE NUMBERS

Positive numbers are greater than 0, and **negative numbers** are less than 0. Both positive and negative numbers can be shown on a **number line**.

Figure 4.3. Number Line

The **absolute value** of a number is the distance the number is from 0. Since distance is always positive, the absolute value of a number is always positive. The absolute value of a is denoted $|a|$. For example, $|-2| = 2$ since -2 is two units away from 0.

Positive and negative numbers can be added, subtracted, multiplied, and divided. The sign of the resulting number is governed by a specific set of rules shown in the table below.

Table 4.1. Operations with Positive and Negative Numbers

Adding Real Numbers		Subtracting Real Numbers	
Positive + Positive = Positive	$7 + 8 = 15$	Negative – Positive = Negative	$-7 - 8 =$ $-7 + (-8) =$ -15
Negative + Negative = Negative	$-7 + (-8) =$ -15	Positive – Negative = Positive	$7 - (-8) =$ $7 + 8 = 15$
Negative + Positive OR Positive + Negative = Keep the sign of the number with larger absolute value and subtract the absolute values of the numbers	$-7 + 8 = 1$ $7 + -8 = -1$	Negative – Negative = Change the subtraction to addition and change the sign of the second number; then use addition rules.	$-7 - (-8) =$ $-7 + 8 = 1$ $-8 - (-7) =$ $-8 + 7 = -1$
Positive × Positive = Positive	$8 \times 4 = 32$	Positive ÷ Positive = Positive	$8 \div 4 = 2$

Multiplying Real Numbers		Dividing Real Numbers	
Negative × Negative = Positive	−8 × (−4) = 32	Negative ÷ Negative = Positive	−8 ÷ (−4) = 2
Positive × Negative OR Negative × Positive = Negative	8 × (−4) = −32 −8 × 4 = −32	Positive ÷ Negative OR Negative ÷ Positive = Negative	8 ÷ (−4) = −2 −8 ÷ 4 = −2

SAMPLE QUESTIONS

7)   Add or subtract the following real numbers:

   A. $-18 + 12$

   B. $-3.64 + (-2.18)$

   C. $9.37 - 4.25$

   D. $86 - (-20)$

Answers:

   A.   Since $|-18| > |12|$, the answer is negative: $|-18| - |12| = 6$. So the answer is **−6**.

   B.   Adding two negative numbers results in a negative number. Add the values: **−5.82**.

   C.   The first number is larger than the second, so the final answer is positive: **5.12**.

   D.   Change the subtraction to addition, change the sign of the second number, and then add: $86 - (-20) = 86 + 20 = $ **106**.

8)   Multiply or divide the following real numbers:

   A. $\left(\frac{10}{3}\right)\left(-\frac{9}{5}\right)$

   B. $\frac{-64}{-10}$

   C. $(2.2)(3.3)$

   D. $-52 \div 13$

Answers:

   A.   Multiply the numerators, multiply the denominators, and simplify: $\frac{-90}{15}$ = **−6**.

   B.   A negative divided by a negative is a positive number: **6.4**.

   C.   The parentheses indicate multiplication: **7.26**.

   D.   Dividing a negative by a positive number gives a negative answer: **−4**.

ORDER OF OPERATIONS

The **order of operations** is simply the order in which operations are performed. **PEMDAS** is a common way to remember the order of operations:

- ▶ Parentheses
- ▶ Exponents
- ▶ Multiplication
- ▶ Division
- ▶ Addition
- ▶ Subtraction

Multiplication and division, and addition and subtraction, are performed together from left to right. So, performing multiple operations on a set of numbers is a four-step process:

1. P: Calculate expressions inside parentheses, brackets, braces, etc.
2. E: Calculate exponents and square roots.
3. MD: Calculate any remaining multiplication and division in order from left to right.
4. AS: Calculate any remaining addition and subtraction in order from left to right.

Always work from left to right within each step when simplifying expressions.

SAMPLE QUESTIONS

9)   Simplify: $2(21 - 14) + 6 \div (-2) \times 3 - 10$

Answer:

$2(21 - 14) + 6 \div (-2) \times 3 - 10$	
$= 2(7) + 6 \div (-2) \times 3 - 10$	Calculate expressions inside parentheses.
$14 + 6 \div (-2) \times 3 - 10$ $= 14 + (-3) \times 3 - 10$ $= 14 + (-9) - 10$	There are no exponents or radicals, so perform multiplication and division from left to right.
$5 - 10 = \mathbf{-5}$	Perform addition and subtraction from left to right.

10)   Simplify: $-(3)^2 + 4(5) + (5 - 6)^2 - 8$

Answer:

$-(3)^2 + 4(5) + (5 - 6)^2 - 8$	
$-(3)^2 + 4(5) + (-1)^2 - 8$	Calculate expressions inside parentheses.
$= -9 + 4(5) + 1 - 8$	Simplify exponents and radicals.

$= -9 + 20 + 1 - 8$	Perform multiplication and division from left to right.
$= 11 + 1 - 8 = 12 - 8$ $= \mathbf{4}$	Perform addition and subtraction from left to right.

11) **Simplify:** $\dfrac{(7 - 9)^3 + 8(10 - 12)}{4^2 - 5^2}$

Answer:

$\dfrac{(7 - 9)^3 + 8(10 - 12)}{4^2 - 5^2}$	
$= \dfrac{(-2)^3 + 8(-2)}{4^2 - 5^2}$	Calculate expressions inside parentheses.
$= \dfrac{-8 + (-16)}{16 - 25}$	Simplify exponents and radicals.
$= \dfrac{-24}{-9}$	Perform addition and subtraction from left to right.
$= \dfrac{\mathbf{8}}{\mathbf{3}}$	Simplify.

Units of Measurement

The standard units for the metric and American systems are shown below, along with the prefixes used to express metric units.

Table 4.2. Units and conversion factors

Dimension	American	SI
length	inch/foot/yard/mile	meter
mass	ounce/pound/ton	gram
volume	cup/pint/quart/gallon	liter
force	pound-force	newton
pressure	pound-force per square inch	pascal
work and energy	cal/British thermal unit	joule
temperature	Fahrenheit	kelvin
charge	faraday	coulomb

Go on

Table 4.3. Metric Prefixes

Prefix	Symbol	Multiplication Factor
tera	T	1,000,000,000,000
giga	G	1,000,000,000
mega	M	1,000,000
kilo	k	1,000
hecto	h	100
deca	da	10
base unit	--	--
deci	d	0.1
centi	c	0.01
milli	m	0.001
micro	μ	0.000001
nano	n	0.000000001
pico	p	0.000000000001

HELPFUL HINT

A mnemonic device to help remember the metric system is *King Henry Drinks Under Dark Chocolate Moon* (KHDUDCM).

Units can be converted within a single system or between systems. When converting from one unit to another unit, a conversion factor (a numeric multiplier used to convert a value with a unit to another unit) is used. The process of converting between units using a conversion factor is sometimes known as dimensional analysis.

Table 4.4. Conversion Factors

1 in. = 2.54 cm	1 lb. = 0.454 kg
1 yd. = 0.914 m	1 cal = 4.19 J
1 mi. = 1.61 km	1 degree F = $\frac{9}{5}$ C + 32 degree C
1 gal. = 3.785 L	1 cm^3 = 1 mL
1 oz. = 28.35 g	1 hr = 3600 s

SAMPLE QUESTIONS

12) **Convert the following measurements in the metric system.**

    A.   4.25 kilometers to meters

    B.   8 m^2 to mm^2

Answers:

A. $4.25 \text{ km} \left(\frac{1000 \text{ m}}{1 \text{ km}} \right) = \textbf{4250 m}$ (because m is a smaller unit than km, multiply by 1000)

B. $\frac{8 \text{ m}^2}{} \times \frac{1000 \text{ mm}}{1 \text{ m}} \times \frac{1000 \text{ mm}}{1 \text{ m}} = \textbf{8,000,000 mm}^2$

Since the units are square units (m²), multiply by the conversion factor twice, so that both meters cancel (and mm × mm = mm²).

13) **Convert the following measurements in the American system.**

A.   12 feet to inches

B.   7 yd² to ft²

Answers:

A. $12 \text{ ft} \left(\frac{12 \text{ in}}{1 \text{ ft}} \right) = \textbf{144 in}$ (since inches is a smaller unit, multiply by 12 inches to get feet)

B. $7 \text{ yd}^2 \left(\frac{9 \text{ ft}^2}{1 \text{ yd}^2} \right) = \textbf{63 ft}^2$

Since the units are square units (ft²), multiply by the conversion factor twice: $\left(\frac{3 \text{ ft}}{1 \text{ yd}} \right) \times \left(\frac{3 \text{ ft}}{1 \text{ yd}} \right) = \left(\frac{9 \text{ ft}^2}{1 \text{ yd}^2} \right)$. Yards squared cancel, leaving square feet.

14) **Convert the following measurements in the metric system to the American system.**

A.   23 meters to feet

B.   10 m² to yd²

Answers:

A. $23 \text{ m}((3.28 \text{ ft})/(1 \text{ m})) = \textbf{75.44 ft}$

B. $\frac{10 \text{ m}^2}{} \times \frac{1.094 \text{ yd}}{1 \text{ m}} \times \frac{1.094 \text{ yd}}{1 \text{ m}} = \textbf{11.97 yd}^2$

15) **Convert the following measurements in the American system to the metric system.**

A.   8 in³ to milliliters

B.   16 kilograms to pounds

Answers:

A. $8 \text{ in}^3 \left(\frac{16.39 \text{ ml}}{1 \text{ in}^3} \right) = \textbf{131.12 mL}$

Because the conversion factor already has cubic units in it, it only needs to be multiplied once.

B. $16 \text{ kg} \left(\frac{2.2 \text{ lb}}{1 \text{ kg}} \right) = \textbf{35.2 lb}$

Decimals and Fractions

Decimals

A **decimal** is a number that contains a decimal point. A decimal number is an alternative way of writing a fraction. The place value for a decimal includes **tenths** (one place after the decimal), **hundredths** (two places after the decimal), **thousandths** (three places after the decimal), etc.

Table 4.5. Place Values		
1,000,000	10^6	millions
100,000	10^5	hundred thousands
10,000	10^4	ten thousands
1,000	10^3	thousands
100	10^2	hundreds
10	10^1	tens
1	10^0	ones
.		decimal
$\frac{1}{10}$	10^{-1}	tenths
$\frac{1}{100}$	10^{-2}	hundredths
1/1000	10^{-3}	thousandths

Decimals can be added, subtracted, multiplied, and divided:

HELPFUL HINT

To determine which way to move the decimal after multiplying, remember that changing the decimal should always make the final answer smaller.

► To add or subtract decimals, line up the decimal point and perform the operation, keeping the decimal point in the same place in the answer.

► To multiply decimals, first multiply the numbers without the decimal points. Then, add the number of decimal places to the right of the decimal point in the original numbers and place the decimal point in the answer so that there are that many places to the right of the decimal.

► When dividing decimals move the decimal point to the right in order to make the divisor a whole number and move the decimal the same number of places in the dividend. Divide the numbers without

$$4.2 \leftarrow \text{quotient}$$
$$2.5\overline{)10.5} \leftarrow \text{dividend}$$
$$\uparrow$$
$$\text{divisor}$$

Figure 4.4. Division Terms

regard to the decimal. Then, place the decimal point of the quotient directly above the decimal point of the dividend.

SAMPLE QUESTIONS

16) Simplify: 24.38 + 16.51 − 29.87

   Answer:

24.38 + 16.51 − 29.87	
24.38 + 16.51 = 40.89	Align the decimals and apply the order of operations left to right.
40.89 − 29.87 = **11.02**	

17) Simplify: (10.4)(18.2)

   Answer:

(10.4)(18.2)	
104 × 182 = 18,928	Multiply the numbers ignoring the decimals.
18,928 → 189.28	The original problem includes two decimal places (one in each number), so move the decimal point in the answer so that there are two places after the decimal point.

   Estimating is a good way to check the answer: 10.4 ≈ 10, 18.2 ≈ 18, and 10 × 18 = 180.

18) Simplify: 80 ÷ 2.5

   Answer:

80 ÷ 2.5	
80 → 800 2.5 → 25	The divisor is 2.5. Move the decimal one place to the right (multiply 2.5 by 10) so that the divisor is a whole number. Since the decimal point of the divisor was moved one place to the right, the decimal point in the dividend must be moved one place right (multiplying it by 10 as well).

$$800 \div 25 = 32 \qquad \Big| \text{Divide normally.}$$

FRACTIONS

A **fraction** is a number that can be written in the form $\frac{a}{b}$, where b is not equal to 0. The a part of the fraction is the **numerator** (top number) and the b part of the fraction is the **denominator** (bottom number).

If the denominator of a fraction is greater than the numerator, the value of the fraction is less than 1 and it is called a **proper fraction** (for example, $\frac{3}{5}$ is a proper fraction). In an **improper fraction**, the denominator is less than the numerator and the value of the fraction is greater than 1 (example: $\frac{8}{3}$ is an improper fraction). An improper fraction can be written as a mixed number. A **mixed number** has a whole number part and a proper fraction part. Improper fractions can be converted to mixed numbers by dividing the numerator by the denominator, which gives the whole number part, and the remainder becomes the numerator of the proper fraction part. (For example, the improper fraction $\frac{25}{9}$ is equal to mixed number $2\frac{7}{9}$ because 9 divides into 25 two times, with a remainder of 7.)

Conversely, mixed numbers can be converted to improper fractions. To do so, determine the numerator of the improper fraction by multiplying the denominator by the whole number, and then adding the numerator. The final number is written as the (now larger) numerator over the original denominator.

Fractions with the same denominator can be added or subtracted by simply adding or subtracting the numerators; the denominator will remain unchanged. To add or subtract fractions with different denominators, find the **least common denominator (LCD)** of all the fractions. The LCD is the smallest number exactly divisible by each denominator. (For example, the least common denominator of the numbers 2, 3, and 8 is 24.) Once the LCD has been found, each fraction should be written in an equivalent form with the LCD as the denominator. To do this, each fraction can be multiplied by 1 in the form $\frac{a}{a}$, where a is the value necessary to convert the denominator to the LCD. Once all fractions have the same denominator, the numerators can be added and the fractions reduced if necessary.

> **HELPFUL HINT**
>
> To convert mixed numbers to improper fractions:
> $$a\frac{m}{n} = \frac{n \times a + m}{n}$$

To multiply fractions, the numerators are multiplied together and denominators are multiplied together. If there are any mixed numbers, they should first be changed to improper fractions. Then, the numerators are multiplied together and the denominators are multiplied together. The fraction can then be reduced if necessary. To divide fractions, multiply the first fraction by the reciprocal of the second.

> **HELPFUL HINT**
>
> $$\frac{a}{b} \pm \frac{c}{b} = \frac{a \pm c}{b}$$
> $$\frac{a}{b} \times \frac{c}{d} = \frac{ac}{bd}$$
> $$\frac{a}{b} \div \frac{c}{d} = \left(\frac{a}{b}\right)\left(\frac{d}{c}\right) = \frac{ad}{bc}$$

Any common denominator can be used to add or subtract fractions. The quickest way to find a common denominator of a set of values is simply to multiply all the values together. The result might not be the least common denominator, but it will get the job done.

SAMPLE QUESTIONS

19) Simplify: $2\frac{3}{5} + 3\frac{1}{4} - 1\frac{1}{2}$

Answer:

$2\frac{3}{5} + 3\frac{1}{4} - 1\frac{1}{2}$	
$= 2\frac{12}{20} + 3\frac{5}{20} - 1\frac{10}{20}$	Change each fraction so it has a denominator of 20, which is the LCD of 5, 4, and 2.
$2 + 3 - 1 = 4$ $\frac{12}{20} + \frac{5}{20} - \frac{10}{20} = \frac{7}{20}$	Add and subtract the whole numbers together and the fractions together.
$\mathbf{4\frac{7}{20}}$	Combine to get the final answer (a mixed number).

20) Simplify: $\frac{7}{8} \times 3\frac{1}{3}$

Answer:

$\frac{7}{8} \times 3\frac{1}{3}$	
$3\frac{1}{3} = \frac{10}{3}$	Change the mixed number to an improper fraction.
$\frac{7}{8}\left(\frac{10}{3}\right) = \frac{7 \times 10}{8 \times 3}$ $= \frac{70}{24}$	Multiply the numerators together and the denominators together.
$= \frac{35}{12}$ $= \mathbf{2\frac{11}{12}}$	Reduce the fraction.

21) Simplify: $4\frac{1}{2} \div \frac{2}{3}$

Answer:

$4\frac{1}{2} \div \frac{2}{3}$	
$4\frac{1}{2} = \frac{9}{2}$	Change the mixed number to an improper fraction.

$\frac{9}{2} \div \frac{2}{3}$ $= \frac{9}{2} \times \frac{3}{2}$ $= \frac{27}{4}$	Multiply the first fraction by the reciprocal of the second fraction.
$= 6\frac{3}{4}$	Simplify.

CONVERTING BETWEEN FRACTIONS AND DECIMALS

A fraction is converted to a decimal by using long division until there is no remainder and no pattern of repeating numbers occurs.

A decimal is converted to a fraction using the following steps:

▸ Place the decimal value as the numerator in a fraction with a denominator of 1.

▸ Multiply the fraction by $\frac{10}{10}$ for every digit in the decimal value, so that there is no longer a decimal in the numerator.

▸ Reduce the fraction.

SAMPLE QUESTIONS

22) **Write the fraction $\frac{7}{8}$ as a decimal.**

Answer:

$$\begin{array}{r} 0.875 \\ 8\overline{)7000} \\ -64\downarrow \\ \hline 60 \\ -56\downarrow \\ \hline 40 \end{array}$$	Divide the denominator into the numerator using long division.

23) **Write the fraction 5/11 as a decimal.**

Answer:

$$\begin{array}{r} 0.4545 \\ 11\overline{)50000} \\ -44\downarrow \\ \hline 60 \\ -55\downarrow \\ \hline 50 \\ -44\downarrow \\ \hline 60 \end{array}$$	Dividing using long division yields a repeating decimal.

24) Write the decimal 0.125 as a fraction.

Answer:

0.125	
$= \frac{0.125}{1}$	Create a fraction with 0.125 as the numerator and 1 as the denominator.
$\frac{0.125}{1} \times \frac{10}{10} \times \frac{10}{10} \times \frac{10}{10} = \frac{125}{1000}$	Multiple by 1 in the form 10/10 three times (one for each numeral after the decimal).
$= \frac{1}{8}$	Simplify.

Alternatively, recognize that 0.125 is read "one hundred twenty-five thousandths" and can therefore be written in fraction form as 125/1000.

ROUNDING AND ESTIMATION

Rounding is a way of simplifying a complicated number. The result of rounding will be a less precise value with which it is easier to write or perform operations. Rounding is performed to a specific place value, for example the thousands or tenths place.

The rules for rounding are as follows:

1. Underline the place value being rounded to.

2. Locate the digit one place value to the right of the underlined value. If this value is less than 5, then keep the underlined value and replace all digits to the right of the underlined value with 0. If the value to the right of the underlined digit is greater than 5, then increase the underlined digit by one and replace all digits to the right of it with 0.

> **HELPFUL HINT**
>
> Estimation can often be used to eliminate answer choices on multiple-choice tests without having to work the problem to completion.

Estimation is when numbers are rounded and then an operation is performed. This process can be used when working with large numbers to find a close, but not exact, answer.

SAMPLE QUESTIONS

25) Round the number 138,472 to the nearest thousands.

Answer:

138,472

138,472 ≈ **138,000**

| The 8 is in the thousands place, and the number to its right is 4. Because 4 is less than 5, the 8 remains and all numbers to the right become 0. |

26) The populations of five local towns are 12,341, 8975, 9431, 10,521, and 11,427. Estimate the total population to the nearest 1000 people.

Answer:

12,341 ≈ 12,000	
8975 ≈ 9000	
9431 ≈ 9000	Round each value to the thousands place.
10,521 ≈ 11,000	
11,427 ≈ 11,000	
12,000 + 9000 + 9000 + 11,000 + 11,000 = **52,000**	Add.

RATIOS

A **ratio** is a comparison of two numbers and can be represented as $\frac{a}{b}$, *a*:*b*, or *a* to *b*. The two numbers represent a constant relationship, not a specific value: for every *a* number of items in the first group, there will be *b* number of items in the second. For example, if the ratio of blue to red candies in a bag is 3:5, the bag will contain 3 blue candies for every 5 red candies. So, the bag might contain 3 blue candies and 5 red candies, or it might contain 30 blue candies and 50 red candies, or 36 blue candies and 60 red candies. All of these values are representative of the ratio 3:5 (which is the ratio in its lowest, or simplest, terms).

To find the *whole* when working with ratios, simply add the values in the ratio. For example, if the ratio of boys to girls in a class is 2:3, the *whole* is five: 2 out of every 5 students are boys, and 3 out of every 5 students are girls.

SAMPLE QUESTIONS

27) There are 10 boys and 12 girls in a first-grade class. What is the ratio of boys to the total number of students? What is the ratio of girls to boys?

Answer:

number of boys: 10 number of girls: 12 number of students: 22	Identify the variables.
number of boys : number of students $= 10 : 22$ $= \frac{10}{22}$ $= \frac{5}{11}$	Write out and simplify the ratio of boys to total students.
number of girls : number of boys $= 12 : 10$ $= \frac{12}{10}$ $= \frac{6}{5}$	Write out and simplify the ratio of girls to boys.

28) A family spends $600 a month on rent, $400 on utilities, $750 on groceries, and $550 on miscellaneous expenses. What is the ratio of the family's rent to their total expenses?

Answer:

rent $= 600$ utilities $= 400$ groceries $= 750$ miscellaneous $= 550$ total expenses $= 600 + 400 + 750 + 550 = 2300$	Identify the variables.
rent : total expenses $= 600 : 2300$ $= \frac{600}{2300}$ $= \frac{6}{23}$	Write out and simplify the ratio of rent to total expenses.

PROPORTIONS

A **proportion** is an equation which states that two ratios are equal. A proportion is given in the form $\frac{a}{b} = \frac{c}{d}$, where the a and d terms are the extremes and the b and c terms are the means. A proportion is solved using cross-multiplication ($ad = bc$) to create an equation with no fractional components. A proportion must have the same units in both numerators and both denominators.

SAMPLE QUESTIONS

29) Solve the proportion for x: $\frac{3x-5}{2} = \frac{x-8}{3}$.

Answer:

$\frac{(3x-5)}{2} = \frac{(x-8)}{3}$	
$3(3x-5) = 2(x-8)$	Cross-multiply.
$9x - 15 = 2x - 16$	
$7x - 15 = -16$	
$7x = -1$	Solve the equation for x.
$x = -\frac{1}{7}$	

30) A map is drawn such that 2.5 inches on the map equates to an actual distance of 40 miles. If the distance measured on the map between two cities is 17.25 inches, what is the actual distance between them in miles?

Answer:

$\frac{2.5}{40} = \frac{17.25}{x}$	Write a proportion where x equals the actual distance and each ratio is written as inches : miles.
$2.5x = 690$	Cross-multiply and divide to solve for x.
$x = 276$	
The two cities are **276 miles apart**.	

31) A factory knows that every 4 out of 1000 parts made will be defective. If in a month there are 125,000 parts made, how many of these parts will be defective?

Answer:

$\frac{4}{1000} = \frac{x}{125{,}000}$	Write a proportion where x is the number of defective parts made and both ratios are written as defective : total.
$1000x = 500{,}000$	Cross-multiply and divide to solve for x.
$x = 500$	
There are **500 defective parts** for the month.	

PERCENTAGES

A **percent** (or percentage) means per hundred and is expressed with a percent symbol (%). For example, 54% means 54 out of every 100. A percent can be converted to a decimal by removing the % symbol and moving the decimal point two places to the left, while a decimal can be converted to a percent by moving the decimal point two places to the right and attaching the % sign. A percent can be converted to a fraction by writing the percent as a fraction with 100 as the denominator and reducing. A fraction can be converted to a percent by performing the indicated division, multiplying the result by 100, and attaching the % sign.

The equation for finding percentages has three variables: the part, the whole, and the percent (which is expressed in the equation as a decimal). The equation, as shown below, can be rearranged to solve for any of these variables.

▶ $part = whole \times percent$

▶ $percent = \dfrac{part}{whole}$

▶ $whole = \dfrac{part}{percent}$

This set of equations can be used to solve percent word problems. All that's needed is to identify the part, whole, and/or percent, and then to plug those values into the appropriate equation and solve.

SAMPLE QUESTIONS

32) **Change the following values to the indicated form:**

   A.   18% to a fraction

   B. $\frac{3}{5}$ to a percent

   C.   1.125 to a percent

   D.   84% to a decimal

   Answers:

   A.   The percent is written as a fraction over 100 and reduced: $\frac{18}{100} = \frac{9}{50}$.

   B.   Dividing 3 by 5 gives the value 0.6, which is then multiplied by 100: **60%**.

   C.   The decimal point is moved two places to the right: $1.125 \times 100 =$ **112.5%**.

   D.   The decimal point is moved two places to the left: $84 \div 100 =$ **0.84**.

33) **In a school of 650 students, 54% of the students are boys. How many students are girls?**

Answer:

Percent of students who are girls = 100% − 54% = 46% percent = 46% = 0.46 whole = 650 students part = ?	Identify the variables.
part = whole × percent = 650 x 0.46 = 299 **There are 299 girls.**	Plug the variables into the appropriate equation.

Percent Change

Percent change problems involve a change from an original amount. Often percent change problems appear as word problems that include discounts, growth, or markups. In order to solve percent change problems, it's necessary to identify the percent change (as a decimal), the amount of change, and the original amount. (Keep in mind that one of these will be the value being solved for.) These values can then be plugged into the equations below:

- ► amount of change = original amount × percent change
- ► percent change = $\dfrac{\text{amount of change}}{\text{original amount}}$
- ► original amount = $\dfrac{\text{amount of change}}{\text{percent change}}$

SAMPLE QUESTIONS

34) An HDTV that originally cost $1,500 is on sale for 45% off. What is the sale price for the item?

Answer:

original amount =$1,500 percent change = 45% = 0.45 amount of change = ?	Identify the variables.
amount of change = original amount × percent change = 1500 × 0.45 = 675	Plug the variables into the appropriate equation.
1500 − 675 = 825 **The final price is $825.**	To find the new price, subtract the amount of change from the original price.

35) **A house was bought in 2000 for \$100,000 and sold in 2015 for \$120,000. What was the percent growth in the value of the house from 2000 to 2015?**

Answer:

original amount = \$100,000 amount of change = 120,000 − 100,000 = 20,000 percent change = ?	Identify the variables.
percent change = $\dfrac{\text{amount of change}}{\text{original amount}}$ $= \dfrac{20{,}000}{100{,}000}$ $= 0.20$	Plug the variables into the appropriate equation.
$0.20 \times 100 = \mathbf{20\%}$	To find the percent growth, multiply by 100.

EXPONENTS AND RADICALS

EXPONENTS

An expression in the form b^n is in an exponential notation where b is the **base** and n is an **exponent**. To perform the operation, multiply the base by itself the number of times indicated by the exponent. For example, 2^3 is equal to $2 \times 2 \times 2$ or 8.

Table 4.6. Operations with Exponents

Rule	Example	Explanation
$a^0 = 1$	$5^0 = 1$	Any base (except 0) to the 0 power is 1.
$a^{-n} = \dfrac{1}{a^n}$	$5^{-3} = \dfrac{1}{5^3}$	A negative exponent becomes positive when moved from numerator to denominator (or vice versa).
$a^m a^n = a^{m+n}$	$5^3 5^4 = 5^{3+4} = 5^7$	Add the exponents to multiply two powers with the same base.
$(a^m)^n = a^{m \times n}$	$(5^3)^4 = 5^{3(4)} = 5^{12}$	Multiply the exponents to raise a power to a power.
$\dfrac{a^m}{a^n} = a^{m-n}$	$\dfrac{5^4}{5^3} = 5^{4-3} = 5^1$	Subtract the exponents to divide two powers with the same base.
$(ab)^n = a^n b^n$	$(5 \times 6)^3 = 5^3 6^3$	Apply the exponent to each base to raise a product to a power.
$\left(\dfrac{a}{b}\right)^n = \dfrac{a^n}{b^n}$	$\left(\dfrac{5}{6}\right)^3 = \dfrac{5^3}{6^3}$	Apply the exponent to each base to raise a quotient to a power.

Table 4.6. Operations with Exponents (continued)

Rule	Example	Explanation
$\left(\frac{a}{b}\right)^{-n} = \left(\frac{b}{a}\right)^{n}$	$\left(\frac{5}{6}\right)^{-3} = \left(\frac{6}{5}\right)^{3}$	Invert the fraction and change the sign of the exponent to raise a fraction to a negative power.
$\frac{a^{m}}{b^{n}} = \frac{b^{-n}}{a^{-m}}$	$\frac{5^{3}}{6^{4}} = \frac{6^{-4}}{5^{-3}}$	Change the sign of the exponent when moving a number from the numerator to denominator (or vice versa).

SAMPLE QUESTIONS

36) **Simplify:** $\frac{(10^{2})^{3}}{(10^{2})^{-2}}$

Answer:

$\frac{(10^{2})^{3}}{(10^{2})^{-2}}$	
$= \frac{10^{6}}{10^{-4}}$	Multiply the exponents raised to a power.
$= 10^{6-(-4)}$	Subtract the exponent in the denominator from the one in the numerator.
$= 10^{10}$ $= \mathbf{10{,}000{,}000{,}000}$	Simplify.

37) **Simplify:** $\frac{(x^{-2}y^{2})^{2}}{x^{3}y}$

Answer:

$\frac{(x^{-2}y^{2})^{2}}{x^{3}y}$	
$= \frac{x^{-4}y^{4}}{x^{3}y}$	Multiply the exponents raised to a power.
$= x^{-4-3}y^{4-1}$ $= x^{-7}y^{3}$	Subtract the exponent in the denominator from the one in the numerator.
$= \frac{y^{3}}{x^{7}}$	Move negative exponents to the denominator.

RADICALS

Radicals are expressed as $\sqrt[b]{a}$, where b is called the **index** and a is the **radicand**. A radical is used to indicate the inverse operation of an exponent: finding the base which can be raised to b to yield a. For example, $\sqrt[3]{125}$ is equal to 5 because $5 \times 5 \times 5$ equals 125. The same operation can be expressed using a fraction exponent, so $\sqrt[b]{a} = a^{\frac{1}{b}}$. Note that when no value is indicated for b, it is assumed to be 2 (square root).

When b is even and a is positive, $\sqrt[b]{a}$ is defined to be the positive real value n such that $n^b = a$ (example: $\sqrt{16} = 4$ only, and not –4, even though $(-4)(-4) = 16$). If b is even and a is negative, $\sqrt[b]{a}$ will be a complex number (example: $\sqrt{-9} = 3i$). Finally if b is odd, $\sqrt[b]{a}$ will always be a real number regardless of the sign of a. If a is negative, $\sqrt[b]{a}$ will be negative since a number to an odd power is negative (example: $\sqrt[5]{-32} = -2$ since $(-2)^5 = -32$).

$\sqrt[n]{x}$ is referred to as the nth root of x.

▶ $n = 2$ is the square root
▶ $n = 3$ is the cube root
▶ $n = 4$ is the fourth root
▶ $n = 5$ is the fifth root

The following table of operations with radicals holds for all cases EXCEPT the case where b is even and a is negative (the complex case).

Table 4.7. Operations with Radicals

Rule	Example	Explanation
$\sqrt[b]{ac} = \sqrt[b]{a}\,\sqrt[b]{c}$	$\sqrt[3]{81} = \sqrt[3]{27}\sqrt[3]{3} = 3\sqrt[3]{3}$	The values under the radical sign can be separated into values that multiply to the original value.
$\sqrt[b]{\dfrac{a}{c}} = \dfrac{\sqrt[b]{a}}{\sqrt[b]{c}}$	$\sqrt{\dfrac{4}{81}} = \dfrac{\sqrt{4}}{\sqrt{81}} = \dfrac{2}{9}$	The b-root of the numerator and denominator can be calculated when there is a fraction under a radical sign.
$\sqrt[b]{a^c} = (\sqrt[b]{a})^c = a^{\frac{c}{b}}$	$\sqrt[3]{6^2} = (\sqrt[3]{6})^2 = 6^{\frac{2}{3}}$	The b-root can be written as a fractional exponent. If there is a power under the radical sign, it will be the numerator of the fraction.
$\dfrac{c}{\sqrt[b]{a}} \dfrac{\sqrt[b]{a^{b-1}}}{\sqrt[b]{a^{b-1}}} = \dfrac{c\sqrt[b]{a^{b-1}}}{a}$	$\dfrac{5}{\sqrt{2}} \dfrac{\sqrt{2}}{\sqrt{2}} = \dfrac{5\sqrt{2}}{2}$	To rationalize the denominator, multiply the numerator and denominator by the radical in the denominator until the radical has been canceled out.
$\dfrac{c}{b - \sqrt{a}} \times \dfrac{b + \sqrt{a}}{b + \sqrt{a}}$ $= \dfrac{c(b + \sqrt{a})}{b^2 - a}$	$\dfrac{4}{3 - \sqrt{2}} \times \dfrac{3 + \sqrt{2}}{3 + \sqrt{2}}$ $= \dfrac{12 + 4\sqrt{2}}{7}$	To rationalize the denominator, the numerator and denominator are multiplied by the conjugate of the denominator.

SAMPLE QUESTIONS

38) Simplify: $\sqrt{48}$

Answer:

$\sqrt{48}$	
$= \sqrt{16 \times 3}$	Determine the largest square number that is a factor of the radicand (48) and write the radicand as a product using that square number as a factor.
$= \sqrt{16}\sqrt{3}$ $= \mathbf{4\sqrt{3}}$	Apply the rules of radicals to simplify.

39) Simplify: $\frac{6}{\sqrt{8}}$

Answer:

$\frac{6}{\sqrt{8}}$	
$= \frac{6}{\sqrt{4}\sqrt{2}}$ $= \frac{6}{2\sqrt{2}}$	Apply the rules of radicals to simplify.
$= \frac{6}{2\sqrt{2}}\left(\frac{\sqrt{2}}{\sqrt{2}}\right)$ $= \mathbf{\frac{3\sqrt{2}}{2}}$	Multiply by $\frac{\sqrt{2}}{\sqrt{2}}$ to rationalize the denominator.

5

Algebra

A lgebra, meaning "restoration" in Arabic, is the mathematical method of finding the unknown. The first algebraic book in Egypt was used to figure out complex inheritances that were to be split among many individuals. Today, algebra is just as necessary when dealing with unknown amounts.

ALGEBRAIC EXPRESSIONS

The foundation of algebra is the **variable**, an unknown number represented by a symbol (usually a letter such as x or a). Variables can be preceded by a **coefficient**, which is a constant (i.e., a real number) in front of the variable, such as $4x$ or $-2a$. An **algebraic expression** is any sum, difference, product, or quotient of variables and numbers (for example $3x^2$, $2x + 7y - 1$, and $\frac{5}{x}$ are algebraic expressions). **Terms** are any quantities that are added or subtracted (for example, the terms of the expression $x^2 - 3x + 5$ are x^2, $3x$, and 5). A **polynomial expression** is an algebraic expression where all the exponents on the variables are whole numbers. A polynomial with only two terms is known as a **binomial**, and one with three terms is a **trinomial**. A **monomial** has only one term.

> **HELPFUL HINT**
>
> Simplified expressions are ordered by variable terms alphabetically with highest exponent first then down to constants.

coefficient

$x^2 + 3y - 12$

variable   constant

Figure 5.1. Polynomial Expression

Evaluating expressions is another way of saying "find the numeric value of an expression if the variable is equal to a certain number." To evaluate the expression, simply plug the given value(s) for the variable(s) into the equation and simplify. Remember to use the order of operations when simplifying:

- ▸ Parentheses
- ▸ Exponents
- ▸ Multiplication
- ▸ Division
- ▸ Addition
- ▸ Subtraction

SAMPLE QUESTION

1) If $m = 4$, find the value of the following expression:
$5(m - 2)^3 + 3m^2 - \frac{m}{4} - 1$

Answer:

$5(m - 2)^3 + 3m^2 - \frac{m}{4} - 1$	
$= 5(4 - 2)^3 + 3(4)^2 - \frac{4}{4} - 1$	Plug the value 4 in for m in the expression.
$= 5(2)^3 + 3(4)^2 - \frac{4}{4} - 1$	Calculate all the expressions inside the parentheses.
$= 5(8) + 3(16) - \frac{4}{4} - 1$	Simplify all exponents.
$= 40 + 48 - 1 - 1$	Perform multiplication and division from left to right.
$= \mathbf{86}$	Perform addition and subtraction from left to right.

Operations with Expressions

Adding and Subtracting

Expressions can be added or subtracted by simply adding and subtracting **like terms**, which are terms with the same variable part (the variables must be the same, with the same exponents on each variable). For example, in the expressions $2x + 3xy - 2z$ and $6y + 2xy$, the like terms are $3xy$ and $2xy$. Adding the two expressions yields the new expression $2x + 5xy - 2z + 6y$. Note that the other terms did not change; they cannot combine because they have different variables.

SAMPLE QUESTION

2) If $a = 12x + 7xy - 9y$ and $b = 8x - 9xz + 7z$, what is $a + b$?

Answer:

$a + b = (12x + 8x) + 7xy - 9y - 9xz + 7z$ $= \mathbf{20x + 7xy - 9y - 9xz + 7z}$	The only like terms in both expressions are 12x and 8x, so these two terms will be added, and all other terms will remain the same.

DISTRIBUTING AND FACTORING

Often simplifying expressions requires distributing and factoring. Distributing and factoring can be seen as two sides of the same coin. **Distribution** multiplies each term in the first factor by each term in the second factor to clear off parentheses. **Factoring** reverses this process, taking a polynomial in standard form and writing it as a product of two or more factors.

When distributing a monomial through a polynomial, the expression outside the parentheses is multiplied by each term inside the parentheses. (coefficients are multiplied, exponents are added, following the rules of exponents). The first step in factoring a polynomial is always to "undistribute" or factor out the **greatest common factor (GCF)** among the terms. The GCF is multiplied by, in parentheses, the expression that remains of each term when the GCF is divided out of each term. Factoring can be checked by multiplying the GCF factor through the parentheses again.

> **HELPFUL HINT**
>
> Operations with polynomials can always be checked by evaluating equivalent expressions for the same value.

When simplifying two polynomials, each term in the first polynomial must multiply each term in the second polynomial. A binomial (two terms) multiplied by a binomial, will require 2×2 or 4 multiplications. For the binomial × binomial case, this process is sometimes called **FOIL**, which stands for *first*, *outer*, *inner*, and *last*. These terms refer to the placement of each term of the expression: multiply the first term in each expression, then the outside terms, then the inside terms, and finally the last terms. A binomial (two terms) multiplied by a trinomial (three terms), will require 2×3 or 6 products to simplify. The first term in the first polynomial multiplies each of the three terms in the second polynomial, then the second term in the first polynomial multiplies each of the three terms in the second polynomial. A trinomial (three terms) by a trinomial will require 3×3 or 9 products, etc.

Figure 5.2. Distribution and Factoring

Factoring is the reverse of distributing: the first step is always to remove ("undistribute") the GCF of all the terms, if there is a GCF (besides 1). The GCF is the product of any constants and/or variables that EVERY term shares. (For example, the GCF of $12x^3$, $15x^2$ and $6xy^2$ is $3x$ because $3x$ evenly divides all three terms). This shared factor can be taken out of each term and moved to the outside of the parentheses, leaving behind a polynomial where each term is the original term divided by the GCF. (The remaining terms for the terms in the example would be $4x^2$, $5x$, and $2xy$.) It may be possible to factor the polynomial in the parentheses further, depending on the problem.

FACTORING TRINOMIALS

If the leading coefficient is $a = 1$, the trinomial is in the form $x^2 + bx + c$ and can often be rewritten in the factored form, as a product of two binomials: $(x + m)(x + n)$. Recall that the product of two binomials can be written in expanded form $x^2 + mx + nx + mn$. Equating this expression with $x^2 + bx + c$, the constant term c would have to equal the product mn. Thus, to work backward from the trinomial to the factored form, consider all the numbers m and n that multiply to make c. For example, to factor $x^2 + 8x + 12$, consider all the pairs that multiply to be 12 ($12 = 1 \times 12$ or 2×6 or 3×4). Choose the pair that will make the coefficient of the middle term (8) when added. In this example 2 and 6 add to 8, so making $m = 2$ and $n = 6$ in the expanded form gives:

$x^2 + 8x + 12 = x^2 + 2x + 6x + 12$	
$= (x^2 + 2x) + (6x + 12)$	Group the first two terms and the last two terms.
$= x(x + 6) + 2(x + 6)$	Factor the GCF out of each set of parentheses.
$= (x + 6)(x + 2)$	The two terms now have the common factor $(x + 6)$, which can be removed, leaving $(x + 2)$ and the original polynomial is factored.

In general:

$x^2 + bx + c = x^2 + mx + nx + mn$, where $c = mn$ and $b = m + n$	
$= (x^2 + mx) + (nx + mn)$	Group.
$= x(x + m) + n(x + m)$	Factor each group.
$= (x + m)(x + n)$	Factor out the common binomial.

Note that if none of the factors of c add to the value b, then the trinomial cannot be factored, and is called **prime**.

If the leading coefficient is not 1 ($a \neq 1$), first make sure that any common factors among the three terms are factored out. If the a-value is negative, factor out -1 first as well. If the a-value of the new polynomial in the parentheses is still not 1, follow this rule: Identify two values r and s that multiply to be ac and add to be b. Then write the polynomial in this form: $ax^2 + bx + c = ax^2 + rx + sx + c$, and proceed by grouping, factoring, and removing the common binomial as above.

There are a few special factoring cases worth memorizing: difference of squares, binomial squared, and the sum and difference of cubes.

▶ **Difference of squares** (each term is a square and they are subtracted):

▷ $a^2 - b^2 = (a + b)(a - b)$

▷ Note that a sum of squares is never factorable.

▸ **Binomial squared**:

▷ $a^2 + 2ab + b^2 = (a + b)(a + b) = (a + b)^2$

▸ **Sum and difference of cubes**:

▷ $a^3 + b^3 = (a + b)(a^2 - ab + b^2)$

▷ $a^3 - b^3 = (a - b)(a^2 + ab + b^2)$

▷ Note that the second factor in these factorizations will never be able to be factored further.

SAMPLE QUESTIONS

3) Factor: $16x^2 + 52x + 30$

Answer:

$16x^2 + 52x + 30$	
$= 2(8x^2 + 26x + 15)$	Remove the GCF of 2.
$= 2(8x^2 + 6x + 20x + 15)$	To factor the polynomial in the parentheses, calculate $ac = (8)(15) = 120$, and consider all the pairs of numbers that multiply to be 120: 1×120, 2×60, 3×40, 4×30, 5×24, 6×20, 8×15, and 10×12. Of these pairs, choose the pair that adds to be the b-value 26 (6 and 20).
$= 2[(8x^2 + 6x) + (20x + 15)]$	Group.
$= 2[2x(4x + 3) + 5(4x + 3)]$	Factor out the GCF of each group.
$= 2[(4x + 3)(2x + 5)]$	Factor out the common binomial.
$\mathbf{2(4x + 3)(2x + 5)}$	

If there are no values r and s that multiply to be ac and add to be b, then the polynomial is prime and cannot be factored.

4) Expand the following expression: $5x(x^2 - 2c + 10)$

Answer:

$5x(x^2 - 2c + 10)$	
$(5x)(x^2) = 5x^3$ $(5x)(-2c) = -10xc$ $(5x)(10) = 50x$	Distribute and multiply the term outside the parentheses to all three terms inside the parentheses.
$\mathbf{= 5x^3 - 10xc + 50x}$	

5)   Expand the following expression: $x(5 + z) - z(4x - z^2)$

Answer:

$x(5 + z) - z(4x - z^2)$	
$= 5x + zx - 4zx + z^3$	Distribute for each set of parentheses. Note that $-z$ is distributed and that $(-z)(-z^2) = +z^3$. <u>Not distributing the negative is a very common error.</u> Note that the xz is a like term with zx (commutative property) and the terms can therefore be combined.
$= z^3 - 3xz + 5x$	Combine like terms and place terms in the appropriate order (highest exponents first).

6)   Expand the following expression: $(x^2 - 5)(2x - x^3)$

Answer:

$(x^2 - 5)(2x - x^3)$	
$(x^2)(2x) = 2x^3$ $(x^2)(-x^3) = -x^5$ $(-5)(2x) = -10x$ $(-5)(-x^3) = 5x^3$	Apply FOIL: first, outside, inside, and last.
$= 2x^3 - x^5 - 10x + 5x^3$	Combine like terms and put them in order.
$= -x^5 + 7x^3 - 10x$	

7)   Factor the expression $16z^2 + 48z$

Answer:

$16z^2 + 48z$ $= 16z(z + 3)$	Both terms have a z, and 16 is a common factor of both 16 and 48. So the greatest common factor is $16z$. Factor out the GCF.

8)   Factor the expression $6m^3 + 12m^3n - 9m^2$

Answer:

$6m^3 + 12m^3n - 9m^2$ $= 3m^2(2m + 4mn - 3)$	All the terms share the factor m^2, and 3 is the greatest common factor of 6, 12, and 9. So, the GCF is $3m^2$.

9) Factor the expression $3b^2 - 30b - 72$

Answer:

$3b^2 - 30b - 72$	
$= 3(b^2 - 10b - 24)$	Factor out 3, since all the terms share the factor 3.
$= 3(b^2 - 12b + 2b - 24)$	Factor the remaining trinomial in the parentheses. Identify all the values that can be multiplied to make -24 ($-24 = 1 \times -24, -1 \times 24, 2 \times -12, -2 \times 12, 3 \times -8, -3 \times 8, 4 \times -6, -4 \times 6$). Choose the factors 2 and -12 because these values add up to the b-value -10. Rewrite $-10b$ as $-12b + 2b$.
$= 3[(b^2 - 12b) + (2b - 24)]$	Group the terms.
$= 3[b(b - 12) + 2(b - 12)]$	Factor each group.
$= \mathbf{3(b - 12)(b + 2)}$	Factor the binomial $(b - 12)$ out of each term.

LINEAR EQUATIONS

An **equation** states that two expressions are equal to each other. Polynomial equations are categorized by the highest power of the variables they contain: the highest power of any exponent of a linear equation is 1, a quadratic equation has a variable raised to the second power, a cubic equation has a variable raised to the third power, and so on.

SAMPLE QUESTION

10) **Which of the following is a linear equation?**

  A. $x + 5$
  B. $x = x^2$
  C. $\frac{x}{x} = 1$
  D. $2y = 3$

Answer:

  A. Incorrect. This is an expression, not an equation.
  B. Incorrect. This is a quadratic equation (the variable is raised to the second power).

C.   Incorrect. It looks like the highest power is 1. However, the *xs* in the fraction cancel, meaning the equation has no variable; it simply states that 1 = 1.

D.   **Correct.** This is the only answer that has a highest power of one and includes an equal sign.

SOLVING LINEAR EQUATIONS

HELPFUL HINT

On multiple choice tests, it is often easier to plug the possible values into the equation and determine which solution makes the equation true than to solve the equation.

Solving an equation means finding the value or values of the variable that make the equation true. To solve a linear equation, it is necessary to manipulate the terms so that the variable being solved for appears alone on one side of the equal sign while everything else in the equation is on the other side.

The way to solve linear equations is to "undo" all the operations that connect numbers to the variable of interest. Follow these steps:

1.   Eliminate fractions by multiplying each side by the least common multiple of any denominators.

2.   Distribute to eliminate parentheses, braces, and brackets.

3.   Combine like terms.

4.   Use addition or subtraction to collect all terms containing the variable of interest to one side, and all terms not containing the variable to the other side.

5.   Use multiplication or division to remove coefficients from the variable of interest.

Sometimes there are no numeric values in the equation or there are a mix of numerous variables and constants. The goal is to solve the equation for one of the variables in terms of the other variables. In this case, the answer will be an expression involving numbers and letters instead of a numeric value.

SAMPLE QUESTIONS

11)   **Solve for *x*:** $\dfrac{100(x + 5)}{20} = 1$

Answer:

$\dfrac{100(x + 5)}{20} = 1$	
$(20)\left(\dfrac{100(x + 5)}{20}\right) = (1)(20)$ $100(x + 5) = 20$	Multiply both sides by 20 to cancel out the denominator.

$100x + 500 = 20$	Distribute 100 through the parentheses.
$100x = -480$	"Undo" the +500 by subtracting 500 on both sides of the equation to isolate the variable term.
$x = \frac{-480}{100}$	"Undo" the multiplication by 100 by dividing by 100 on both sides to solve for x.
$= -4.8$	

12) Solve for x: $2(x + 2)^2 - 2x^2 + 10 = 42$

Answer:

$2(x + 2)^2 - 2x^2 + 10 = 42$	
$2(x + 2)(x + 2) - 2x^2 + 10 = 42$	Simplify the left-hand side of the equation using the order of operations and combining like terms. Begin with the exponent.
$2(x^2 + 4x + 4) - 2x^2 + 10 = 42$	Apply FOIL.
$2x^2 + 8x + 8 - 2x^2 + 10 = 42$	Distribute the 2.
$8x + 18 = 42$	Combine like terms on the left-hand side.
$8x = 24$	Isolate the variable. "Undo" + 18 by subtracting 18 on both sides.
$x = 3$	"Undo" multiplication by 8 by dividing both sides by 8.

13) Solve the equation for D: $\frac{A(3B + 2D)}{2N} = 5M - 6$

Answer:

$\frac{A(3B + 2D)}{2N} = 5M - 6$	
$3AB + 2AD = 10MN - 12N$	Multiply both sides by $2N$ to clear the fraction, and distribute the A through the parentheses.
$2AD = 10MN - 12N - 3AB$	Isolate the term with the D in it by moving $3AB$ to the other side of the equation.
$D = \frac{(10MN - 12N - 3AB)}{2A}$	Divide both sides by $2A$ to get D alone on the right-hand side.

GRAPHS OF LINEAR EQUATIONS

The most common way to write a linear equation is **slope-intercept form**, $y = mx + b$. In this equation, m is the slope, which describes how steep the line is, and b is the y-intercept. Slope is often described as "rise over run" because it is calculated as the difference in y-values (rise) over the difference in x-values (run). The slope of the line is also the rate of change of the dependent variable y with respect to the independent variable x. The y-intercept is the point where the line crosses the y-axis, or where x equals zero.

To graph a linear equation, identify the y-intercept and place that point on the y-axis. If the slope is not written as a fraction, make it a fraction by writing it over 1 $\left(\frac{m}{1}\right)$. Then use the slope to count up (or down, if negative) the "rise" part of the slope and over the "run" part of the slope to find a second point. These points can then be connected to draw the line. To find the equation of a line, identify the y-intercept, if possible, on the graph and use two easily identifiable points to find the slope. If the y-intercept is not easily identified, identify the slope by choosing easily identifiable points; then choose one point on the graph, plug the point and the slope values into the equation, and solve for the missing value b.

- ▶ slope: $m = \dfrac{y_2 - y_1}{x_2 - x_1}$
- ▶ standard form: $Ax + By = C$
- ▶ $m = -\dfrac{A}{B}$
- ▶ x-intercept $= \dfrac{C}{A}$
- ▶ y-intercept $= \dfrac{C}{B}$

Another way to express a linear equation is standard form: $Ax + By = C$. In order to graph equations in this form, it is often easiest to convert them to point-slope form. Alternately, it is easy to find the x- or y-intercept from this form, and once these two points are known, a line can be drawn through them. To find the x-intercept, simply make $y = 0$ and solve for x. Similarly, to find the y-intercept, make $x = 0$ and solve for y.

SAMPLE QUESTIONS

14) What is the equation of the following line?

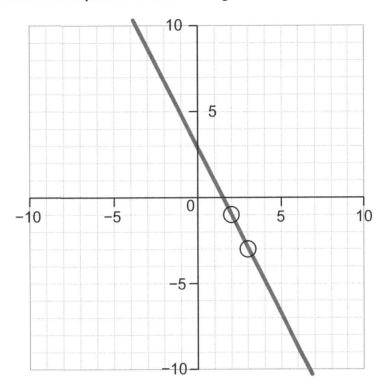

Answer:

$b = 3$	The y-intercept can be identified on the graph as $(0, 3)$.
$m = \dfrac{(-3) - (-1)}{3 - 2} = \dfrac{-2}{1} = -2$	To find the slope, choose any two points and plug the values into the slope equation. The two points chosen here are $(2, -1)$ and $(3, -3)$.
$y = -2x + 3$	Counting squares and verifying the line goes down 2 and over 1 to get from one point on the line to another point on the line gives the same result. Replace m with -2 and b with 3 in $y = mx + b$

15) What is the slope of the line whose equation is $6x - 2y - 8 = 0$?

Answer:

$6x - 2y - 8 = 0$

	Rearrange the equation into slope-intercept form by solving the equation for *x*.
$-2y = -6x + 8$	"Undo" 6*x* by subtracting 6*x* on both sides of the equation.
$y = \dfrac{-6x + 8}{-2}$	"Undo" multiplication of −2 by *y* by dividing both sides by −2.
$y = 3x - 4$	Simplify the fractions.
= 3	The slope is 3, the value attached to *x*.

16)   **What is the equation of the following graph?**

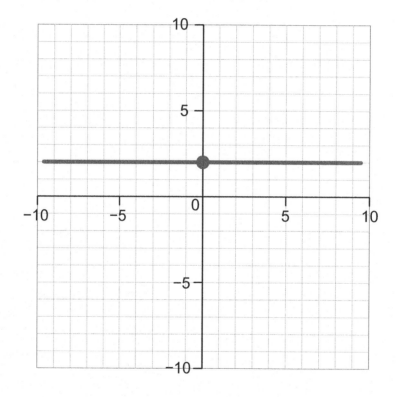

Answer:

	The line has a rise of 0 and a run of 1, so the slope is $\frac{0}{1} = 0$. There is no *x*-intercept. The *y*-intercept is (0, 2), meaning that the *b*-value in the slope-intercept form is 2.
$y = 0x + 2$, or $y = 2$	

17)   **Write the equation of the line going through the points (−2, 5) and (−5, 3).**

Answer:

$(-2, 5)$ and $(-5, 3)$	
$m = \dfrac{3 - 5}{(-5) - (-2)}$ $= \dfrac{-2}{-3}$ $= \dfrac{2}{3}$	Calculate the slope.
$5 = \dfrac{2}{3}(-2) + b$ $5 = \dfrac{-4}{3} + b$ $b = \dfrac{19}{3}$	To find b, plug into the equation $y = mx + b$ the slope for m and a set of points for x and y.
$y = \dfrac{2}{3}x + \dfrac{19}{3}$	Replace m and b to find the equation of the line.

18) The revenue of a company in the year 2010 was \$50,000. The revenue five years later was \$125,000. Assuming that the revenue grew in a linear manner, what was the rate of change of revenue per year?

Answer:

rate of change = slope $= \dfrac{125{,}000 - 50{,}000}{5 - 0} = \dfrac{75{,}000}{5} = 15{,}000$	The rate of change is just the slope. It is helpful to represent year 2010 as $t = 0$. Then the two points given are $(0, 50000)$ and $(5, 125000)$.
The rate of change of revenue is \$15,000 per year.	

BUILDING EQUATIONS

In word problems, it is often necessary to translate a verbal description of a relationship into a mathematical equation. No matter the problem, this process can be done using the same steps:

1. Read the problem carefully and identify what value needs to be solved for.

2. Identify the known and unknown quantities in the problem, and assign the unknown quantities a variable.

3. Create equations using the variables and known quantities.

4. Solve the equations.

5. Check the solution: Does it answer the question asked in the problem? Does it make sense?

> **HELPFUL HINT**
>
> Use the acronym STAR to remember word-problem strategies: Search the problem, Translate into an expression or equation, Answer, and Review.

SAMPLE QUESTIONS

19) A school is holding a raffle to raise money. There is a $3 entry fee, and each ticket costs $5. If a student paid $28, how many tickets did he buy?

Answer:

Number of tickets = x Cost per ticket = 5 Cost for x tickets = $5x$ Total cost = 28 Entry fee = 3	Identify the quantities.
$5x + 3 = 28$	Set up equations. The total cost for x tickets will be equal to the cost for x tickets plus the $3 flat fee.
$5x + 3 = 28$ $5x = 25$ $x = 5$	Solve for the equation.

The student bought **5 tickets**.

20) Kelly is selling shirts for her school swim team. There are two prices: a student price and a nonstudent price. During the first week of the sale, Kelly raised $84 by selling 10 shirts to students and 4 shirts to nonstudents. She earned $185 in the second week by selling 20 shirts to students and 10 shirts to nonstudents. What is the student price for a shirt?

Answer:

Student price = s Nonstudent price = n	Assign variables.
$10s + 4n = 84$ $20s + 10n = 185$	Create two equations using the number of shirts Kelly sold and the money she earned.
$10s + 4n = 84$ $10n = -20s + 185$ $n = -2s + 18.5$ $10s + 4(-2s + 18.5) = 84$ $10s - 8s + 74 = 84$ $2s + 74 = 84$ $2s = 10$ $s = 5$	Solve the system of equations using substitution. Since the question asks for the student price, the goal is to solve for s. Therefore, solve one of the equations for n, so that when the expression is substituted for n, n will be eliminated and s will remain.

The student cost for shirts is **$5**.

LINEAR INEQUALITIES

An **inequality** shows the relationship between two expressions, much like an equation. However, the equal sign is replaced with an inequality symbol that expresses the following relationships:

- ▶ < less than
- ▶ ≤ less than or equal to
- ▶ > greater than
- ▶ ≥ greater than or equal to

Inequalities are read from left to right. For example, the inequality $x \leq 8$ would be read as "x is less than or equal to 8," meaning x has a value smaller than or equal to 8. The set of solutions of an inequality can be expressed using a number line.

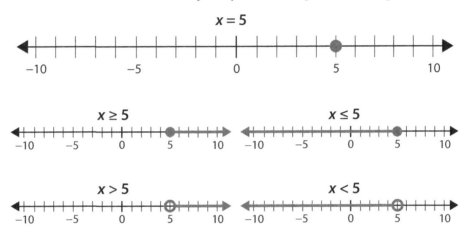

Figure 5.3. Inequalities on a Number Line

The shaded region on the number line represents the set of all the numbers that make an inequality true. One major difference between equations and inequalities is that equations generally have one or two solutions, while inequalities generally have infinitely many solutions (an entire interval on the number line containing infinitely many values).

SOLVING LINEAR INEQUALITIES

Linear inequalities can be solved in the same way as linear equations, with one exception. When multiplying or dividing both sides of an inequality by a negative number, the direction of the inequality sign must reverse—"greater than" becomes "less than" and "less than" becomes "greater than."

SAMPLE QUESTIONS

21) Solve for z: $3z + 10 < -z$

Answer:

Solve the inequality using the same steps used to solve equations.

$3z + 10 < -z$	
$3z < -z - 10$	Collect nonvariable terms to one side.
$4z < -10$	Collect variable terms to the other side.
$z < -2.5$	Isolate the variable.

−2.5

22)   Solve for x: $2x - 3 > 5(x - 4) - (x - 4)$

Answer:

$2x - 3 > 5(x - 4) - (x - 4)$	
$2x - 3 > 5x - 20 - x + 4$	Distribute 5 through the parentheses and −1 through the parentheses.
$2x - 3 > 4x - 16$	Combine like terms.
$-2x > -13$	Collect x-terms to one side, and constant terms to the other side.
$x < 6.5$	Divide both sides by −2; since dividing by a negative, reverse the direction of the inequality.

6.5

GRAPHING LINEAR INEQUALITIES IN TWO VARIABLES

Linear inequalities in two variables can be graphed in much the same way as linear equations. Start by graphing the corresponding equation of a line (temporarily replace the inequality with an equal sign, and then graph). This line creates a boundary line of two half-planes. If the inequality is a "greater/ less than," the boundary should not be included and a dotted line is used. A solid line is used to indicate that the boundary should be included in the solution when the inequality is "greater/less than or equal to."

One side of the boundary is the set of all points (x,y) that make the inequality true. This side is shaded to indicate that all these values are solutions. The simplest method to determine which side should be shaded is to choose a point (*x*,*y*) on one side of the boundary and evaluate the inequality, plugging in this *x*- and *y*- value. If the point makes the inequality true, that side should be shaded; if it does not, it is not a solution, so the other side should be shaded. A second point can be tested as a check. Any point on the shaded side should make the inequality true.

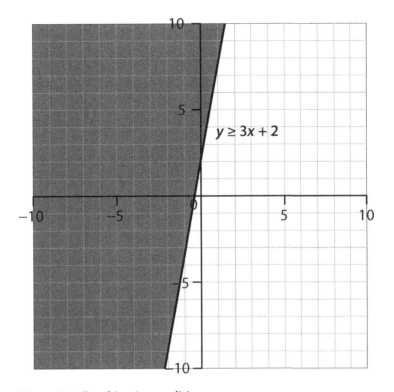

Figure 5.4. Graphing Inequalities

A set of two or more linear inequalities is a **system of inequalities**. Solutions to the system are all the values of the variables that make every inequality in the system true. Systems of inequalities are solved graphically by graphing all the inequalities in the same plane. The region where all the shaded solutions overlap is the solution to the system.

SAMPLE QUESTIONS

23) Graph the following inequality: $3x + 6y \leq 12$

Answer:

The easiest way to graph this line is to find the *x*- and *y*-intercepts. Find the *y*-intercept by making $x = 0$ and solving for *y*. This gives $(0, 2)$ as the *y*-intercept. Find the *x*-intercept by making $y = 0$ and solving for *x*. This give $(4, 0)$ as the *x*-intercept. Knowing these two points, the line can be drawn. Because the inequality says "or equal to," the boundary line is included and is represented by a solid line. To determine which side to shade, choose a value on one side of the boundary, plug it in, and determine if it is a solution. For

example, choosing the origin $(0,0)$ and plugging it into the inequality gives
$3(0) + 6(0)$, which gives 0, which is less than 12, so it must be a solution.
Therefore, ALL the solutions lie on the same side as $(0,0)$. Shade the side that
includes $(0,0)$.

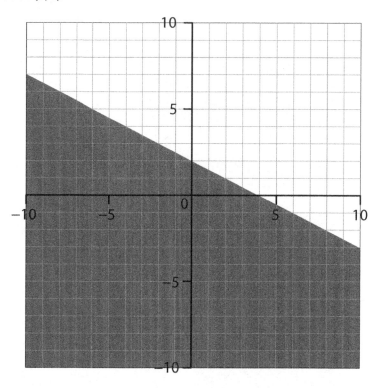

24)   **What is the inequality represented on the graph below?**

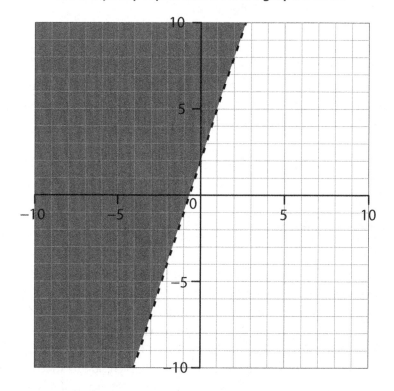

Answer:

y-intercept: (0,2) slope: 3 $y = 3x + 2$	The line crosses the y-axis at $y = 2$. To arrive at another point on the line, go up 3 (rise) and right 1 (run). Determine the equation of the boundary line.
$y > 3x + 2$	Replace the equal sign with the appropriate inequality: the line is dotted and the shading is above the line, indicating that the symbol should be "greater than." Check a point: for example (1, 5) is a solution since $5 > 3(-1) + 2$.

25) **Graph the system of inequalities:** $-x + y \leq 1, x \geq 1, y > 2x - 4$

Answer:

To solve the system, graph all three inequalities in the same plane; then identify the area where the three solutions overlap. All points (x, y) in this area will be solutions to the system since they satisfy all three inequalities. The first inequality is a solid line with slope 1, and the area below that line is shaded. The second inequality is a vertical line and the area to the right of that line is shaded. The third inequality is the dashed line with slope 2 and the area above that line is shaded. The overlapping area is the shaded triangle in the middle. To check the solution, choose one point in that area. It looks like (0, 0) is a solution and plugging that point into each inequality confirms that it is a solution.

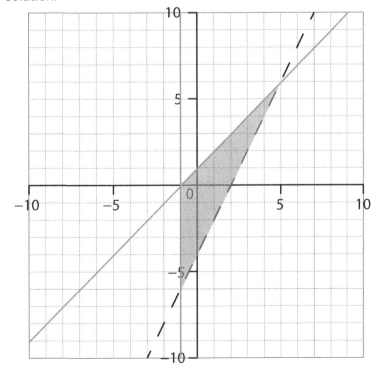

FUNCTIONS

WORKING WITH FUNCTIONS

Functions can be thought of as a process: when something is put in, an action (or operation) is performed, and something different comes out. A **function** is a relationship between two quantities (for example x and y) in which, for every value of the independent variable (usually x), there is exactly one value of the dependent variable (usually y). Briefly, each input has *exactly one* output. Graphically this means the graph passes the **vertical line test**: anywhere a vertical line is drawn on the graph, the line hits the curve at exactly one point. The notation $f(x)$ or $g(t)$, etc., is often used when a function is being considered. This is **function notation.** The

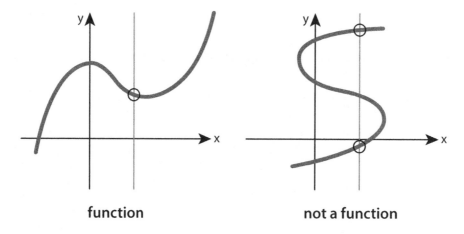

function   not a function

Figure 5.5. Vertical Line Test

input value is x and the output value y are written as $y = f(x)$. Thus, $f(2)$ represents the output value (or y value) when $x = 2$, and $f(2) = 5$ means that when $x = 2$ is plugged into the $f(x)$ function, the output (y value) is 5. In other words, $f(2) = 5$ represents the point $(2,5)$ on the graph of $f(x)$.

Every function has an **input domain** and **output range**. The domain is the set of all the possible x values that can be used as input values (these are found along the horizontal axis on the graph), and the range includes all the y values or output values that result from applying $f(x)$ (these are found along the vertical axis on the graph). Domain and range are usually intervals of numbers and are often expressed as inequalities.

A function $f(x)$ is **even** if $f(-x) = f(x)$. Even functions have symmetry across the y-axis. An example of an even function is the parent quadratic $y = x^2$, because any value of x (for example, 3) and its opposite $-x$ (for example, -3) have the same y value (for example, $3^2 = 9$ and $(-3)^2 = 9$). A function is **odd** if $f(-x) = -f(x)$. Odd functions have symmetry about the origin. For example, $f(x) = x^3$ is an odd function because $f(3) = 27$, and $f(-3) = -27$. A function may be even, odd, or neither.

even   odd

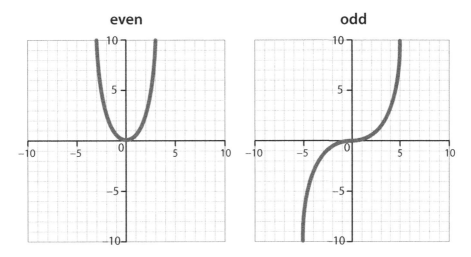

Figure 5.6. Even and Odd Function

SAMPLE QUESTIONS

26) **What is the domain and range of the following function?**

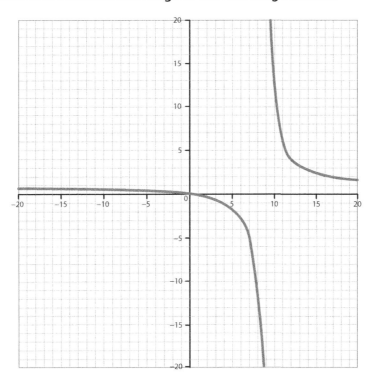

Answer:

This function has an asymptote at $x = 8$, so is not defined there. Exclude 8 from the domain. Otherwise, the function is defined for all other values of x. The proper way to write the domain is:

D: $-\infty < x < 8$ or $8 < x < \infty$

Another way to state the domain is "all real numbers except 8." Sometimes interval notations are used: $(-\infty, 8) \cup (8, \infty)$. The round brackets indicate that 8 is not included; square brackets [ ] would indicate that the value is included in the domain. The U symbol simply means *or*.

Since the function has a horizontal asymptote at $y = 1$ that it never crosses, the function never takes the value 1, so the range is all real numbers except 1, or **R**: $-\infty < y < 1 \; or \; 1 < y < \infty$.

27)   **Evaluate:** $f(4) \; if \; f(x) = x^3 - 2x + \sqrt{x}$

Answer:

$f(4) \; if \; f(x) = x^3 - 2x + \sqrt{x}$	
$f(4) = (4)^3 - 2(4) + \sqrt{(4)}$	Plug in 4.
$= 64 - 8 + 2$	Follow the PEMDAS order of operations.
$= 58$	

28)   **Which of the following represents a function?**

A.

x	$g(x)$
0	0
1	1
2	2
1	3

B.

x	$f(x)$
0	1
0	2
0	3
0	4

C.

t	$f(t)$
1	1
2	2
3	3
4	4

D.

x	$f(x)$
0	0
5	1
0	2
5	3

Answer:

For a set of numbers to represent a function, every input must generate a unique output. Therefore, if the same input (x) appears more than once in the table, determine if that input has two different outputs. If so, then the table does not represent a function.

A.   Incorrect. This table is not a function because input value 1 has two different outputs (1 and 3).

B. Incorrect. Table B is not function because 0 is the only input and results in four different values.

C. **Correct.** Each input has one output.

D. Incorrect. This table also has one input going to two different values.

29) **What is the domain and the range of the following graph?**

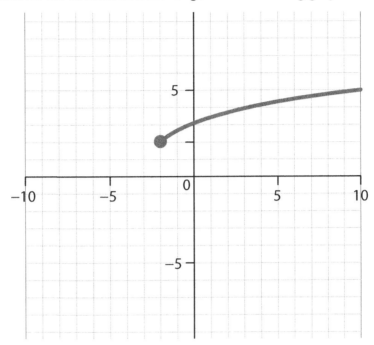

Answer:

For the domain, this graph goes on to the right to positive infinity. Its leftmost point, however, is $x = -2$. Therefore, its domain is all real numbers equal to or greater than -2, **D: $-2 \leq x < \infty$.** In interval notation, write **[–2, ∞).**

The lowest range value is $y = 2$. Although it has a decreasing slope, this function continues to rise and there is no reason to think it will stop rising. Therefore, the domain is all real numbers greater than 2, **R: $2 \leq y < \infty$.**

Also notice that this is indeed a graph of a function, since there is no x-value that has more than one y-value. It passes the vertical line test, since any vertical line drawn anywhere in the domain of the function results in hitting the curve only once.

6

Geometry

Geometry is the study of shapes, angles, volumes, areas, lines, points, and the relationships among them. It is normally approached as an axiomatic system; that is, a small number of entities are taken for granted as true, and everything else is derived logically from them.

PROPERTIES OF SHAPES

BASIC DEFINITIONS

The basic figures from which many other geometric shapes are built are points, lines, and planes. A point is a location in a plane. It has no size or shape, but is represented by a dot. It is labeled using a capital letter.

Two points may be connected by a **line** that extends indefinitely in both directions. There are infinitely many points on a line. A line is a one-dimensional figure. Lines are represented by any two points (say, *A* and *B*) on the line and the line symbol: ($\overleftrightarrow{AB}$). For any two points, a line can be defined that goes through the points. Any points on the same line are co-linear. If two lines are parallel, they will never touch. Parallel lines have the exact same slopes. Two lines with different slopes intersect at a point. If two lines are perpendicular, they intersect at 90° angles.

A **line segment** has two endpoints and a finite length. The length of a segment, called the measure of the segment, is the distance from *A* to *B*. A line segment is a subset of a line, and is also denoted with two points, but with a segment symbol: ($\overline{AB}$). The midpoint of a line segment is the point at which the segment is divided into two equal parts. A line, segment, or plane that passes through the midpoint of a segment is called a bisector of the segment, since it cuts the segment into two equal segments.

A **ray** has one endpoint and extends indefinitely in one direction. It is defined by its endpoint, followed by any other point on the ray: ($\overrightarrow{AB}$). It is important that the first letter represents the endpoint. A ray is sometimes called a half line.

Term	Dimensions	Graphic	Symbol
Table 6.1. Basic Geometric Figures			
point	zero	●	$\cdot A$
line segment	one	A ——— B	$\overline{AB}$
ray	one	A ——→ B	$\overrightarrow{AB}$
line	one	←——→	$\overleftrightarrow{AB}$
plane	two	▱	Plane M

A **plane** is a flat sheet that extends indefinitely in two directions (like an infinite sheet of paper). A plane is a two-dimensional (2D) figure. A plane can ALWAYS be defined through any three noncollinear points in three-dimensional (3D) space. A plane is named using any three points that are in the plane (for example, plane **ABC**). Any points lying in the same plane are said to be coplanar. When two planes intersect, the intersection is a line.

SAMPLE QUESTION

1) Which points and lines are not contained in plane *M* in the diagram below?

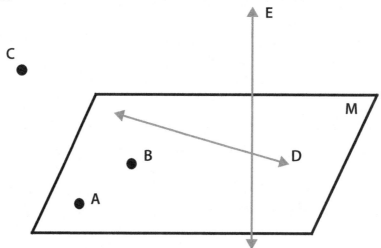

Answer:

Points *A* and *B* and line *D* are all on the same plane, as is the ray beginning at *D*. Point *C* is above the plane, and line *E* cuts through the plane and thus is on a more vertical plane. The point at which line *E* intersects plane *M* is on plane *M* but the line as a whole is not.

ANGLES

Angles are formed when two rays share a common endpoint. They are named using three letters, with the vertex point in the middle (for example ∠**ABC**, where *B* is the vertex). They can also be labeled with a number or named by their vertex alone (if it is clear to do so). Angles are commonly measured in degrees or radians. They are also classified based on their angle measure. A **right angle** has a measure of exactly 90°. **Acute angles** have measures that are less than 90°, whereas **obtuse angles** have measures that are greater than 90°.

Any two angles that add to make 90° are called **complementary angles**. A 30° angle would be complementary to a 60° angle. **Supplementary angles** add up to 180°. A supplementary angle to a 60° angle would be a 120° angle; likewise, 60° is the **supplement** of 120°. The complement and supplement of any angle must always be positive. For example, a 140 degree has no complement. Angles that are next to each other and share a common ray are called **adjacent angles**. Angles that are adjacent and supplementary are called a **linear pair** of angles. Their nonshared rays form a line (thus the *linear* pair). Note that angles that are supplementary do not need to be adjacent; their measures simply need to add to 180°.

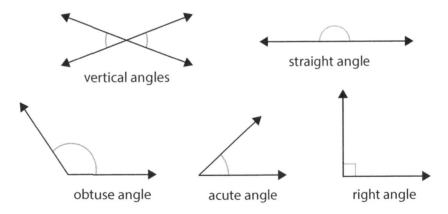

Figure 6.1. Types of Angles

Vertical angles are formed when two lines intersect. Four angles will be formed; the vertex of each angle is at the intersection point of the lines. The vertical angles across from each other will be equal in measure. The angles adjacent to each other will be linear pairs and therefore supplementary.

A ray, line, or segment that divides an angle into two equal angles is called an **angle bisector**.

SAMPLE QUESTIONS

2)   How many pairs of supplementary angles are there in the following figure?

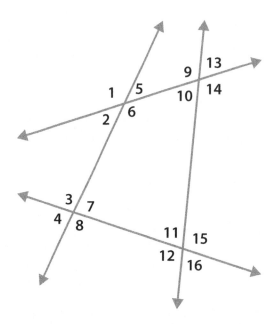

Answers:

Any two angles that are adjacent to one another on a line are supplementary. Therefore, there are **sixteen supplementary pairs** here (∠1 and ∠5, ∠2 and ∠6, ∠5 and ∠6, ∠2 and ∠1, and so on).

3)   If angles *M* and *N* are supplementary and ∠*M* is 30° less than twice ∠*N*, what is the degree measurement of each angle?

Answer:

This problem requires a system of equations to solve:

∠*M* + ∠*N* = 180°

∠*M* = 2∠*N* − 30°

Replacing ∠*M* with 2∠*N* − 30° gives:

2∠*N* − 30° + ∠*N* = 180°	Substitute.
3∠*N* − 30° = 180°	Combine like terms.
3∠*N* = 210°	Add 30 to both sides.
∠*N* = 70°	Divide by 3.

Since ∠*N* and ∠*M* are supplementary, ∠*M* must be 110°. Work can be checked by using the second equation: 110 = 2(70) − 30 verifies the answers.

CIRCLES

Circles are a fundamental shape in geometry. A **circle** is the set of all the points in a plane that are the same distance from a fixed point (called the **center**). The distance from the center to any point on the circle is the **radius** of the circle. The distance around the circle (the perimeter) is called the **circumference**.

The ratio of a circle's circumference to its diameter is a constant value called pi (π), an irrational number which is commonly rounded to 3.14. The formula to find a circle's circumference is $C = 2\pi r$. The formula to find the enclosed area of a circle is $A = \pi r^2$.

Circles have a number of unique parts and properties:

▸ The **diameter** is the largest measurement across a circle. It passes through the circle's center, extending from one side of the circle to the other. The measure of the diameter is twice the measure of the radius.

▸ A line that cuts across a circle and touches it twice is called a **secant** line.

▸ A line that touches a circle or any curve at one point is **tangent** to the circle or the curve. These lines are always exterior to the circle. A line tangent to a circle and a radius drawn to the point of tangency meet at a right angle (90°).

▸ An **arc** is any portion of a circle between two points on the circle. The **measure** of an arc is in degrees, whereas the **length of the arc** will be in linear measurement (such as centimeters or inches). A **minor arc** is the small arc between the two points (it measures less than 180°), whereas a **major arc** is the large arc between the two points (it measures greater than 180°).

▸ An angle with its vertex at the center of a circle is called a **central angle**. For a central angle, the measure of the arc intercepted by the sides of the angle (in degrees) is the same as the measure of the angle.

▸ The part of a secant line that lies within a circle is called a **chord**.

▸ A **sector** is the part of a circle *and* its interior that is inside the rays of a central angle (its shape is like a slice of pie). The formula for area of a sector using θ in degrees is *sector area* $= \frac{\theta}{360}\pi r^2$ (note that this formula is simply the total area of the circle multiplied by $\frac{\theta}{360}$, the fraction of the complete circle area that the sector contains). If θ is in radians, then *sector area* $= \frac{r^2\theta}{2}$.

▸ The formula to find the **arc length** (measured in linear units like centimeters, inches, or feet) is *arc length* $= s = \frac{\theta}{360}(2\pi\alpha) = \frac{\theta}{180}(\pi\alpha)$, where

α is the central angle forming the arc, measured in degrees. Again, this is just the fraction of the total circumference. The formula to find the length of the arc if α is measured in radians is *arc length s = rα*.

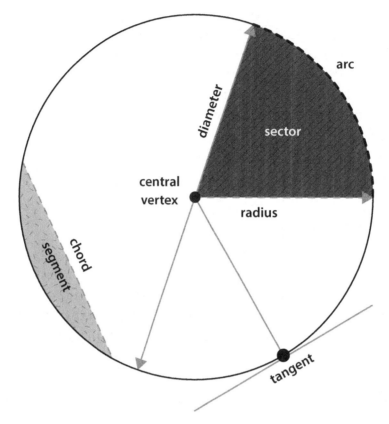

Figure 6.2. Parts of a Circle

▶ An **inscribed angle** has a vertex on the circle and is formed by two chords that share that vertex point. The angle measure of an inscribed angle is one-half the angle measure of the central angle with the same endpoints on the circle (in the diagram below right, $\theta = \frac{\alpha}{2}$).

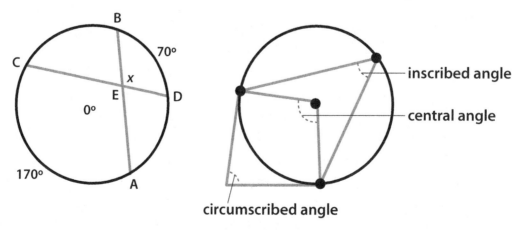

Figure 6.3. Angles in a Circle

▸ A **circumscribed angle** has rays tangent to the circle. The angle lies outside of the circle.

▸ Any angle outside the circle, whether formed by two tangent lines, two secant lines, or a tangent line and a secant line, is equal to half the difference of the intercepted arcs.

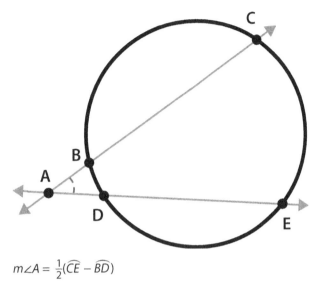

$$m\angle A = \tfrac{1}{2}(\widehat{CE} - \widehat{BD})$$

Figure 6.4. Angles Outside a Circle

▸ Angles are formed within a circle when two chords intersect in the circle. The measure of the smaller angle formed is half the sum of the two smaller arc measures (in degrees). Likewise, the larger angle is half the sum of the two larger arc measures (think: average the arc measures).

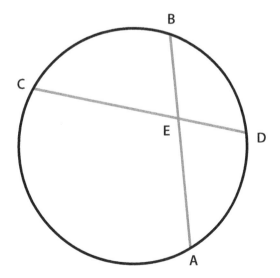

$$m\angle E = \tfrac{1}{2}(\widehat{AC} + \widehat{BD})$$

Figure 6.5. Intersecting Chords

▶ If a chord intersects a line tangent to the circle, the angle formed by this intersection measures one half the measurement of the intercepted arc (in degrees).

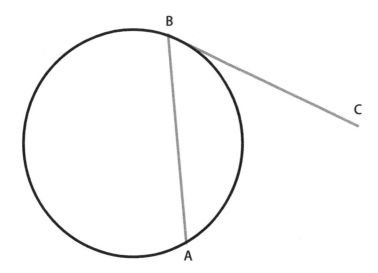

$$m\angle ABC = \tfrac{1}{2}m\widehat{AB}$$

Figure 6.6. Intersecting Chord and Tangent

SAMPLE QUESTIONS

4) Find the area of the sector *NHS* of the circle below with center at *H*:

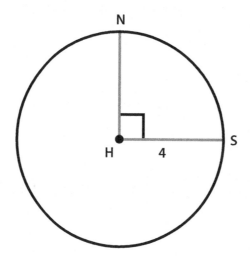

Answer:

$A = \pi 4^2 = 16\pi$	First, determine the area of the entire circle.
$\dfrac{x}{16\pi} = \dfrac{90°}{360°}$	Next, write a proportion.
$x = 4\pi$	Solve.

This answer makes sense because the sector in question is a quarter of the circle, and the area is one quarter of the total area.

5) **In the circle below with center O, the minor arc ACB measures 5 feet. What is the measurement of m∠AOB?**

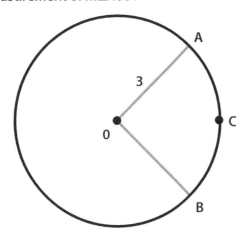

Answer:

The circumference of this circle is $C = 2\pi r = 2\pi(3) = 6\pi$ or 18.84. Now a proportion can be set up, equating the ratio of the arc lengths to the ratio of the angle measures:

$\dfrac{5}{18.84} = \dfrac{x}{360°}$	
$x = \mathbf{95.54°}$	Multiply both sides by 360 to solve.

6) **In the circle below with center A, there are two congruent chords. Solve for x.**

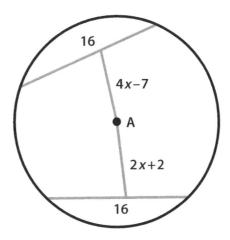

Answer:

A circle's chords are equal only if they are the same distance from the circle. This means that the two segments expressed in terms of x are equal. The equation that must be solved is:

$$4x - 7 = 2x + 2$$
$$2x = 9$$
$$\mathbf{\textit{x} = 4.5}$$

TRIANGLES

Much of geometry is concerned with **triangles** as they are commonly used shapes. A good understanding of triangles allows decomposition of other shapes (specifically polygons) into triangles for study.

Triangles have three sides, and the three interior angles always sum to 180°. The formula for the area of a triangle is $A = \frac{1}{2}bh$ or one-half the product of the base and height (or altitude) of the triangle.

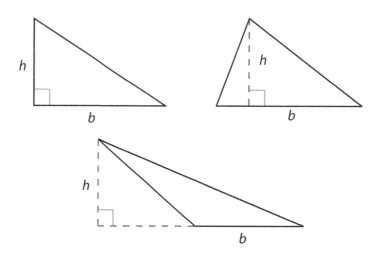

Figure 6.7. Finding the Base and Height of Triangles

Some important segments in a triangle include the angle bisector, the altitude, and the median. The **angle bisector** extends from the side opposite an angle to bisect that angle. The **altitude** is the shortest distance from a vertex of the triangle to the line containing the **base side** opposite that vertex. It is perpendicular to that line and can occur on the outside of the triangle. The **median** extends from an angle to bisect the opposite side.

Angle Bisector
Divides angle in half

Altitude
Shortest distance to side

Median
Divides opposite side
in half

Figure 6.8. Important Segments in a Triangle

Triangles have two "centers." The **orthocenter** is formed by the intersection of a triangle's three altitudes. The **centroid** is where a triangle's three medians meet.

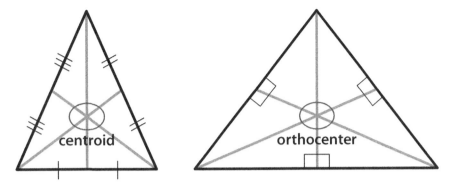

Figure 6.9. Centroid and Orthocenter of a Triangle

Triangles can be classified in two ways: by sides and by angles.

A **scalene triangle** has no equal sides or angles. An **isosceles triangle** has two equal sides and two equal angles, often called **base angles**. In an **equilateral triangle**, all three sides are equal as are all three angles. Moreover, because the sum of the angles of a triangle is always 180°, each angle of an equilateral triangle must be 60°.

Triangles Based on Sides

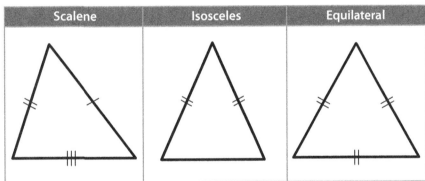

Triangles Based on Angles

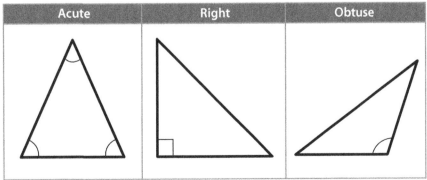

Figure 6.10. Types of Triangles

A **right triangle** has one right angle (90°) and two acute angles. An **acute triangle** has three acute angles (all angles are less than 90°). An **obtuse triangle** has one obtuse angle (more than 90°) and two acute angles.

For any triangle, the side opposite the largest angle will have the longest length, while the side opposite the smallest angle will have the shortest length. The **triangle inequality theorem** states that the sum of any two sides of a triangle must be greater than the third side. If this inequality does not hold, then a triangle cannot be formed. A consequence of this theorem is the **third-side rule**: if b and c are two sides of a triangle, then the measure of the third side a must be between the sum of the other two sides and the difference of the other two sides: $c - b < a < c + b$.

HELPFUL HINT

Trigonometric functions can be employed to find missing sides and angles of a triangle.

Solving for missing angles or sides of a triangle is a common type of triangle problem. Often a right triangle will come up on its own or within another triangle. The relationship among a right triangle's sides is known as the **Pythagorean theorem**: $a^2 + b^2 = c^2$, where c is the hypotenuse and is across from the 90° angle. Right triangles with angle measurements of 90° – 45° – 45° and 90° – 60° – 30° are known as *special* right triangles and always have the following relationship between legs and hypotenuse:

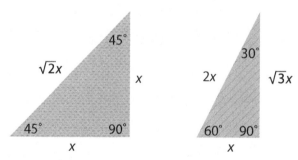

Figure 6.11. Special Right Triangles

SAMPLE QUESTIONS

7) **What are the minimum and maximum values of the third side of the triangle, x, to the nearest hundredth?**

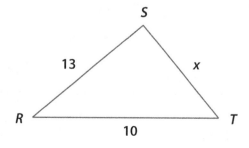

Answers:

The sum of two sides is 23 and their difference is 3. To connect the two other sides and enclose a space, *x* must be less than the sum and greater than the difference (that is, $3 < x < 23$). Therefore, **x's minimum value to the nearest hundredth is 3.01 and its maximum value is 22.99.**

8) Examine and classify each of the following triangles:

1.

2.

3.

4.
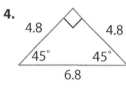

Answers:

Triangle 1 is an equilateral triangle (since all 3 sides are equal, and all 3 angles are equal)

Triangle 2 is a scalene, right triangle (since all 3 sides are different, and there is a 90° angle)

Triangle 3 is an obtuse isosceles triangle (since there are 2 equal sides and, consequently, 2 equal angles)

Triangle 4 is a right, isosceles triangle (since there are 2 equal sides and a 90° angle)

9) **Given the diagram, if *XZ* = 100, *WZ* = 80, and *XU* = 70, then *WY* = ?**

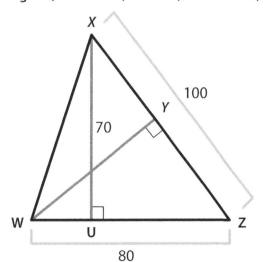

Answer:

WY can be seen as one of the legs of a right triangle, but from the given information it is unclear how that segment divides *XZ* (we cannot assume that it splits in exactly in two since the triangle is not necessarily isosceles). Another approach is required. Since altitude *XU* and base *WZ* are given values, the area of the triangle can be written in two different ways and equated.

$A = \frac{1}{2}(80)(70) = 2800$	The height *XU* = 70 and base *WZ* = 80 give the area of triangle *XWZ*.
$A = \frac{1}{2}(100)(WY)$	The area of triangle *XWZ* can also be written using *XZ* = 100 and height *WY*.
$2800 = \frac{1}{2}(100)(WY)$	Since both these represent the same area, these may be equated, and *WY* can be solved for.

WY = 56

Quadrilaterals

All closed, four-sided shapes are **quadrilaterals**. The sum of all internal angles in a quadrilateral is always 360°. (Think of drawing a diagonal to create two triangles. Since each triangle contains 180°, two triangles, and therefore the quadrilateral, must contain 360°.) The **area of any quadrilateral** is $A = bh$, where *b* is the base and *h* is the height (or altitude).

> **HELPFUL HINT**
>
> All squares are rectangles and all rectangles are parallelograms; however, not all parallelograms are rectangles and not all rectangles are squares.

A **parallelogram** is a quadrilateral with two pairs of parallel sides. A rectangle is a parallelogram with two pairs of equal sides and four right angles. A **kite** also has two pairs of equal sides, but its equal sides are consecutive. Both a **square** and a **rhombus** have four equal sides. A square has four right angles, while a rhombus has a pair of acute opposite angles and a pair of obtuse opposite angles. A **trapezoid** has exactly one pair of parallel sides.

Table 6.2 Properties of Parallelograms

Term	Shape	Properties
Parallelogram		Opposite sides are parallel.
		Consecutive angles are supplementary.
		Opposite angles are equal.
		Opposite sides are equal.
		Diagonals bisect each other.

Term	Shape	Properties
Rectangle		All parallelogram properties hold. Diagonals are congruent *and* bisect each other. All angles are right angles.
Square		All rectangle properties hold. All four sides are equal. Diagonals bisect angles. Diagonals intersect at right angles and bisect each other.
Kite		Kites have exactly one pair of opposite equal angles and two pairs of equal consecutive sides. Diagonals meet at right angles.
Rhombus		All four sides are equal. Diagonals bisect angles. Diagonals intersect at right angles and bisect each other.
Trapezoid		Trapezoids have exactly one pair of parallel sides (called bases). Bases have different lengths. Isosceles trapezoids have a pair of equal sides (and base angles).

SAMPLE QUESTIONS

10) **Figure *WEST* is a parallelogram. Determine each of the following:**

$\overline{TW} =$ _____

$\overline{EM} \cong$ _____

$\overline{TM} = \frac{1}{2}$ _____

$\angle STW \cong \angle$ _____

$\angle EST + \angle$ _____ $= 180°$.

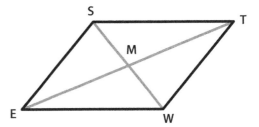

Answer:

Line $\overline{TW}$ is parallel to $\overline{SE}$ (opposite sides are equal); $\overline{EM}$ is congruent to $\overline{TM}$; $\overline{TM}$ is one half of $\overline{TE}$ (since diagonals bisect each other); $\angle STW$ is congruent to $\angle SEW$ (opposite sides are equal); and the sum of angles $\angle EST$ and $\angle STW$ is 180° (consecutive angles are supplementary); $\angle SEW$ would also work.

11) In parallelogram *ABCD*, the measure of the exterior angle at *C* is $m° = 260°$. What is the measure of *n*°?

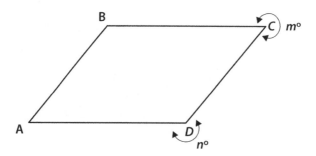

Answers:

The two variables are exterior angles. If these two angles were to be added to the interior angles (*A* and *D*) the sum of each pair would be 360°. Since *ABCD* is a parallelogram, these two consecutive interior angles are supplementary. The problem can be solved with this information:

$260° + m\angle C = 360°$

$m\angle C + m\angle D = 180°$

$m\angle D + n = 360°$

It follows from the first equation that $m\angle C = 100°$. Substituting that value in for $\angle C$ in the second equation yields $m\angle D = 80°$. Substituting 80° in for $m\angle D$ in the third equation gives $\boldsymbol{n = 280°}$.

12) A rectangular section of a football field has dimensions of *x* and *y* and an area of 1000 square feet. Three additional lines drawn vertically divide the section into four smaller rectangular areas as seen in the diagram below. If all the lines shown need to be painted, calculate the total number of linear feet, in terms *x*, to be painted.

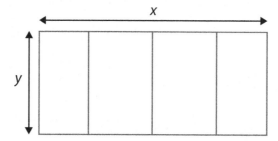

Answer:

Since the area is 1000 square feet, $xy = 1000$. The total perimeter of the larger rectangle is $2x + 2y$. In addition, the three interior lines, each of length *y*, need to be painted for a total of $2x + 2y + 3y$ or $2x + 5y$. To express the total in terms of *x*, solve $xy = 1000$ for *y*, and substitute:

$y = \frac{1000}{x}$	Solve for y.
$P = 2x + 5y$	
$= 2x + 5\left(\frac{1000}{x}\right)$	Solve for the perimeter.
$= 2x + \frac{5000}{x}$	

POLYGONS

Any closed shape made up of three or more line segments is a polygon. In addition to triangles and quadrilaterals, **hexagons** and **octagons** are two common polygons:

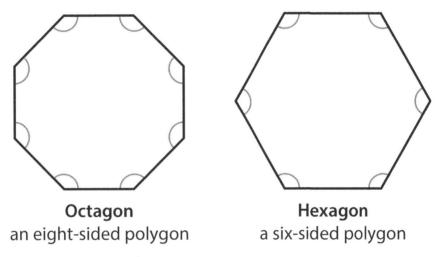

Octagon
an eight-sided polygon

Hexagon
a six-sided polygon

Figure 6.12. Common Polygons

The two polygons depicted above are **regular polygons**, meaning that they are equilateral (all sides having equal lengths) and equiangular (all angles having equal measurements). Angles inside a polygon are **interior angles**, whereas those formed by one side of the polygon and a line extending outside the polygon are **exterior angles**:

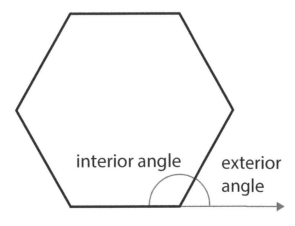

interior angle

exterior angle

Figure 6.13. Interior and Exterior Angles

The sum of the all the exterior angles of a polygon is always 360°. Dividing 360° by the number of a polygon's sides finds the measure of the polygon's exterior angles.

To determine the sum of a polygon's interior angles, choose one vertex and draw diagonals from that vertex to each of the other vertices, decomposing the polygon into multiple triangles. For example, an octagon has six triangles within it, and therefore the sum of the interior angles is 6 × 180° = 1080°. In general, the formula for finding the sum of the angles in a polygon is sum of angles = $(n - 2) \times 180°$, where n is the number of sides of the polygon.

To find the measure of a single interior angle in a regular polygon, simply divide the sum of the interior angles by the number of angles (which is the same as the number of sides). So, in the octagon example, each angle is $\frac{1080}{8} = 135°$.

In general, the formula to find the measure of a regular polygon's interior angles is: *interior angle* $= \frac{(n - 2)}{n} \times 180°$ where n is the number of sides of the polygon.

To find the area of a polygon, it is helpful to know the perimeter of the polygon (p), and the **apothem** (a). The apothem is the shortest (perpendicular) distance from the polygon's center to one of the sides of the polygon. The formula for the area is: *regular polygon area* $= \frac{ap}{2}$.

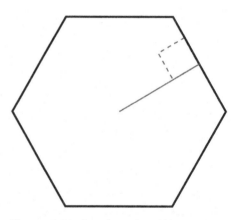

Finally, there is no universal way to find the perimeter of a polygon (when the side length is not given). Often, breaking the polygon down into triangles and adding the base of each triangle all the way around the polygon is the surest way to calculate the perimeter.

Figure 6.14. Apothem in a Hexagon

SAMPLE QUESTIONS

13) **What is the measure of an exterior angle and an interior angle of a regular 400-gon?**

Answer:

The sum of the exterior angles is 360°. Dividing this sum by 400 gives $\frac{360°}{400} = \textbf{0.9°}$. Since an interior angle is supplementary to an exterior angle, all the interior angles have measure 180 − 0.9 = **179.1°**. Alternately, using the formula for calculating the interior angle gives the same result:

interior angle $= \frac{400 - 2}{400} \times 180° = 179.1°$

14) The circle and hexagon below both share center point T. The hexagon is entirely inscribed in the circle. The circle's radius is 5. What is the area of the shaded area?

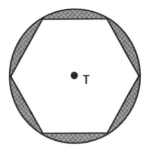

Answer:

The area of the circle (with radius $r = 5$) is:

$A = 5^2\pi = 25\pi = 78.54$

To find the hexagon's area, the perimeter must be calculated. The key is using the interior angle formula to find the measure of the interior angles: $\frac{(6-2)}{6}(180°) = 120°$. Six triangles can be drawn by drawing segments from the center of the hexagon to each vertex. Since these triangles are all the same (congruent), and isosceles, they divide each $120°$ angle exactly in half. Thus, each of the three angles of each triangle is $60°$. Moreover the triangles are, in fact, equilateral. The side length of the hexagon is therefore 5 units, and the perimeter is 30. Drawing a perpendicular to the side and using special triangles to find the side opposite the $60°$ angle calculates the apothem:

The apothem is $2.5\sqrt{3}$, and the area can now be calculated as $area = \frac{ap}{2}$ $= \frac{(2.5\sqrt{3})(30)}{2} = \frac{75\sqrt{3}}{2} = 64.95$.

The shaded area constitutes only parts of the circle that are not in the polygon. The difference between the circle's area and the polygon's area is $78.54 - 64.95 = \textbf{13.59}$.

THREE-DIMENSIONAL SHAPES

Three-dimensional shapes have depth in addition to width and length. The sides of three-dimensional shapes exist on a flat plane, so questions concerning these shapes require the use of the properties discussed above.

Volume is expressed as the number of cubic units any solid can hold—that is, what it takes to fill it up. Surface area is the sum of the areas of the two-dimensional figures that are found on its surface. Three-dimensional shapes have unique formulas:

Table 6.3. Three-Dimensional Shapes and Formulas

Term	Shape	Formula	
Prism		$V = Bh$ $SA = 2lw + 2wh + 2lh$ $SA = 2B + lateral\ area$	B = area of base h = height l = length w = width d = longest diagonal
Cube		$V = s^3$ $SA = 6s^2$ $d^2 = a^2 + b^2 + c^2$	s = cube edge
Sphere		$V = \frac{4}{3}\pi r^3$ $SA = 4\pi r^2$	r = radius
Cylinder		$V = Bh = \pi r^2 h$ $SA = 2\pi r^2 + 2\pi rh$	B = area of base h = height r = radius
Cone		$V = \frac{1}{3}\pi r^2 h$ $SA = \pi r^2 + \pi rl$	r = radius h = height l = slant height
Pyramid		$V = \frac{1}{3}Bh$ $SA = B + \frac{1}{2}(p)l$	B = area of base h = height p = perimeter l = slant height

SAMPLE QUESTIONS

15) A sphere has a radius z. If that radius is increased by t, by how much is the surface area increased? Write the answer in terms of z and t.

Answer:

$SA_1 = 4\pi z^2$	The original surface area is:
$SA_2 = 4\pi(z + t)^2$	The increased surface area is:
$= 4\pi(z^2 + 2zt + t^2)$	
$= 4\pi z^2 + 8\pi zt + 4\pi t^2$	

	To find the difference between the two, subtract the original from the increased surface area:
$4\pi z^2 + 8\pi zt + 4\pi t^2 - 4\pi z^2$	
$= 4\pi t^2 + 8\pi zt$	The surface area increased by $4\pi t^2 + 8\pi zt$.

16) **The length of the base of a rectangular pyramid measures 4 feet, and the width of the base is half of the pyramid's height. What is the pyramid's volume in terms of height?**

Answer:

The length of the base is $l = 4$. The width of the base is $w = \frac{1}{2}h$.

The base of the pyramid is rectangular and thus has area:

$B = lw = 4\left(\frac{1}{2}h\right) = 2h$

Plugging this information into a pyramid's volume equation provides the answer:

$V = \frac{1}{3}Bh = \frac{1}{3}(2h)h = \frac{2h^2}{3}$

17) **A cube with volume 27 cubic meters is inscribed within a sphere and all of the cube's vertices touch the sphere. What is the length of the sphere's radius?**

Answer:

Since the cube's volume is 27, each side length is equal to $\sqrt[3]{27} = 3$. The long diagonal distance from one of the cube's vertices to its opposite vertex will provide the sphere's diameter. Using the super Pythagorean theorem, it is found that:

$d = \sqrt{3^2 + 3^2 + 3^2} = \sqrt{27} = 5.2$

This is the diameter of the sphere. Half of this length is the radius, which is **2.6 meters**.

TRANSFORMATIONS OF GEOMETRIC FIGURES

TRANSLATIONS, ROTATIONS, REFLECTIONS, AND CONGRUENCE

Geometric figures are often drawn in the coordinate xy-plane, with the vertices or centers of the figures indicated by ordered pairs. Important understandings about the nature of a figure can be examined by performing **transformations**, which are manipulations of the shape in the plane. The original shape is called the **pre-image**, and the shape after a transformation is applied is called the **image**.

A **translation** transforms a shape by moving it right or left, or up or down. Translations are sometimes called slides. The image under this transformation is identical in size and shape to the pre-image. In other words, the image is **congruent**, or identical in size, to the pre-image. All corresponding pairs of angles are congruent, and all corresponding side lengths are congruent.

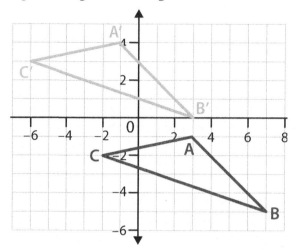

The translation moved triangle ABC left 4 units
and up 6 units to produce triangle A'B'C'.

Figure 6.15. Translation

Translations are often written with pointy brackets: $\{-x, y\}$. The first number represents the change in the *x* direction (left/right), while the second number shows the change in the *y* direction (up/down). The symbol $\cong$ is read "congruent."

Similarly, rotations and reflections preserve the size and shape of the figure, so congruency is preserved. A **rotation** takes a pre-image and rotates it about a fixed point (often the origin) in the plane. Although the position or orientation of the shape changes, the angles and side lengths remain the same.

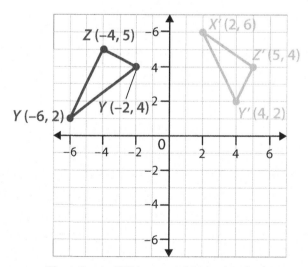

The triangle XYZ is rotated 90 in the clockwise
direction about the origin (0, 0).

Figure 6.16. Rotation

A **reflection** takes each point in the pre-image and flips it over a point or line in the plane (often the *x*- or *y*-axis, but not necessarily). The image is congruent to the pre-image. When a figure is flipped across the *y*-axis, the signs of all *x*-coordinates will change. The *y*-coordinates change sign when a figure is reflected across the *x*-axis.

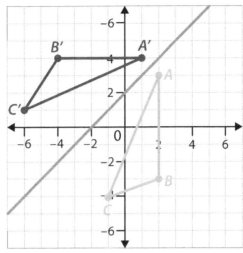

The triangle ABC is reflected over the line to produce the triangle A'B'C'.

Figure 6.17. Reflection

SAMPLE QUESTIONS

18) If quadrilateral *ABCD* has vertices *A* (−6, 4), *B* (−6, 8), *C* (2, 8), and *D* (4, −4), what are the new vertices if *ABCD* is translated 2 units down and 3 units right?

Answer:

Translating two units down decreases each *y*-value by 2, and moving 3 units to the right increases the *x*-value by 3. The new vertices are *A* (−3, 2), *B* (−3, 6), *C* (5, 6), and *D* (7, −6).

19) If quadrilateral *ABCD* has vertices *A* (−6, 4), *B* (−6, 8), *C* (2, 8), and *D* (4, −4), what are the new vertices if *ABCD* is rotated 270° and then reflected across the *x*-axis?

Answer:

When a figure is rotated 270°, the coordinates change: $(a, b) \rightarrow (b, -a)$ (see the summary of rotation coordinate changes in the next section). After the rotation, the new coordinates are (4, 6), (8, 6), (8, −2), and (−4, −4). Reflecting across the *x*-axis requires that every *y*-value is multiplied by −1 to arrive at the completely transformed quadrilateral with vertices of (4, −6), (8, −6), (8, 2), and (−4, 4).

Dilations and Similarity

The last transformations of interest are dilations. A **dilation** increases (or decreases) the size of a figure by some **scale factor**. Each coordinate of the points that make up the figure is multiplied by the same factor. If the factor is greater than 1, multiplying all the factors enlarges the shape; if the factor is less than 1 (but greater than 0), the shape is reduced in size.

In addition to the scale factor, a dilation needs a **center of dilation**, which is a fixed point in the plane about which the points are multiplied. Usually, but not always, the center of dilation is the origin (0,0). For dilations about the origin, the image coordinates are calculated by multiplying each coordinate by the scale factor k. Thus, point $(x, y) \rightarrow (kx, ky)$. Although dilations do not result in congruent figures, the orientation of the figure is preserved; consequently, corresponding line segments will be parallel.

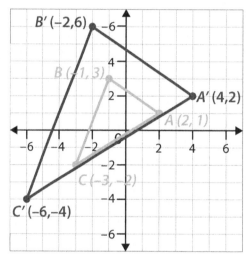

The triangle ABC is dilated by the scale factor 2 to produce triangle A'B'C'.

Fiure 6.18. Dilation

Importantly, dilations do NOT create images that are congruent to the original because the size of each dimension is increased or decreased (the only exception being if the scale factor is exactly 1). However, the shape of the figure is maintained. The corresponding angle measures will be congruent, but the corresponding side lengths will be **proportional**. In other words, the image and pre-image will be **similar** shapes.

Considering congruent and similar shapes as a consequence of transformations is helpful in understanding what is meant by congruence and similarity. Often, however, the fact that two shapes are congruent or similar is given as a fact, unrelated to a transformation. In that case, much information is being given in a single statement. For example, given that $\triangle ABC \sim \triangle PQR$ (~ is read *is similar to*) tells the reader that $\angle A \cong \angle P$, $\angle B \cong \angle Q$, $\angle C \cong \angle R$, and $\frac{AB}{PQ} = \frac{BC}{QR} = \frac{AC}{PR} = k$ (where k is the constant of proportionality).

TRANSFORMING COORDINATES

Transformations in a plane can actually be thought of as functions. An input pair of coordinates, when acted upon by a transformation, results in a pair of output coordinates. Each point is moved to a unique new point (a one-to-one correspondence).

Table 6.4. How Coordinates Change for Transformations in a Plane

Type of Transformation	Coordinate Changes
Translation right m units and up n units	$(x, y) \rightarrow (x + m, y + n)$
Rotations about the origin in positive (counterclockwise) direction	
Rotation 90°	$(x, y) \rightarrow (-y, x)$
Rotation 180°	$(x, y) \rightarrow (-x, -y)$
Rotation 270°	$(x, y) \rightarrow (y, -x)$
Reflections about the	
x-axis	$(x, y) \rightarrow (x, -y)$
y-axis	$(x, y) \rightarrow (-x, y)$
line **y = x**	$(x, y) \rightarrow (y, x)$
Dilations about the origin by a factor of k	
0 < k < 1 → size reduced	
k > 1 → size enlarged	$(x, y) \rightarrow (kx, ky)$

SAMPLE QUESTIONS

20) Triangle *ABC* with coordinates $(2, 8)$, $(10, 2)$, and $(6, 8)$ is transformed in the plane as shown in the diagram. What transformations result in the image triangle *A'B'C'*?

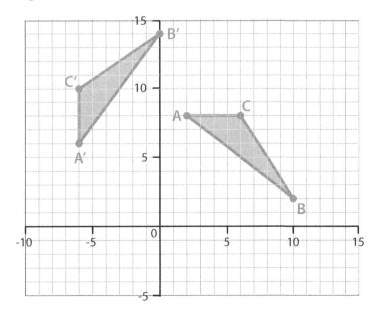

Answer:

Since the orientation of the triangle is different from the original, it must have been rotated. A counterclockwise rotation of 90° about the point *A* (2, 8) results in a triangle with the same orientation. Then the triangle must be translated to move it to the image location. Pick one point, say *A*, and determine the translation necessary to move it to point *A'*. In this case, each point on the pre-image must be translated 8 units left and 2 units down. **This could be written {−8, −2}.** Note that other transformations could also result in the same image. For example, triangle ABC could be rotated clockwise 270° and then translated.

21) If quadrilateral *ABCD* has vertices *A* (−6, 4), *B* (−6, 8), *C* (2, 8), and *D* (4, −4), what are the new vertices if *ABCD* is increased by a factor of 5 about the origin?

Answer:

Changing coordinates to account for a dilation transformation requires that all the coordinates be multiplied by the scale factor. The new vertices are **A (−30, 20), B (−30, 40), C (10, 40), and D (20, −20).**

TRANSFORMATIONS AND COORDINATE GEOMETRY PROOF

Using transformation and coordinates can be a powerful method of proving geometric theorems. For example, the image of a line in a plane that has been translated within the plane is clearly parallel to its pre-image. This can be proven using transformations.

Consider any line with slope $m = \frac{\Delta y}{\Delta x} = \frac{\text{rise}}{\text{run}}$, as shown in Figure 6.19. The Δy can be represented with a vertical segment, and the Δx with a horizontal segment, which forms a triangle as shown. When the line is shifted vertically down 4 units (or in any direction, really), the triangle representing slope will be congruent to the original slope triangle. Thus, the rise and run are equivalent, and the slopes must be equal. This proves that lines are parallel if and only if they have equal slopes.

Similarly, a rotation transformation can prove that two lines are perpendicular if and only if they have opposite, reciprocal slopes. This is facilitated by using a line that goes through (0,0) and rotating about that point.

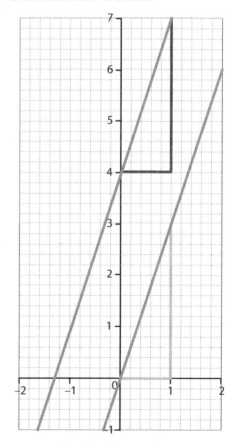

Figure 6.19. Translation of a Line in a Plane

This can be assumed since any line can be translated to the origin without changing its slope, as seen in the previous example.

If the line with positive slope in this diagram contains points (0,0) and (*a,b*), then the slope of this line is $\frac{b}{a}$. When the line is rotated 90° about the origin, point (*a,b*) → (–*b,a*), according to the rules of rotations. Thus, the image line passes through (0,0) and (–*b,a*) and has slope $\frac{a}{-b} = -\frac{a}{b}$. Notice that the slope of the image line is the opposite, reciprocal (flip) of the pre-image line. This proves the theorem.

In the Figure 3.20, the slope of the pre-image line is 3, whereas the slope of the perpendicular image line is $-\frac{1}{3}$.

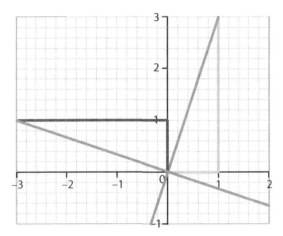

Figure 6.20. Rotation of a Line in a Plane

Another theorem that can be proven using coordinate geometry is that **all circles are similar to one another**. Suppose that circle 1 has radius r_1 and center (*h,k*), and circle 2 has radius r_2 ($r_2 > r_1$) and center (*a,b*). Circle 2 can be re-centered to (*h,k*) by doing a horizontal translation of *h* – *a* and a vertical translation *k* – *b*. Then a dilation can be performed about the center with a scale factor of $\frac{r_1}{r_2}$. This results in the image of circle 2 landing right on top of circle 1, showing that the circles are similar.

All equations for two-dimensional lines have a slope, a zero slope, or an undefined slope. A horizontal line has zero slope and a vertical line has undefined slope (since its slope would be the opposite, reciprocal of a horizontal line, which would require division by 0).

SAMPLE QUESTIONS

22) **Identify three lines perpendicular to** *y* = 3*x* + 3.

Answer:

There are an infinite number of lines perpendicular to this line since the line does not stop. Three possibilities are $y = -\frac{1}{3}x + 3$, $y = -\frac{1}{3}x$, and $y = -\frac{1}{3}x - 3$. These four equations are depicted below. The original equation is the only line with a positive slope. Note that all of the lines perpendicular to *y* = 3*x* + 3 are parallel to one another. Any

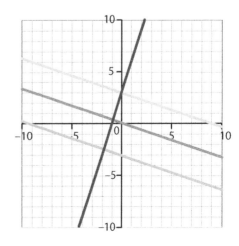

line with the form $y = -\frac{1}{3}x + b$, where b is any real number, is perpendicular to the original line.

23) If one line has a slope of $\frac{k}{6}$ and a line parallel to that line has a slope of $\frac{k-10}{12}$, what is the slope of a line perpendicular to both these lines?

Answer:

Since the slopes of the two given lines are equal, x can be solved for by setting these two equations equal to one another:

$\frac{k}{6} = \frac{k-10}{12}$

$12k = 6k - 60$

$6k = -60$

$k = -10$

If k is equal to -10, then the slope of these parallel lines is $-\frac{5}{3}$. **A line perpendicular to both of these lines would have a slope of $\frac{3}{5}$.**

7

Statistics and Probability

The statistics and probability sections below will provide multiple ways to collect, interpret, and display data. **Data** is simply the result of an observation or measurement. Data is often collected when an experiment or survey is performed. Conclusions are drawn from this data using various mathematical formulas.

To collect data, investigators run experiments or observe behavior. In an **experiment**, a treatment is applied to a group (of people, animals, plants, etc.), and the effect of that treatment is observed. In a **randomized experiment**, the subjects are randomly split into two groups (by a flip of a coin or a random number generator, for example). One group is a **control** group and does not receive the treatment, and the other group does receive the treatment. Then measurements are conducted on each group, and results are compared. In an **observational study** no treatment is applied, but researchers observe and measure some variable of interest. An example of an observational study is studying the relationship between left- or right-handedness and industrial accidents. No treatment would be applied to either group in this situation.

Information is frequently used to make statements about an entire population. In these cases, because collecting data from every member of the population is impossible, statisticians collect data from a small, random, but specific subset of the entire population. This random **sample** enables inferences to be made about the entire population. There are a variety of methods of creating a representative sample that are beyond the scope of this text, but it is important to note that statistics are only as good as the experiment and sampling methods used. Too small a sample will not represent the larger population, and a sample that is not representative of the population introduces **bias** into the experiment. For example, if a survey was to be conducted about Americans' feelings on race relations, bias could occur if the sample did not include people of different races, sexes, and geographical locations (including urban, suburban, and rural locations).

Describing Sets of Data

Measures of Central Tendency

If there are more than two measurements of a certain event or phenomenon, central values help identify trends in the entirety of measurements. There are three such **central tendencies** that describe the "center" of the data in different ways. The **mean** is the arithmetic average and is found by dividing the sum of all measurements by the number of measurements. The equation for the mean, can be written as follows:

$$\text{population mean} = \mu = \frac{x_1 + x_2 + ...x_N}{N} = \frac{\Sigma x}{N} \qquad \text{sample mean} = \bar{x} = \frac{x_1 + x_2 + ...x_n}{n} = \frac{\Sigma x}{n}$$

The data points are represented by xs with subscripts; the sum is denoted using the Greek letter sigma $(\Sigma)x$; N is the number of data points in the entire population; and n is the number of data points in a sample set.

The **median** divides the measurements into two equal halves. The median is the measurement right in the middle of an odd set of measurements (the fifth-largest in nine measurements) or the average of the two middle numbers in an even data set (the average of the fifth- and sixth-largest measurements of ten total measurements). When calculating the median, it is important to order the data values from least to greatest before attempting to locate the middle value. The **mode** is simply the measurement that occurs most often. There can be many modes in a data set, or no mode. Since measures of central tendency describe a *center* of the data, all three of these measures will be between the lowest and highest data values (inclusive).

Unlike the mean, the median is not affected by very large or very small unusual measurements (**outliers**). Notice that in the following sample questions, both have the same data points, but the median is not skewed by the single large value. That is, the median is much closer to the terms in the data set than the mean is. If there is a high outlier, the mean will be greater than the median; if there is a low or negative outlier, the mean will be lower than the median. When outliers are present, the median is a better measure of the center of the data than the mean is.

SAMPLE QUESTIONS

1) **What is the mean of the following data set? {1000, 0.1, 10, 1}**

   Answer:

   The mean to the nearest hundredth is found as follows:

   $\frac{1000 + 0.1 + 10 + 1}{4} = \textbf{252.78}$

2) **What is the median of the following data set? {1000, 10, 1, 0.1}**

   Answer:

   Since there are an even number of data points in the set, the median will be the mean of the two middle numbers. Order the numbers from least to greatest: 0.1, 1, 10, and 1000. The two middle numbers are 1 and 10, and their mean is:

$$\frac{1 + 10}{2} = \textbf{5.5}$$

3) **Josey has an average of 81 on four equally weighted tests she has taken in her statistics class. She wants to determine what grade she must receive on her fifth test so that her mean is 83, which will give her a B in the course, but she does not remember her other scores. What grade must she receive on her fifth test?**

Answer:

Even though Josey does not know her test scores, she knows her average. Therefore it can be assumed that each test score was 81, since four scores of 81 would average to 81. To find the score, x, that she needs:

$$\frac{4(81) + x}{5} = 83$$

$$324 + x = 415$$

$$x = 91$$

Josey must score a 91 on the last test to have a mean score of 83.

MEASURES OF VARIATION

The values in a data set can be very close together (close to the mean), or very spread out. This is called the **spread** or **dispersion** of the data. Sometimes most of the data is close to the mean, but there are one or more values far from the mean. These are called **outliers**. There are a few **measures of variation** (or **measures of dispersion**) that quantify the spread within a data set. **Range** is the difference between the largest and smallest data points in a set:

R = largest data point – smallest data point

Notice range depends on only two data points, the two extremes. Sometimes these data points are outliers; regardless, for a large data set, relying on only two data points is not an exact tool. The understanding of the data set can be improved by calculating **quartiles**. To calculate quartiles, first arrange the data in ascending order and find the set's median (also called quartile 2 or Q2). Then find the median of the lower half of the data, called quartile 1 (Q1), and the median of the upper half of the data, called quartile 3 (Q3). These three points divide the data into four equal groups of data (thus the word *quartile*). Each quartile contains 25% of the data.

Interquartile range (IQR) provides a more reliable range that is not as affected by extremes. IQR is the difference between the third quartile data point and the first quartile data point:

$$IQR = Q_3 - Q_1$$

The interquartile range gives the spread of the middle 50% of the data.

A measure of variation that depends on the mean is **standard deviation**, which uses every data point in a set and basically calculates the average distance of each data point from the mean of the data. Standard deviation can be computed for an entire population, if the data set is not too large, or for a sample of the population. The formula for standard deviation is slightly different based on whether it is a population standard deviation (denoted by σ or lowercase sigma) or a sample standard deviation (denoted by the letter s):

$$\sigma = \sqrt{\frac{\Sigma(x_i - \mu)^2}{N}} \qquad s = \sqrt{\frac{\Sigma(x_i - \bar{x})^2}{n-1}}$$

Thus, to calculate standard deviation, the difference between the mean μ or $\bar{x}$ or and each data point x_i is calculated. Each of these differences is squared (this is done mostly to make all the differences positive). The average of the squared values is computed by summing the squares and dividing by N or $(n-1)$. (The reason for dividing by $n-1$ and not just n is beyond the scope of this text.) Then the square root is taken, to "undo" the previous squaring.

The **variance** of a data set is simply the square of the standard variation:

$$V = \sigma^2 = \frac{1}{N}\sum_{i=1}^{N}(x_i - \mu)^2$$

Variance measures how narrowly or widely the data points are distributed. A variance of zero means every data point is the same; a large variance means the data is widely spread out.

SAMPLE QUESTIONS

4) **What are the range and interquartile range of the following set? {3, 9, 49, 64, 81, 100, 121, 144, 169}**

Answer:

The range is the difference between the largest and smallest data points:

$R = 169 - 3 = 166$

The set's median is 81, which is Q_2. The median of the bottom half of the data is midway between 9 and 49, which, averaging those two numbers, is 29. This is Q_1. The median of the upper half of the data is midway between 121 and 144, which, averaging those two numbers, is 132.5. This is Q_3. Thus, the $IQR = Q_3 - Q_1 = 132.5 - 29 = $ **103.5**.

5) **In a group of 7 people, 1 person has no children, 2 people have 1 child, 2 people have 2 children, 1 person has 5 children, and 1 person has 17 children. To the nearest hundredth of a child, what is the standard deviation in this group? What is the variance?**

Answer:

$\{0, 1, 1, 2, 2, 5, 17\}$	Create a data set out of this scenario.
$\mu = \dfrac{0 + 1 + 1 + 2 + 2 + 5 + 17}{7} = 4$	Calculate the population mean.
$(0 - 4)^2 = (-4)^2 = 16$ $(1 - 4)^2 = (-3)^2 = 9$ $(1 - 4)^2 = (-3)^2 = 9$ $(2 - 4)^2 = (-2)^2 = 4$ $(2 - 4)^2 = (-2)^2 = 4$ $(5 - 4)^2 = (1)^2 = 1$ $(17 - 4)^2 = (13)^2 = 169$	Find the square of the difference of each term and the mean $(x_i - \mu)^2$.
$\sigma = \sqrt{\dfrac{212}{7}} = \sqrt{30.28} = 5.50$	Plug the sum (Σ) of these squares, 212, into the standard deviation formula.

The standard deviation is 5.50 and the variance is 30.28. Notice that both the mean and the standard deviation are greatly skewed by the outlier value 17. Of the 7 people, 5 have fewer than 3 children, but the mean number of children is 4. Most of the people have within 1 or 2 children of one another, but the deviation is more than 5 children. An outlier seriously skews statistics, especially in a small data set.

6) **What happens to the mean and the standard deviation of a data set if all *n* values of the data set are increased by the same amount? What if each data value is multiplied by the same value?**

Answer:

When all the members of a data set are increased by the same amount, the sum of the data is increased by the product of that number times the number of values *n*. For example, if each member of a data set with ten values were increased by 4, the sum would be increased by 40. To calculate the new mean:

$$new\ mean = \frac{3a + 3b + 3c + 3d}{4} = \frac{3(a + b + c + d)}{4} = 3\left(\frac{a + b + c + d}{4}\right) = 3\ (old\ mean)$$

The new mean is just shifted up by the amount each data value is increased. Since each data value is shifted up the same amount, and the mean is also shifted up by that amount, the deviation between each value and the mean will be unchanged.

Thus, when the same value is added to each element of a data set, the mean increases by the same value and the standard deviation is unchanged.

When all the members of a data set are multiplied by the same amount, the sum of the values will be multiplied by that amount due to the distributive property, and the mean will also be multiplied by the same value. Say there are four values, a, b, c, and d, and each is multiplied by 3:

In the standard deviation formula, since each of the differences will also be multiplied by 3, the squares of the difference will be multiplied by 9, so the variance is multiplied by 9. But after the square root of the variance is taken to calculate the standard deviation, standard deviation is changed by a factor of 3.

Thus both the mean and the standard deviation of a data set is changed by the same factor (k) when each value of the data set is multiplied by some factor k.

Box Plots

A **box plot** depicts the median and quartiles along a scaled number line. A box plot is meant to summarize the data in a visual manner and emphasize central trends while decreasing the pull of outlier data. To construct a box plot:

1.   Create a number line that begins at the lowest data point and terminates at the highest data point.

2.   Find the quartiles of the data: Q_1, the median (Q_2), and Q_3. Create a horizontal rectangle (the "box") whose left border is Q_1 and right border is Q_3.

3.   Draw a vertical line within the box to mark the median.

4.   Draw a horizontal line going from the left edge of the box to the smallest data value.

5.   Draw a horizontal line going from the right edge of the box to the largest data value.

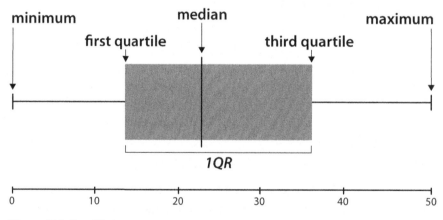

Figure 7.1. Box Plot

When reading a box plot, the following stands out:

▶   The length of the box is the IQR, $Q_3 - Q_1$, hence the middle 50% of the data.

▶   Each of the four pieces (the whiskers and two pieces in the box) represent 25% of the data.

▶ The horizontal lines (whiskers) show by their length whether the data higher or lower than the middle 50% is more or less prominent.

▶ Reading from left to right: the horizontal line (whisker) shows the spread of the first quarter; the box's left compartment shows the spread of the second quarter; the box's right compartment shows the spread of the third quarter; and the right horizontal line (whisker) shows the spread of the fourth quarter.

SAMPLE QUESTION

7) **A recent survey asked 8 people how many pairs of shoes they wear per week. Their answers are in the following data set: {1, 3, 5, 5, 7, 8, 12}. Construct a box plot from this data.**

Answer:

Create a number line that begins at 1 and ends at 12. Q_1 is 3, the median (Q_2) is 5, and Q_3 is 8. A rectangle must be drawn whose length is 5 and that borders on Q_1 and Q_3. Mark the median of 5 within the rectangle. Draw a horizontal line going left to 1. Draw a horizontal line going right to 12.

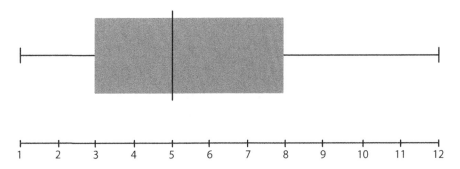

GRAPHS, CHARTS, AND TABLES

PIE CHARTS

Pie charts summarize the prominence of categories in a data set. Appropriate uses of pie charts may include budgets, production breakdowns, population analyses, and data that is best expressed as percentages. A pie chart simply states the proportion of each category within the whole. To construct a pie chart, the categories of a data set must be determined. The frequency of each category must be found and that frequency converted to a percent of the total. To draw the pie chart, determine the angle of each slice by multiplying the percentage by 360°.

8)   A firm is screening applicants for a job by education-level attainment. There are 125 individuals in the pool. By the highest level of education attained in the pool, 5 have a doctorate, 20 have a master's degree, 40 have a bachelor's degree, 30 have an associate degree, and the remaining only have a high school degree. Construct a pie chart showing the highest level of education attained by the applicants.

Answer:

The total given to us is 125, meaning there are 30 applicants with just a high school degree. Next, a frequency table must be created. The percent is found by dividing the frequency of a specific category by the total (125). Multiply that percent by 360° to get the angle measure:

Category	Frequency	Percent	Angle Measure
High School	30	24%	86.4
Associate	30	24%	86.4
Bachelor's	40	32%	115.2
Master's	20	16%	57.6
Doctorate	5	4%	14.4

The pie chart below expresses the table's data.

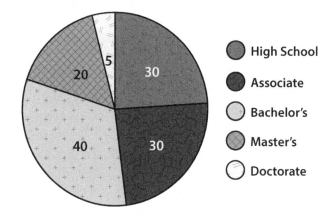

SCATTER PLOTS

A scatter plot is displayed in the first quadrant of the *xy*-plane where all numbers are positive. A scatter plot is an easy way to tell if there is a correlation between two variables in a data set. Data points are plotted as ordered pairs, with one variable along the horizontal axis and the other along the vertical axis. Constructing a scatter plot requires the plotting of every point on a domain and range that includes every data outcome. Often, but not always, the data points will show a linear tendency. There is a **positive correlation** (expressed as a positive slope) if increasing one variable appears to result in an increase in the other variable. A **negative correlation** (expressed as a negative slope) occurs when an increase in one variable causes a decrease in the other. If the scatter plot shows no discernible pattern, then there is no correlation (a zero, mixed, or indiscernible slope). Scatter plots are often used for lab experiments and any attempt to establish a causal link.

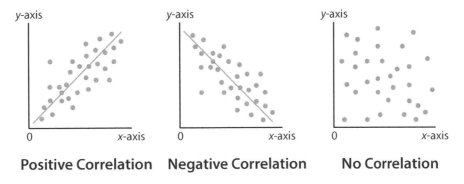

Positive Correlation   Negative Correlation   No Correlation

Figure 7.2. Scatter Plots and Correlation

Working from data points, or using the regression feature of a calculator, a regression equation can be created that encapsulates the directionality of the scatter plot. If the regression equation is graphed, the resulting line (or curve) is known as a regression line (or curve). This is also known as the "line of best fit." To figure out how well the regression line (or curve) fits every data point on a scatter plot, the equation's **correlation coefficient** (r) can be considered. The formula for computing the correlation coefficient is complex, but the calculator will provide this number along with the regression line if the diagnostics feature is on. The value of r is between –1 and 1. The closer r is to 1 (if the line has a positive slope) or –1 (if the line has a negative slope), the better the regression line fits the data. The closer the r value is to 0, the weaker the correlation between the line and the data. Generally, if the absolute value of the correlation coefficient is 0.8 or higher, then it is considered to be a strong correlation, while an $|r|$ value of less than 0.5 is considered a weak correlation.

To determine which curve is the "best fit" for a set of data, **residuals** are calculated. The calculator automatically calculates and saves these values to a list called RESID. These values are all the differences between the actual y-value of data points and the y-value calculated by the best-fit line or curve for that x-value. These values can be plotted on an xy-plane with the x-values along the x-axis and the residuals along the y-axis. This is called a **residual plot**. The residual plot helps determine if a line is the best model for the data. Residual points that are randomly dispersed above and below the horizontal indicate that a linear model is appropriate, while a u shape or upside-down u shape indicate a nonlinear model would be more appropriate.

Once a best-fit line (or curve) is established, it can be used to estimate output values given an input value within the domain of the data. For a short extension outside that domain, reasonable predictions may be possible. However, the further from the domain of the data the line is extended, the greater the reduction in the accuracy of the prediction. For example, a model is created from the growth data of a city over a twenty-year period; that model will not be a good predictor of the population of the city in one hundred years.

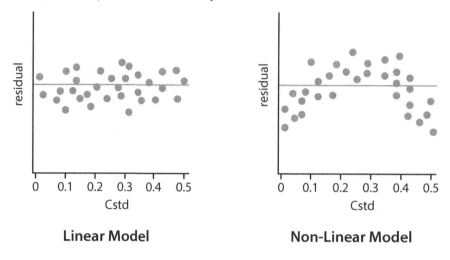

Figure 7.3. Residual Plots

It is important to note here that just because two variables have a strong positive or negative correlation, it cannot necessarily be inferred that those two quantities have a **causal** relationship—that is, that one variable changing *causes* the other quantity to change. There are often other factors that play into their relationship. For example, a positive correlation can be found between the number of ice cream sales and the number of shark attacks at a beach. It would be incorrect to say that selling more ice cream *causes* an increase in shark attacks. It is much more likely that on hot days more ice cream is sold, and many more people are swimming, so one of them is more likely to get attacked by a shark. Confusing correlation and causation is one of the most common statistical errors people make.

SAMPLE QUESTION

9) Based on the scatter plot, where the *x*-axis represents hours spent studying per week and the *y*-axis represents the average percent grade on exams during the school year, is there a correlation between the amount of studying for a test and test results?

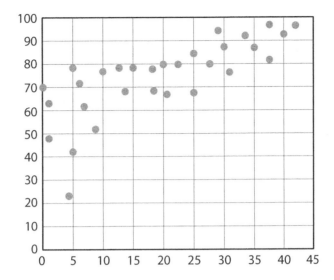

Answer:

There is a somewhat weak positive correlation. As the number of hours spent studying increases, the average percent grade also generally increases.

LINE GRAPHS

Line graphs are used to display a relationship between two variables, such as change over time. Like scatter plots, line graphs exist in quadrant 1 of the *xy*-plane. Line graphs are constructed by graphing each point and connecting each point to the next consecutive point by a line. To create a line graph, it may be necessary to consolidate data into single bivariate data points. Thus, a line graph is a function, with each *x*-value having exactly one *y*-value, whereas a scatter plot may have multiple *y*-values for one *x*-value.

Figure 7.4. Line Graph

SAMPLE QUESTION

10) Create a line graph based on the following survey values, where the first column represents an individual's age and the other represents that individual's reported happiness level on a 20-point scale (0 being the least happy that person has been and 20 being the happiest). Then interpret the resulting graph to determine whether the following statement is true or false: *On average, middle-aged people are less happy than young or older people are.*

Age	Happiness
12	16
13	15
20	18
15	12
40	5
17	17
18	18
19	15
42	7
70	17
45	10
60	12
63	15
22	14
27	15
36	12
33	10
44	8
55	10
80	10
15	13
40	8
17	15
18	17
19	20
22	16
27	15
36	9
33	10
44	6

Answer:

To construct a line graph, the data must be ordered into consolidated categories by averaging the data of people who have the same age so that the data is one-to-one. For example, there are two twenty-two-year-olds who are reporting. Their average happiness level is 15. When all the data has been consolidated and ordered from least to greatest, the table and graph below can be presented.

Age	Happiness
12	16
13	15
15	12.5
17	16
18	17.5
19	17.5
20	18
22	15
27	15
33	10
36	10.5
40	6.5
42	7
44	7
45	10
55	10
60	12
63	15
70	17
80	10

Average Happiness Rating Versus Age

The statement that, on average, middle-aged people are less happy than young or older people appears to be true. According to the graph, people in their thirties, forties, and fifties are less happy than people in their teens, twenties, sixties, and seventies.

BAR GRAPHS

Like line graphs, **bar graphs** compare changes between groups or over time. The data here is grouped into certain ranges and represented by rectangles (a bar graph's rectangles can be vertical or horizontal, depending on whether the dependent variable is placed on the *x*- or *y*-axis). Instead of the *xy*-plane, however, one axis is made up of types of categories. Bar graphs are useful because the differences between categories are easy to see. Reading a bar graph requires understanding that the width or height (depending on vertical or horizontal orientation) of each rectangle indicates the total within that category, and the difference among the rectangles shows the difference year to year.

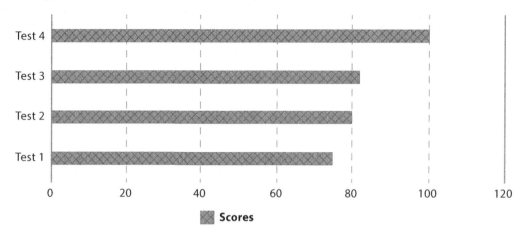

Figure 7.5. Bar Graph

SAMPLE QUESTION

11) **A company X had a profit of $10,000 in 2010, $12,000 in 2011, and each of the following two years saw a 30% increase in profits. Create a bar graph displaying the profit from each of these four years.**

Answer:

If 2012 saw a 30% increase from 2011, that year's profit is 1.3($12,000) = $15,600; by the same method, the profit in 2013 was $20,280. The bar graph below captures this data:

STEM-AND-LEAF PLOTS

Stem-and-leaf plots are ways of organizing large amounts of data by grouping it into classes. All data points are broken into two parts: a stem and a leaf. For instance, the number 512 might be broken into a stem of 5 and a leaf of 12. All data in the

500 range would appear in the same row (this group of data is a class). Usually a simple key is provided to explain how the data is being represented. For instance, 5|12 = 512 would show that the stems are representing hundreds. The advantage of this display is that it shows general density and shape of the data in a compact display, yet all original data points are preserved and available. It is also easy to find medians and quartiles from this display.

Stem	Leaf
0	5
1	6, 7
2	8, 3, 6
3	4, 5, 9, 5, 5, 8, 5
4	7, 7, 7, 8
5	5, 4
6	0

Figure 7.6. Stem and Leaf Plot

SAMPLE QUESTION

12) The table gives the weights of wrestlers (in pounds) for a certain competition. What is the mean, median, and IQR of the data?

2	05, 22, 53, 40
3	07, 22, 29, 45, 89, 96, 98
4	10, 25, 34
6	21

Key: 2|05 = 205 pounds

Answer:

$\mu = \frac{\Sigma x}{N}$ $= \frac{5281}{15}$ $= \textbf{353.1 lbs.}$	Find the mean using the equation for the population mean.
Q1 = 253 Q2 = 345 Q3 = 410 IQR = 410 − 253 = 157 **The median is 345 lbs.** **The IQR is 157 lbs.**	Find the median and IQR by counting the leaves and identifying Q1, Q2, and Q3.

FREQUENCY TABLES AND HISTOGRAMS

The frequency of a particular data point is the number of times that data point occurs. Constructing a frequency table requires that the data or data classes be arranged in ascending order in one column and the frequency in another column.

A histogram is used to compare the frequency of specified ranges of data. It is a graphical representation of a frequency table. A histogram is constructed in quadrant I of the *xy*-plane, with data in each equal-width class presented as a bar and the height of each bar representing the frequency of that class. Unlike bar graphs, histograms cannot have gaps between bars. A histogram is used to determine the distribution of data among the classes. Examples of histograms include population statistics, arrivals and departures at airports, and ecological studies such as the average temperature over a year.

Histograms can be symmetrical, skewed left or right, or multimodal (data spread around). Note that **skewed left** means the peak of the data is on the *right*, with a tail to the left, while **skewed right** means the peak is on the *left*, with a tail to the right. This seems counterintuitive to many; the "left" or "right" always refers to the tail of the data. This is because a long tail to the right, for example, means there are high outlier values that are skewing the data to the right.

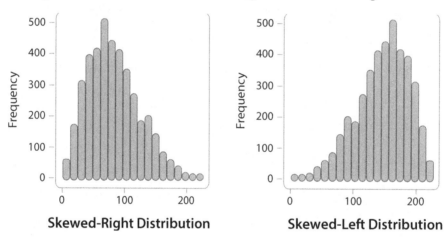

Figure 7.7. Histograms

A **two-way frequency table** compares **categorical data** (data in more than one category) of two related variables (bivariate data). Two-way frequency tables are also called **contingency tables** and are often used to analyze survey results. One category is displayed along the top of the table and the other category down along the side. Rows and columns are added and the sums appear at the end of the row or column. The sum of all the row data must equal the sum of all the column data. From a two-way frequency table, the **joint relative frequency** of a particular category can be calculated by taking the number in the row and column of the categories in question and dividing by the total number surveyed. This gives the percent of the total in that particular category. Sometimes the **conditional relative frequency** is of interest. In this case, calculate the relative frequency confined to a single row or column, because a condition was given that restricts the data examined.

Students by Grade and Gender

	9th grade	**10th grade**	**11th grade**	**12th grade**	**Total**
Male	57	63	75	61	256
Female	54	42	71	60	227
Total	111	105	146	121	483

Figure 7.8. Two-Way Frequency Table

SAMPLE QUESTIONS

13) A café owner tracked the number of customers he had over a twelve-hour period one day in the frequency table below. Display the data in a histogram and determine what kind of distribution there is in the data.

Time	**Number of Customers**
6 a.m. – 8 a.m.	5
8 a.m. – 9 a.m.	6
9 a.m. – 10 a.m.	5
10 a.m. – 12 p.m.	23
12 p.m. – 2 p.m.	24
2 p.m. – 4 p.m.	9
4 p.m. – 6 p.m.	4

Answer:

Since time is the independent variable, it is on the *x*-axis and the number of customers is on the *y*-axis. For the histogram to correctly display data continuously, categories on the *x*-axis must be equal 2-hour segments. The 8 a.m. – 9 a.m. and 9 a.m. – 10 a.m. categories must be combined for a total of 11 customers in that time period. The correct graph is displayed below. Although not perfectly symmetrical, the amount of customers peaks in the middle and is therefore considered symmetrical.

14) In a class of 30 students, 10% got an A, 30% got a B, 30% received a C, 10% received a D, and the remainder received an F on a recent exam (the minimum possible grade recorded was a 50). Create a frequency table summarizing this data. Estimate the average (mean) grade on the exam by using the midpoint of each class of grade.

Answer:

Frequency tables deal with total frequency. Every percent then must be multiplied by 30 students to figure out the total number of students in each grade category. Additionally, the number of students with an F can be found by multiplying the remaining percent by 30: $(1 - 0.10 - 0.30 - 0.30 - 0.10)$ $(30) = 6$.

Grade	Number of Students
A (90 – 100)	3
B (80 – 89)	9
C (70 – 79)	9
D (60 – 69)	3
F (50 – 59)	6

An estimate of the class average using approximate midpoints of each class and computing the weighted average:

$$\frac{3(95) + 9(85) + 9(75) + 3(65)\ 6(55)}{30} = \frac{2250}{3.0} = \mathbf{75}.$$

15) Cineflix movie theater polled its moviegoers on a weeknight to determine their favorite type of movie. The results are in the two-way frequency table below.

Moviegoers	Comedy	Action	Horror	Totals
Male	15	25	21	61
Female	8	18	17	43
Totals	23	43	38	104

Determine whether each of the following statements is true or false.

A. Action films are the most popular type of movie

B. About 1 in 5 moviegoers prefers comedy films

C. Men choose the horror genre more frequently than women do

Answers:

A. **True**. More people (42) chose action movies than comedy (23) or horror (38).

B. **True**. Find the ratio of total number of people who prefer comedy to total number of people. $\frac{23}{103} = 0.22$; 1 in 5 is 20%, so 22% is about the same.

C. **False**. The percentage of men who choose horror is less than the percentage of women who do.

   $part = number\ of\ men\ who\ prefer\ horror = 21$

   $whole = number\ of\ men\ surveyed = 60$

   $percent = \frac{part}{whole}$

   $= \frac{21}{60} = 0.35 = 35\%$

   $part = number\ of\ women\ who\ prefer\ horror = 17$

   $whole = number\ of\ women\ surveyed = 43$

   $percent = \frac{part}{whole}$

   $= \frac{17}{43} = 0.40 = 40\%$

COUNTING PRINCIPLES

THE FUNDAMENTAL COUNTING PRINCIPLE

An **outcome** is any possible result of an experiment, such as the outcome "heads" in a coin toss. The set of all possible outcomes for a specific experiment is called the **sample space**. The sample space for tossing a single coin is {H = heads, T = tails}. Any outcome's probability is based on all the unique possibilities that could occur, so being able to calculate all the possible outcomes is critical to finding probabilities. The number of unique possible outcomes for any sequence of events is often calculated by the **fundamental counting principle**. This principle states that the total number of possible outcomes is the product of the total possible number of outcomes in each trial. Suppose a coin is tossed three times. Each toss of the coin is a trial. Each trial has two possible outcomes. By the fundamental counting principle, the total number of possibilities (the number of elements in the sample space) when a coin is tossed three times is $2 \times 2 \times 2 = 8$. They are {HHH, HHT, HTT, HTH, TTH, THH, THT, TTT}.

SAMPLE QUESTIONS

16) **A personal assistant is struggling to pick a shirt, tie, and cufflink set that go together. If his client has 70 shirts, 2 ties, and 5 cufflinks, how many possible combinations does he have to consider?**

Answer:

The formula is always the same. The total number of combinations is (70)(2)(5) = 700. **There are 700 shirt, tie, and cufflink combinations.**

17) **A bank requires a four-digit personal identification number (PIN) for access to an automated teller machine. If only numbers 1 – 9 are allowed, how many different four-digit PIN numbers are there?**

Answer:

Assuming repeat digits are allowed, there are 9 possible numbers for each of the 4 digits (each digit is a "trial"). Thus, there are $9 \times 9 \times 9 \times 9 = $ **6561 possible PIN codes.**

18) **How many ways can four distinct books be arranged on the shelf?**

Answer:

As in the previous problem, there are four slots to be filled. Unlike the previous problem, however, each slot does not have the same number of choices. For the first slot, there are four book choices. Once one book is chosen to be put on the shelf, there are only three book choices for the second slot, two for the third slot, and one for the last. The total number of ways to arrange the four books is $4 \times 3 \times 2 \times 1 = $ **24.**

COMBINATIONS AND PERMUTATIONS

Combinations and permutations are arrangements of a set of objects. In **combinations**, the order of the arrangement or selection does not matter. For **permutations**, the order of the arrangement or selection is important. A "combination lock" is therefore *misnamed*—it really should be a *permutation lock*, since the order in which the numbers are dialed is important. An example of a question calling for a combination would be, "How many ways can a committee of three people be chosen from twelve people?" The order in which the people are chosen is not relevant if all the positions on the committee are exactly the same.

The formulas for calculating the number of permutations or combinations both use factorials. Factorials are expressed by an integer, followed by an exclamation point (!). Recall that a factorial $n!$ is the product of n times $(n - 1)$, times $(n - 2)$, etc., until n is multiplied by 1. For example, $3! = 3 \times 2 \times 1 = 6$. Zero factorial is defined to 1, that is $0! = 1$.

Also recall that factorial expressions, when divided, can be simplified. For example,

$$10! \div 8! = \frac{10 \times 9 \times 8 \times 7 \times 6 \times 5 \times 4 \times 3 \times 2 \times 1}{8 \times 7 \times 6 \times 5 \times 4 \times 3 \times 2 \times 1} = 10 \times 9 = 90$$

since all the number from 8 down to 1 cancel. In the following two formulas, rep-resents the total amount of items or actions and represents the total number of these items that are to be selected or ordered.

Permutation Formula	Combination Formula
$P(n,k) = \dfrac{n!}{(n-k)!}$	$C(n,k) = \dfrac{n!}{(n-k)!\,k!}$

Figure 7.9. Permutation and Combination Formulas

The only difference between the two formulas is the k! in the combination denominator. This is to account for redundancy of data with the same values just in a different order. Dividing by this k! reduces the number of possibilities.

The example from the previous section about ordering four books on a shelf is actually a permutation problem. Since each book is unique, when arranging them, the order matters. Using the permutation formula with $n = 4$ items, all $k = 4$ of which are being ordered, yields $P(4,4) = \dfrac{4!}{(4-4)!} = \dfrac{4!}{0!} = \dfrac{4 \times 3 \times 2 \times 1}{1} = 24$, which is the same answer arrived at before.

SAMPLE QUESTIONS

19) **If there are twenty applicants for three open positions, in how many different ways can a team of three be hired?**

Answer:

In this problem, $n = 20$ and $k = 3$. Since the three positions are presumably identical, the order of hiring is not important, so this is a combination problem. Using the combination formula:

$C(20, 3) = \dfrac{20!}{(20-3)!\,3!} = \dfrac{20!}{17!\,3!} = \dfrac{(20)(19)(18)}{3!} = 1140$

There are **1140 different three-person teams** that can be hired.

Another way to think about this problem is to calculate all the ways that a three-spot team can be created and then divide by how many ways that team of three can be arranged. For the first spot, 20 people can be chosen; for the second, 19; for the third, 18. This gives (20)(19)(18) = 6840 teams of three. But this is too many since the order of those three chosen does not matter, so it is necessary to divide by the number of ways possible to order three people = 3 × 2 × 1 = 6. Dividing, 6840 by 6 gives 1140.

20) **At a sandwich shop, a customer has a choice of ten toppings he can add to his sandwich. If three distinct toppings are added, how many three-topping sandwiches are possible?**

Answer:

This question is a combination problem—the order does not matter, only that each item added be distinct. Plugging the appropriate values into the equation, it is found that:

$$C(10, 3) = \frac{10!}{(10 - 3)! \, 3!} = 120$$

There are **120 possible sandwiches** with three toppings added out of ten possible ingredients to add.

21) **Calculate the number of unique permutations that can be made out of all the letters in the word *pickle*, the number of unique permutations that can be made out of all the letters in the word *cheese*, and the number of unique permutations that can be made out of all the letters in the word *blueberry*.**

Answer:

To find the number of unique permutations of the letters of *pickle*, use the permutation formula with the total number of letters $n = 6$, and the number to be arranged $k = 6$.

$$P(6, 6) = \frac{6!}{(6 - 6)!} = \frac{720}{1} = 720$$

(Or think of it as six slots that need to be filled; in the first there are six choices, the second five choices, etc., giving 6! as the answer.)

There are 720 distinct arrangements of the letters in the word *pickle*.

The word *cheese* has the letter *e* that repeats three times. Thus, some permutations of the six letters will be indistinguishable from others, as the reader will be unable to tell one *e* from another. The number of permutations must be divided by the number of ways the three *e*s can be arranged, 3! = 6. The formula is:

total number of permutations = number of ways to arrange 6 letters/number of ways to arrange 3 letters $= \frac{6!}{3!} = 6 \times 5 \times 4 = 120$

There are 120 distinct arrangements of the letters in the word *cheese*.

The word *blueberry* repeats *b* two times, *e* two times, and *r* two times. To calculate the number of unique arrangements of all nine letters, calculate the number of ways to arrange nine items, and divide by the number of ways the *b*s can be arranged (2!), the *e*s can be arranged (2!), and the *r*s can be arranged (2!):

total number of permutations $= \frac{9!}{2! \, 2! \, 2!} = \frac{9!}{8} = 45,360.$

There are 45,360 distinct arrangements of all the letters in the word *blueberry*.

22) Suppose 7 runners are lining up for a race. 3 runners are women and 4 are men. How many ways can they line up if they can line up in any order? How many ways can they line up if the women must be beside each other, and the men must be grouped together?

Answer:

If all 7 can be arranged in any order, there are 7! = **5040 arrangements**. If the women must stay together, and the men must stay together, there are 2 groups that can be arranged in exactly 2 ways (women on the left and men on the right, or vice-versa). Within these groups, the women can be arranged 3! ways and the men 4! ways. Using the fundamental counting principle:

total number of arrangements with men grouped and women grouped =
$2 \times 3! \times 4! = 2 \times 6 \times 24 = $ **288**.

PROBABILITY

PROBABILITY OF A SINGLE EVENT

Probability is the likelihood of one or a certain number of specific events occurring. The probability of a single event occurring is the number of outcomes in which that event occurs (called **favorable events**) divided by the number of items in the sample space (total possible outcomes):

$$P \text{ (an event)} = \frac{number\ of\ favorable\ outcomes}{total\ number\ of\ possible\ outcomes}$$

The probability of any event occurring will always be a fraction or decimal between 0 and 1. It may also be expressed as a percent. An event with 0 probability will never occur and an event with a probability of 1 is certain to occur. The probability of an event not occurring is referred to as that event's **complement**. The sum of an event's probability and the probability of that event's complement will always be 1.

SAMPLE QUESTIONS

23) In an experiment to see if a certain drug works correctly, it is determined that there are 10 distinct equally likely outcomes that would show the drug works incorrectly and 1 that it does work correctly. All else being equal, what is the probability that the experiment shows the drug in question works correctly?

Answer:

The problem specified there are 11 equally likely possible outcomes: 10 negatives and 1 positive. Therefore, the probability of the 1 positive occurring is:

$P \text{ (drug working correctly)} = \frac{1}{11}$

24) **What is the difference between the probability that when a six-sided die is rolled an even number outcome results and the probability that the die lands on the number 5?**

Answer:

In both of these probabilities, the denominator is 6. There are 3 even numbers possible in the first event. There is just 1 possible favorable outcome in the other. The two probabilities are:

P (rolling even) = $\frac{3}{6}$

P (rolling 5) = $\frac{1}{6}$

The difference then is $\frac{2}{6}$ or $\frac{1}{3}$.

25) **Only 20 tickets were issued in a raffle. If someone were to buy 6 tickets, what is the probability that person would not win the raffle?**

Answer:

If 6 tickets were purchased, that means 14 remain. Thus, the probability of not winning the raffle is:

P (not winning) = $\frac{14}{20}$

Notice that the sum of the probability of winning, $\frac{6}{20}$, and the probability of losing, $\frac{14}{20}$, is **1**. Since these events are complements of each other, one of these must occur (the raffle participant either wins or loses).

Probability of Multiple Events

If events are **independent events**, the probability of one occurring does not affect the probability of the other event occurring. If events are **dependent events**, the probability of one occurring changes the probability of the other event occurring. Rolling a die and getting one number does not change the probability of getting any particular number on the next roll. The number of faces has not changed, so these are independent events. When drawing two cards from a deck of cards, it is important to pay attention to whether the card is *replaced* or not. If the cards are drawn *with replacement*, then the second draw of a card is independent of the first draw (assuming the cards are shuffled). If the cards are drawn *without replacement*, then the probability of the second draw is affected by the first draw, and the events are dependent.

The probability of two independent events occurring is the product of the two events' probabilities:

$$P \text{ (}A \text{ and } B\text{)} = P(A) \times P(B)$$

The probability of one event *or* another occurring can be found using the following formula:

$$P \text{ (}A \text{ or } B\text{)} = P(A) + P(B) - P \text{ (}A \text{ and } B\text{)}$$

Notice this is exactly the same as finding in set theory. These topics are closely related. Two events that are **mutually exclusive** *cannot* happen at the same time. This is similar to disjoint sets in set theory. In that case, $P(A \text{ and } B) = 0$ and $P(A \text{ or } B) = P(A) + P(B)$. For example, if a single die is to be rolled one time, event A represents getting an even number, and event B represents getting the number 5, then these events are mutually exclusive and $P(A \text{ and } B) = 0$. Also, the probability of one or the other event occurring is $P(A \text{ or } B) = P(A) + P(B) = \frac{1}{2} + \frac{1}{6} = \frac{4}{6} = \frac{2}{3}$.

Conditional probability is the probability of an event (A) occurring given that another event (B) has occurred. Above, the formula did not specify that an event had already occurred. Conditional probability deals with a fact of past occurrence. The example of calculating the probability of drawing a second card from a deck when the first card was not replaced is an example of conditional probability.

The notation $P(B|A)$ represents the probability that event B occurs, given that event A has already occurred (it is read "probability of B, given A"). For example, suppose 2 cards are drawn from a deck of 10 cards, numbered 1 through 10, without replacement. Let event A be drawing a 7 on the first draw; then $P(A) = \frac{1}{10}$. Let event B be drawing a 5 on the second draw. The probability that a 5 is now drawn given that 7 was already drawn is $P(B|A) = \frac{1}{9}$, since there are now only 9 cards from which to draw. The probability of both events occurring is $P(A \text{ and } B) = \frac{1}{10} \times \frac{1}{9} = P(A) \times P(B|A)$. Note that the $P(B)$ just represents the probability of drawing a 7 out of 10 cards, so it is incorrect to say $P(A \text{ and } B) = P(A) \times P(B)$. The fact that the 7 has already been drawn prior to the second event must be taken into account. In general,

$$P(A \text{ and } B) = P(B|A)P(A) = P(A|B)P(B)$$

This formula can be rearranged to solve for any of the three quantities on the right side, if necessary. If A and B are independent events, then the left side becomes $P(A) \times P(B)$ and the above equation simplifies to:

$$P(B|A) = P(B) \text{ or } P(A|B) = P(A)$$

for A and B independent.

SAMPLE QUESTIONS

26) **A group of ten individuals is drawing straws. There are 30 straws and 2 of them are short. If the straws are not replaced, what is the probability, as a percentage, that none of the first three individuals to draw straws will draw a short straw?**

Answer:

Drawing straws in this scenario is a sequence of dependent events. The total number of possible outcomes diminishes after each person draws. Therefore, the first person has a probability of 28 normal-sized straws out of 30 straws. The second person, however, only has 27 normal straws out of 29, since the first person took out, and did not replace, 1 straw. The third person's probability is even lower, at 26 out of the 28. Thus,

P (3 people not drawing short straws) $= \frac{28}{30} \times \frac{27}{29} \times \frac{26}{28} = \frac{117}{145} = 0.81$

There is an **81% chance** that none of the first three people to draw will get a short straw.

27) **A used car dealership is selling 30 cars, and 2 of these cars are defective. One individual buys a car that is defective. What is the probability of the next person at the dealership buying a car that is not defective?**

Answer:

These two events are dependent and conditional since one already occurred. The probability of the first event occurring was $\frac{2}{30}$. Since one of the defective cars was purchased, the probability that the next car purchased is not defective is 28 properly functioning cars over 29 defective and properly functioning cars. The conditional probability is:

P (not defective car | defective car) $= \dfrac{P\,(\text{defective AND 2nd not defective})}{P\,(\text{defective})} =$

$\dfrac{\frac{2}{30} \times \frac{28}{29}}{\frac{2}{30}} = \mathbf{\dfrac{28}{29}}$

28) **Alyssa has 2 blue blouses out of 13 total. The likelihood of her wearing blue slacks if she is wearing a blue blouse is $\frac{1}{10}$. What is the likelihood that she wears blue slacks and a blue blouse?**

Answer:

$P(B) = \frac{2}{13}$	Let $P(B)$ stand for the chance of wearing a blue blouse.
$P(S|B) = \frac{1}{10}$	Let $P(S|B)$ the probability of her wearing blue slacks, given that she is wearing a blue blouse.
$P(S|B) = \frac{P(B \text{ and } S)}{P(B)}$ $\frac{1}{10} = \frac{P(B \text{ and } S)}{\frac{2}{13}}$ $P(B \text{ and } S) = \frac{2}{130}$ $= \frac{1}{65}$	Plug what is known into the conditional probability formula.

Thus, the probability of Alyssa wearing blue slacks and a blue blouse is $\frac{1}{65}$.

Practice Test

READING

After reading the passage or table, choose the best answer to each question.

The odds of success for any new restaurant are slim. Competition in the city is fierce, and the low margin of return means that aspiring restaurateurs must be exact and ruthless with their budget and pricing. The fact that The Hot Dog has lasted as long as it has is a testament to its owners' skills.

1

Based on information presented in the selection, it is reasonable to infer that:

A. The Hot Dog offers the best casual dining in town.

B. The Hot Dog has a well-managed budget and prices items on its menu appropriately.

C. The popularity of The Hot Dog will likely fall as new restaurants open in the city.

D. The Hot Dog has a larger margin of return than other restaurants in the city.

Table 8.1. Distributor Cost Structure

Wholesale Books	$100 for the first 25 books; $80 for every 25 additional books
The Book Barn	$98 for every 25 books
Books and More	$3.99 per book
Quarter Price Books	$3.99 per book for the first 25 books; $2.99 for each additional book

2

A school wants to buy seventy-five textbooks. Based on the pricing chart, which of the following distributors would offer the cheapest price for the books?

A.   Wholesale Books

B.   The Book Barn

C.   Books and More

D.   Quarter Price Books

3

A teacher wants to buy an additional twenty-five books for her classroom. If she orders her books separately, which distributor would offer the cheapest price?

A.   Wholesale Books

B.   The Book Barn

C.   Books and More

D.   Quarter Price Books

The social and political discourse of America continues to be permeated with idealism. An idealistic viewpoint asserts that the ideals of freedom, equality, justice, and human dignity are the truths that Americans must continue to aspire to. Idealists argue that truth is what should be, not necessarily what is. In general, they work to improve things and to make them as close to ideal as possible.

4

The writer's main purpose in the selection is to:

A.   advocate for freedom, equality, justice, and human rights

B.   explain what an idealist believes in

C.   explain what's wrong with social and political discourse in America

D.   persuade readers to believe in certain truths

Throughout the history of psychology, researchers have sought to relieve human suffering. From the earliest forms of psychotherapy to the cognitive-behavioral therapies of recent decades, nearly all efforts in the study of psychology have been aimed at helping individuals overcome or learn to manage mental illness and extreme emotional distress. In the early twenty-first century, however, a new perspective on psychology emerged when Dr. Martin E. P. Seligman received funding to begin research into an idea that he referred to as positive psychology, a field that would be concerned with understanding the factors that contribute not to psychological distress but to an individual's ability to live a happy, fulfilling, productive life.

According to Seligman's 2011 book *Flourish: A Visionary New Understanding of Happiness and Well-being*, positive psychology began as an inquiry into the experiences that contribute to life satisfaction. Through his theory of authentic happiness,

Seligman posited that human happiness could be understood in terms of three elements, all of which we pursue for their <u>inherent</u> value—positive emotions (like joy, amusement, and gratitude), engagement (the tendency to lose oneself in activity), and meaning (the extent to which one believes his or her life has purpose). These elements together could be evaluated through an individual's assessment of his or her life satisfaction.

More than a decade after the publication of his first theory, however, Seligman views positive psychology somewhat differently. He argues that there are a number of flaws with his initial theory, especially in its intense focus on the topic of happiness. The term *happiness*, by today's usage, is inadequate for describing all that contributes to a fulfilling life: the term does not typically refer to the elements of engagement and meaning at all, and "feeling cheerful or merry," writes Seligman, "is a far cry from what Thomas Jefferson declared that we have the right to pursue[.]" In addition, life satisfaction measures are too dependent on mood to be considered useful in evaluating an individual's overall welfare, and the three elements of happiness as initially defined are too limited.

As a result of these insufficiencies, Seligman has published a new theory that he hopes will drive positive psychology in a different direction: well-being theory. Unlike authentic happiness theory, well-being theory addresses not only life satisfaction but also the extent to which one flourishes in his or her life: the term *well-being* refers not to a specific thing that can be evaluated (like life satisfaction) but to a <u>composition</u> of elements that ultimately shape one's overall sense of fulfillment. According to this theory, an individual's well-being is determined by—in addition to subjective experiences like positive emotions, engagement, and meaning—external factors like constructive relationships and personal achievement.

Though positive psychology is a relatively young field within the social sciences, it has already made great strides in attracting attention from researchers and practitioners in the field. Further, it has already begun to gain popular attention, proving that it is on its way to meeting the goal that Dr. Seligman initially set out to accomplish—to have a positive impact on the lives of everyday people who might otherwise have no motivation to seek therapy.

5

In the first paragraph, the author indicates that positive psychology was distinct from other psychological perspectives in that it:

A.   did not necessitate psychotherapeutic or cognitive-behavioral treatments

B.   is one of the oldest perspectives of psychology still in use today

C.   would be focused on understanding and increasing positive experiences rather than minimizing the effects of negative experiences

D.   required the practitioner to focus only on the challenges, rather than the strengths, of his or her clients

6

Which word best defines the word *inherent* as it is used in the selection?

A. genetic

B. instinctive

C. intrinsic

D. integral

7

According to the selection, authentic happiness theory was inadequate as a tool in positive psychology because it:

A. does not adhere to the definition that is described in the Declaration of Independence

B. did not allow practitioners to understand the subjective experience of their clients

C. cannot be observed quantitatively

D. was overly reliant on fluctuating, subjective measures

8

According to authentic happiness theory, life satisfaction could be understood by examining:

A. subjective measures of enjoyment, engagement, and fulfillment.

B. positive feelings of joy, amusement, and gratitude and negative feelings of sadness and anger.

C. the number of times per week that the client experienced complete engagement.

D. one's perception of his or her life's purpose.

9

Which word best defines the word *composition* as it is used in the selection?

A. combination

B. configuration

C. alignment

D. masterpiece

10

The major difference between authentic happiness and well-being theories is that:

A.   Authentic happiness theory focuses primarily on the impact of positive emotions on an individual's overall life satisfaction.

B.   Well-being theory attempts to understand welfare more holistically by taking into account external measures of prosperity.

C.   Well-being theory does not take into account the impact of positive emotions, engagement, or fulfillment.

D.   Authentic happiness theory seeks to explain the correlation between happiness and financial prosperity.

11

Based on information presented in the last paragraph, it is reasonable to infer that the author believes which statement?

A.   Individuals who do not seek therapy in response to their life challenges should consider doing so.

B.   The popularity of positive psychology discounts it in the eyes of many professionals.

C.   Positive psychology is intended for a broad audience both within and outside the field of psychology.

D.   There is no reason for individuals who are already in therapy to take an interest in positive psychology.

William James, 1842 – 1910, was an influential American philosopher and psychologist who studied the human psyche. He taught that the function of thought is to guide action; his central focus was practical effects of knowledge. James urges teachers to use the principles suggested by psychology, the science of the mind, as guidelines in the same way the science of logic or ethics offers a set of standards or rules to help govern specific choices. James stated, "A science only lays down lines within which the rules of the art must fall, laws which the follower of the art must not transgress; but what particular thing he shall positively do within those lines is left exclusively to his own genius. One genius will do his work well and succeed in one way, while another succeeds as well quite differently; yet neither will transgress the lines."

The three principles include: First, engage the interest of students by determining what they need to know and being aware of what they already know and what they do not know. Second, make what is presented memorable. Third, build student curiosity about what will be next. James explained, "you must simply work your pupil into such a state of interest in what you are going to teach him that every other object of attention is banished from his mind; then reveal it to him so impressively that he will remember the occasion to his dying day; and finally fill him with devouring curiosity to know what the next steps in connection with the subject are." Within these practical guidelines, a teacher must apply creativity, awareness of student knowledge, and perception of student interests and needs.

12

Which statement best expresses the main idea of the selection?

A.   Teachers must plan their lessons with the interests of their students in mind.

B.   To engage student interest, teachers must arouse the curiosity of their students about the subject of the lesson.

C.   The science of the mind is similar to the science of logic in the sense that both sciences examine the way thought guides action.

D.   Psychology has established principles for teachers to follow, but leaves the details of the actual lessons to the creativity of the teachers.

13

According to the selection, what question should a teacher ask before planning a lesson?

A.   What is my objective?

B.   How can I introduce this information in a way that is meaningful and targeted to my students?

C.   What will the learning outcomes of this lesson be?

D.   How will students behave if I ask them to remember this information?

14

Based on information presented in the selection, it is reasonable to infer that the author would agree with which statement?

A.   Teachers need to think of creative ways to make sure the information they present leaves a lasting impression on the minds of their students.

B.   Education is a science that considers the sequence of skills or steps that teachers need to present, reinforce, and assess.

C.   Teachers need to focus instruction on developing thinking and organizational habits in students.

D.   Teachers must insist on their students paying attention and banishing other concerns from their minds.

It has now been two decades since the introduction of thermonuclear fusion weapons into the military inventories of the great powers, and more than a decade since the United States, Great Britain, and the Soviet Union ceased to test nuclear weapons in the atmosphere. Today our understanding of the technology of thermonuclear weapons seems highly advanced, but our knowledge of the physical and biological consequences of nuclear war is continuously evolving.

15

Which of the following best expresses the topic of the selection?

A.   the impact of thermonuclear weapons on the military

B.   the technology of thermonuclear weapons

C.   atmospheric testing of nuclear weapons

D.   the physical and biological consequences of nuclear war

American Cowslip: This plant grows spontaneously in Virginia and other parts of North America. It flowers in the beginning of May, and the seeds ripen in July, soon after which the stalks and leaves decay, so that the roots remain inactive till the following spring. It is <u>propagated</u> by offsets, which the roots put out freely when they are in a loose moist soil and a shady situation; the best time to remove the roots, and take away the offsets, is in August, after the leaves and stalks are decayed, that they may be fixed well in their new situation before the frost comes on.

16

According to the selection, which of the following is the best time to remove the roots of American Cowslip?

A.   August

B.   May

C.   July

D.   December

17

Which word best defines the word *propagated* as it is used in the selection?

A.   killed

B.   multiplied

C.   extracted

D.   concealed

The greatest changes in sensory, motor, and perceptual development happen in the first two years of life. When babies are first born, most of their senses operate in a similar way to those of adults. For example, babies are able to hear before they are born; studies show that babies turn toward the sound of their mothers' voices just minutes after being born, indicating they recognize the mother's voice from their time in the womb.

The exception to this rule is vision. A baby's vision changes significantly in its first year of life; initially it has a range of vision of only 8 – 12 inches and no depth perception. As a result, infants rely primarily on hearing; vision does not become the dominant sense until around the age of 12 months. Babies also prefer faces to other objects. This preference, along with their limited vision range, means that their sight is initially focused on their caregiver.

18

Which statement is an accurate summary of the passage?

A. Babies have no depth perception until 12 months, which is why they focus only on their caregivers' faces.

B. Babies can recognize their mothers' voices when born, so they initially rely primarily on their sense of hearing.

C. Babies have senses similar to those of adults except for their sense of sight, which doesn't fully develop until 12 months.

D. Babies' senses go through many changes in the first year of their lives.

19

According to the selection, which of the following senses do babies primarily rely on?

A. vision

B. hearing

C. touch

D. smell

20

Which of the following best describes the purpose of the passage?

A. expository

B. narrative

C. persuasive

D   descriptive

East River High School has released its graduation summary for the class of 2016. Out of a total of 558 senior students, 525 (94 percent) successfully completed their degree program and graduated. Of these, 402 (representing 72 percent of the total class) went on to attend to a two- or four-year college or university. The distribution of students among the four main types of colleges and universities—small or large private and small or large public—is shown in the figure below. As the data shows, the majority of East River High School's college-attending graduates chose a large, public institution.

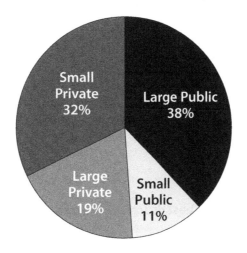

21

According to the figure, how many students from East River High School will attend a small, public college or university?

A.   4

B.   44

C.   440

D.   4400

22

Which of the following best describes the tone of the passage?

A.   professional

B.   casual

C.   concerned

D.   congratulatory

The best friend a man has in the world may turn against him and become his enemy. His son or daughter that he has reared with loving care may prove ungrateful. Those who are nearest and dearest to us, those whom we trust with our happiness and our good name may become traitors to their faith. The money that a man has, he may lose. It flies away from him, perhaps when he needs it most. A man's reputation may be sacrificed in a moment of ill-considered action.

The one absolutely unselfish friend that man can have in this selfish world, the one that never deserts him, the one that never proves ungrateful or treacherous is his dog. A man's dog stands by him in prosperity and in poverty, in health and in sickness. He will sleep on the cold ground, where the wintry winds blow and the snow drives fiercely, if only he may be near his master's side. He will kiss the hand that has no food to offer. He will lick the wounds and sores that come in encounters with the roughness of the world. He guards the sleep of his pauper master as if he were a prince. When all other friends desert, he remains.

23

Which of the following best describes the organization of the text?

A.   chronology

B.   cause and effect

C.   problem and solution

D.   contrast

24

Which of the following best describes the topic of this passage?

A.   loyal friends

B.   misfortune

C.   human treachery

D.   feeling safe

25

Based on information presented in the selection, it is reasonable to infer that the author believes which statement?

A.   Those closest to you will always betray you.

B.   Friendships with other people are pointless.

C.   Someone who wants a loyal friend should get a dog.

D.   Only a dog can help a person through the rough times in his or her life.

26

The writer's main purpose in the selection is to:

A.   inform

B.   entertain

C.   describe

D.   persuade

As NASA missions explore our solar system and search for new worlds, they are finding water in surprising places. Water is but one piece of our search for habitable planets and life beyond Earth, yet it links many seemingly unrelated worlds in surprising ways.

"NASA science activities have provided a wave of amazing findings related to water in recent years that inspire us to continue investigating our origins and the fascinating possibilities for other worlds, and life, in the universe," said Ellen Stofan, chief scientist for the agency. "In our lifetime, we may very well finally answer whether we are alone in the solar system and beyond."

The chemical elements in water, hydrogen and oxygen, are some of the most abundant elements in the universe. Astronomers see the signature of water in giant molecular clouds between the stars, in disks of material that represent newborn planetary systems, and in the atmospheres of giant planets orbiting other stars.

There are several worlds thought to possess liquid water beneath their surfaces, and many more that have water in the form of ice or vapor. Water is found in primitive bodies like comets and asteroids, and dwarf planets like Ceres. The atmospheres and interiors of the four giant planets—Jupiter, Saturn, Uranus and Neptune—are thought to contain enormous quantities of the wet stuff, and their moons and rings have substantial water ice.

Perhaps the most surprising water worlds are the five icy moons of Jupiter and Saturn that show strong evidence of oceans beneath their surfaces: Ganymede, Europa and Callisto at Jupiter, and Enceladus and Titan at Saturn.

Scientists using NASA's Hubble Space Telescope recently provided powerful evidence that Ganymede has a saltwater, sub-surface ocean, likely sandwiched between two layers of ice.

Europa and Enceladus are thought to have an ocean of liquid water beneath their surface in contact with mineral-rich rock, and may have the three ingredients needed for life as we know it: liquid water, essential chemical elements for biological processes, and sources of energy that could be used by living things.

Understanding the distribution of water in our solar system tells us a great deal about how the planets, moons, comets and other bodies formed 4.5 billion years ago from the disk of gas and dust that surrounded our sun. The space closer to the sun was hotter and drier than the space farther from the sun, which was cold enough for water to condense. The dividing line, called the "frost line," sat around Jupiter's present-day orbit. Even today, this is the approximate distance from the sun at which the ice on most comets begins to melt and become "active." Their brilliant spray releases water ice, vapor, dust and other chemicals, which are thought to form the <u>bedrock</u> of most worlds of the frigid outer solar system.

Scientists think it was too hot in the solar system's early days for water to condense into liquid or ice on the inner planets, so it had to be delivered—possibly by comets and water-bearing asteroids. NASA's Dawn mission is currently studying Ceres, which is the largest body in the asteroid belt between Mars and Jupiter. Researchers think Ceres might have a water-rich composition similar to some of the bodies that brought water to the three rocky, inner planets, including Earth.

The amount of water in the giant planet Jupiter holds a critical missing piece to the puzzle of our solar system's formation. Jupiter was likely the first planet to form, and it contains most of the material that wasn't incorporated into the sun. The leading theories about its formation rest on the amount of water the planet soaked up.

It's easy to forget that the story of Earth's water, from gentle rains to raging rivers, is intimately connected to the larger story of our solar system and beyond. But our water came from somewhere—every world in our solar system got its water from the same shared source. So it's worth considering that the next glass of water you drink could easily have been part of a comet, or an ocean moon, or a long-vanished sea on the surface of Mars. And note that the night sky may be full of exoplanets formed by similar processes to our home world, where gentle waves wash against the shores of alien seas.

Moons of Jupiter and Saturn

Name (description)	Distance from Sun (in astronomical units)	Ocean World Status
Europa (moon of Jupiter)	5.2 AU	Active
Ganymede (moon of Jupiter)	5.2 AU	Locked (under ice)
Callisto (moon of Jupiter)	5.2 AU	Locked (under ice)
Enceladus (moon of Saturn)	9.5 AU	Active
Titan (moon of Saturn)	9.5 AU	Locked (under ice)

27

In the third paragraph, the author provides details in order to:

A. pique the reader's curiosity about celestial bodies and events

B. discount the assertion that the elements found in water are plentiful within our solar system

C. remind the reader of the relative size of Earth in comparison to the rest of our solar system

D. illustrate the widespread availability of hydrogen and oxygen in space

28

Based on information presented in the selection, it is reasonable to infer that water:

A. can be found across our solar system in various forms

B. is the most precious resource within our solar system

C. is only available on our planet and the planets nearest to us

D. is not a renewable resource

29

According to the passage, water distribution in our solar system provides:

A. an efficient system for recycling the precious resource

B. an important clue about the formation of celestial bodies

C. proof that life cannot survive outside the "frost line"

D. plentiful opportunities for transporting the substance across great distances

30

According to the passage, in addition to liquid water, terrestrial forms of life also require:

A.   certain chemical elements and useable energy sources in order to survive

B.   substantial amounts of hydrogen and oxygen in order to survive

C.   at least some sunlight in order to survive

D.   frozen water in order to survive

31

According to the passage, the frost line is:

A.   a dividing line outside of which planets cannot sustain life

B.   the only location in our solar system where liquid water and frozen water can exist simultaneously

C.   the location at which most new bodies in our solar system form

D.   the distance from the sun at which liquid water begins to freeze

32

Which word best defines the word *bedrock* as it is used in the selection?

A.   pedestal.

B.   heart.

C.   anchor.

D.   foundation.

33

According to the passage, Earth's liquid water was most likely:

A.   recycled from other planets

B.   transported here by traveling, water-rich bodies like comets

C.   found on Jupiter before it was carried across the solar system by comets

D.   in the form of vapor until it reached our atmosphere

34

Based on information presented in the selection and table, it is reasonable to infer that:

A.   Celestial bodies that exist outside of the frost line are not likely to contain water in any form.

B.   Jupiter's distance from the sun prevents it from hosting liquid water.

C.   Evidence of water in some form has been found on a number of celestial bodies as far from the sun as Saturn.

D.   Water is a rare and valuable substance in our solar system.

In the eleven years that separated the Declaration of the Independence of the United States from the completion of that act in the ordination of our written Constitution, the great minds of America were bent upon the study of the principles of government that were essential to the preservation of the liberties which had been won at great cost and with heroic labors and sacrifices. Their studies were conducted in view of the imperfections that experience had developed in the government of the Confederation, and they were, therefore, practical and thorough.

35

Based on information presented in the selection, it is reasonable to infer what about the writers of the Constitution?

A.   The writers studied principles of government in relation to the government of the Confederation; their goal was to write a Constitution that would secure liberty in America.

B.   The writers worked to make sure that Americans would never lose the freedom that they fought to achieve.

C.   The writers of the Constitution were both thorough and practical as they wrote the Constitution.

D.   The writers studied the government of the Confederation and worked very hard to take into account the imperfections of this government.

I say moreover that you make a great, a very great mistake, if you think that psychology, being the science of the mind's laws, is something from which you can deduce definite programs and schemes and methods of instruction for immediate schoolroom use. Psychology is a science, and teaching is an art; and sciences never generate arts directly out of themselves. An intermediary inventive mind must make the application, by using its originality.

36

The writer's main purpose in the selection is to:

A.   explain that psychology is a science

B.   emphasize that the science of psychology cannot determine educational programs and methods

C.   describe the artistic nature of educational practices, programming, and step-by-step planning

D.   compare the values of art to those of science

AMERICAN COWSLIP: This plant grows spontaneously in Virginia and other parts of North America. It flowers the beginning of May, and the seeds ripen in July, soon after which the stalks and leaves decay, so that the roots remain inactive till the following spring. It is propagated by offsets, which the roots put out freely when they are in a loose moist soil and a shady situation; the best time to remove the roots, and take away the offsets, is in August, after the leaves and stalks are decayed, that they may be fixed well in their new situation before the frost comes on.

37

Based on information presented in the selection, it is reasonable to infer that American Cowslip grows spontaneously because:

A.   the seeds ripen quickly

B.   the roots remain inactive

C.   soil is moist most of the year

D.   the roots put out offsets

The most important part of brewing coffee is getting the right water. Choose a water that you think has a nice, neutral flavor. Anything with too many minerals or contaminants will change the flavor of the coffee, and water with too few minerals won't do a good job of extracting the flavor from the coffee beans. Water should be heated to between 195 and 205 degrees Fahrenheit. Boiling water (212 degrees Fahrenheit) will burn the beans and give your coffee a scorched flavor.

While the water is heating, grind your beans. Remember, the fresher the grind, the fresher the flavor of the coffee. The number of beans is entirely dependent on your personal taste. Obviously, more beans will result in a more robust flavor, while fewer beans will give your coffee a more subtle taste. The texture of the grind should be not too fine (which can lead to bitter coffee) or too large (which can lead to weak coffee).

Once the beans are ground and the water has reached the perfect temperature, you're ready to brew. A French press (which we recommend), allows you to control brewing time and provide a thorough brew. Pour the grounds into the press, then pour the hot water over the grounds and let it steep. The brew shouldn't require more than 5 minutes, although those of you who like your coffee a bit harsher can leave it longer. Finally, use the plunger to remove the grounds and pour.

38

According to the selection, which of the following lists the steps for brewing coffee in the correct sequence?

A.   Choose a water that doesn't have too many or two few minerals. Then, heat water to boiling and pour over coffee grounds.

B.   Grind the beans to the appropriate texture and pour into the French press. Then, heat water to boiling and pour over the ground beans. Finally, use the plunger to remove the grounds and pour.

C.   Grind beans to the appropriate texture, and then heat water to 195 degrees Fahrenheit. Next, pour water over the grounds and steep for no more than five minutes. Finally, remove the grounds using the plunger.

D.   Choose the right type of water and heat it to the correct temperature. Next, grind the beans and put them in the French press. Then, pour the hot water over the grounds and let the coffee steep.

39

Which of the following best describes the organization of the text?

A.   chronological

B.   cause and effect

C.   problem and solution

D.   contrast

40

Which sentence from the selection expresses an opinion rather than a fact?

A.   While the water is heating, grind your beans.

B.   A French press (which we recommend), allows you to control brewing time and provide a thorough brew.

C.   Anything with too many minerals or contaminants will change the flavor of the coffee, and water with too few minerals won't do a good job of extracting the flavor from the coffee beans.

D.   Finally, use the plunger to remove the grounds and pour.

41

Based on information presented in the selection, it is reasonable to infer that:

A.   Coffee should never be brewed for longer than 5 minutes.

B.   It's better to use too many coffee beans when making coffee than too few.

C.   Brewing quality coffee at home is too complicated for most people to do well.

D.   The best way to brew coffee is often determined by personal preferences.

42

Which of the following would be an appropriate title for this passage?

A.   How to Brew the Perfect Cup of Coffee

B.   Why Drinking Coffee Is the Best Way to Start the Day

C.   How to Use a French Press to Make Coffee

D.   The Importance of Grinding Coffee Beans

The bacteria, fungi, insects, plants, and animals that live together in a habitat have evolved to share a pool of limited resources. They've competed for water, minerals, nutrients, sunlight, and space—sometimes for thousands or even millions of years. As these communities have evolved, the species in them have developed complex, long-term interspecies interactions known as symbiotic relationships.

Ecologists characterize these interactions based on whether each party benefits. In mutualism, both individuals benefit, while in synnecrosis, both organisms are harmed. A relationship where one individual benefits and the other is harmed is known as parasitism. Examples of these relationships can easily be seen in any ecosystem. Pollination, for example, is mutualistic—pollinators get nutrients from the flower, and the plant is able to reproduce—while tapeworms, which steal nutrients from their host, are parasitic.

There's yet another class of symbiosis that is <u>controversial</u> among scientists. As it's long been defined, commensalism is a relationship where one species benefits and the other is unaffected. But is it possible for two species to interact and for one to remain completely unaffected? Often, relationships described as commensal include one species that feeds on another species' leftovers; remoras, for instance, will attach themselves to sharks and eat the food particles they leave behind. It might seem like the shark gets nothing from the relationship, but a closer look will show that sharks in fact benefit from remoras, which clean the sharks' skin and remove parasites. In fact, many scientists claim that relationships currently described as commensal are just mutualistic or parasitic in ways that haven't been discovered yet.

43

Which word best defines the word *controversial* as it is used in the selection?

A.   debatable

B.   objectionable

C.   confusing

D.   upsetting

44

The writer's main purpose in the selection is to:

A.   argue that commensalism isn't actually found in nature

B.   describe the many types of symbiotic relationships

C.   explain how competition for resources results in long-term interspecies relationships

D.   provide examples of the many different ways individual organisms interact

45

Which of the following is NOT a fact stated in the passage?

A.   Mutualism is an interspecies relationship where both species benefit.

B.   Synnecrosis is an interspecies relationship where both species are harmed.

C.   The relationship between plants and pollinators is mutualistic.

D.   The relationship between remoras and sharks is parasitic.

46

Epiphytes are plants that attach themselves to trees and derive nutrients from the air and surrounding debris. Sometimes, the weight of epiphytes can damage the trees on which they're growing. The relationship between epiphytes and their hosts would be described as:

A.   mutualism

B.   commensalism

C.   parasitism

D.   synnecrosis

47

According to the selection, why is commensalism controversial among scientists?

A.   Many scientists believe that an interspecies interaction where one species is unaffected does not exist.

B.   Some scientists believe that relationships where one species feeds on the leftovers of another should be classified as parasitism.

C.   Because remoras and sharks have a mutualistic relationship, no interactions should be classified as commensalism.

D.   Only relationships among animal species should be classified as commensalism.

48

Based on information presented in the selection, it is reasonable to infer what about symbiotic relationships?

A.   Scientists cannot decide how to classify symbiotic relationships among species.

B.   The majority of interspecies interactions are parasitic because most species do not get along.

C.   If two species are involved in a parasitic relationship, one of the species will eventually become extinct.

D.   Symbiotic relationships evolve as the species that live in a community adapt to their environments and each other.

It is painfully evident, upon experiment, that not many of the books which come teeming from our presses every year are meant to be read. They are meant, it may be, to be pondered; it is hoped, no doubt, they may instruct, or inform, or startle, or arouse, or reform, or provoke, or amuse us; but we read, if we have the true reader's zest and plate, not to grow more knowing, but to be less pent up and bound within a little circle—and not as those who laboriously seek instruction—as a means of seeing and enjoying the world of men and affairs. We wish companionship and renewal of spirit, enrichment of thought and the full adventure of the mind; and we desire fair company, and a larger world in which to find them.

When you say that a book was meant to be read, you mean, for one thing, of course, that it was not meant to be studied. You do not study a good story, or a haunting poem, or a battle song, or a love ballad, or any moving narrative, whether it be out of history or out of fiction—nor any argument, even, that moves vital in the field of action. You do not have to study these things; they reveal themselves, you do not stay to see how. They remain with you, and will not be forgotten or laid by. They cling like a personal experience, and become the mind's intimates. You devour a book meant to be read, not because you would fill yourself or have an anxious care to be nourished, but because it contains such stuff as it makes the mind hungry to look upon. Neither do you read it to kill time, but to lengthen time, rather, adding to its natural usury by living the more abundantly while it lasts, joining another's life and thought to your own.

49

Based on information presented in the selection, it is reasonable to infer that the author views a book "to be read" as an experience that:

A. compels the reader to reread and to analyze the author's meaning

B. offers both instruction and new ideas

C. leaves the reader changed

D. provides a feeling of being refreshed and energized

50

The writer's main purpose in the selection is to:

A. list the many reasons people read

B. explain what it means to read a book

C. describe the difficulties readers have with most of the books available

D. identify a solution for readers who are bored by most books

51

According to the selection, which of the following is one effect of the kind of book read for pleasure?

A. amusement

B. personal improvement

C. companionship

D. a sense of knowing

Credit scores, which range from 300 to 850, are a single value that summarizes an individual's credit history. Pay your bills late? Your credit score will be lower than someone who gets that electric bill filed on the first of every month. Just paid off your massive student loans? You can expect your credit score to shoot up. The companies that compile credit scores actually keep track of all the loans, credit cards, and bill payments in your name. This massive amount of information is summed up in a credit report, which is then <u>distilled</u> to a single value: your credit score.

Credit scores are used by many institutions that need to evaluate the risk of providing loans, rentals, or services to individuals. Banks use credit scores when deciding whether to hand out loans; they can also use them to determine the terms of the loan itself. Similarly, car dealers, landlords, and credit card companies will likely all access your credit report before agreeing to do business with you. Even your employer can access a modified version of your credit report (although it will not have your actual credit score on it).

When it comes to credit, everyone begins with a clean slate. The first time you access any credit—be it a credit card, student loan, or rental agreement—information begins to accumulate in your credit report. Thus, having no credit score can often be just as bad as having a low one. Lenders want to know that you have a history of borrowing money and paying it back on time. After all, if you've never taken out a loan, how can a bank know that you'll pay back its money? So, having nothing on your credit report can result in low credit limits and high interest rates.

With time, though, credit scores can be raised. With every payment, your credit report improves and banks will be more likely to loan you money. These new loans will in turn raise your score even further (as long as you keep making payments, of course).

In general, you can take a number of basic steps to raise your credit score. First, ensure that payments are made on time. When payments are past due, it not only has a negative impact on your score, but new creditors will be reluctant to lend while you are delinquent on other accounts.

Being smart about taking on debt is another key factor in keeping your credit score high. As someone who is just starting off in the financial world, there will be multiple offers to open accounts, say, for an introductory credit card or short-term loan. You may also find that as your score increases, you will receive offers for larger and larger loans. (Predatory lenders are a scourge on the young as well as the old.) But just because banks are offering you those loans doesn't make them a good idea. Instead, you should only take on debt you know you can pay back in a reasonable amount of time.

Lastly, keep an eye on unpaid student loans, medical bills, and parking tickets, all of which can take a negative toll on your credit score. In fact, your credit score will take a major hit from any bill that's sent to a collection agency, so it's in your best interest to avoid letting bills get to that point. Many organizations will agree to keep bills away from collection agencies if you set up a fee payment system.

52

The writer's main purpose in the selection is to:

- A.   help readers understand and improve their credit scores
- B.   warn banks about the dangers of lending to people with no credit score
- C.   persuade readers to take out large loans to improve their credit scores
- D.   explain to readers how the process of taking out a bank loan works

53

According to the selection, which individual is likely to have the highest credit score?

- A.   someone who has had medical bills sent to a collection agency
- B.   someone who is in the process of paying back his student loans
- C.   someone who has never borrowed any money but pays his bills on time
- D.   someone who has borrowed a large amount of money and paid it back on time

54

Which statement is an accurate summary of the passage?

- A.   Individuals with low credit scores will likely have trouble getting credit cards and loans. However, they can improve their credit scores over time.
- B.   Having no credit score can often be worse than having a low credit score, so it's important to sign up for credit cards and loans early in life.
- C.   Credit scores summarize an individual's credit history and are used by many businesses. They can be improved by making smart financial decisions.
- D.   Credit scores can be raised by paying bills on time, taking out reasonably sized loans, and avoiding collection agencies.

55

Which sentence from the selection expresses an opinion rather than a fact?

- A.   Credit scores, which range from 300 to 850, are a single value that summarizes an individual's credit history.
- B.   Many organizations will agree to keep bills away from collection agencies if you set up a fee payment system.
- C.   After all, if you've never taken out a loan, how can a bank know that you'll pay back its money?
- D.   Predatory lenders are a scourge on the young as well as the old.

56

Based on information presented in the selection, it is reasonable to infer that:

A.   It's possible to wipe your credit report clean and start over with a blank slate.

B.   People with a large amount of debt can likely get a loan with a low interest rate because they have demonstrated they are trustworthy.

C.   Someone who has borrowed and paid back large sums of money will get a loan with more favorable terms than someone who has never borrowed money before.

D.   A college student with no credit cards or debt likely has a high credit score.

57

Which statement is NOT a detail from the passage?

A.   In general, you can take a number of basic steps to raise your credit score.

B.   When it comes to credit, everyone begins with a clean slate.

C.   Employers can access your credit score before hiring you.

D.   Predatory lenders are a scourge on the young as well as the old.

58

Which word best defines the word *distilled* as it is used in the selection?

A.   to refine to its essence

B.   to explain at length

C.   to keep records of

D.   to undergo substantial change

Alan —

I just wanted to drop you a quick note to let you know I'll be out of the office for the next two weeks. Elizabeth and I are finally taking that trip to France we've been talking about for years. It's a bit of a last-minute decision, but since we had the vacation time available, we figured it was now or never.

Anyway, my team's been briefed on the upcoming meeting, so they should be able to handle the presentation without any hiccups. If you have any questions or concerns, you can direct them to Joanie, who'll be handling my responsibilities while I'm out.

Let me know if you want any special treats. I don't know if you can take chocolate and cheese on the plane, but I'm going to try!

Best regards,

Michael

59

Which of the following most likely describes the relationship between the author and Alan?

A.   familial

B.   formal

C.   friendly

D.   strained

60

The writer's main purpose in the selection is to:

A.   ask Alan if he wants any special treats from France

B.   brag to Alan about his upcoming vacation

C.   inform Alan that he will be out of the office

D.   help Alan prepare for the upcoming meeting

WRITING

SELECTED RESPONSE

Read the selection below; then answer the questions that follow.

Selection One

(1) The Grand Canyon is a landmark <u>who's</u> enormity cannot truly be understood until it is experienced. (2) The canyon, <u>which</u> was formed by millions of years of erosion by the Colorado River, is over one mile deep, nearly twenty miles wide, and over 250 miles long. (3) It is located in northern Arizona and falls primarily inside Grand Canyon National Park, <u>which</u> bisects the Kaibab National Forest. (4) <u>Adjacent</u> to the park are three Indian reservations—the Hualapai, the Kaibab Paiute, and the Navajo. (5) Management of this enormous landmark is achieved through the cooperation of many different groups. (6) The tribal nations <u>that</u> reside in the area work alongside governmental organizations, like the National Park Service to ensure that the lands are protected and tourists are kept _____.

(7) <u>In fact</u>, the Grand Canyon is one of the most popular tourist attractions in the world, it draws upwards of five million visitors every year. (8) People come from all over the world to see the massive landmark, so activities and attractions are generous. (9) Outdoor activities like hiking, rafting, and camping are popular, especially during the cooler months of spring and autumn. (10) Despite this, other activities like airplane and helicopter flyovers allow visitors a broader perspective of the canyon.

(11) Most activities at the Grand Canyon, <u>however</u>, are extremely limited by the weather, which varies significantly based on season. (12) Even daytime and nighttime temperatures can vary substantially, so it is important for visitors to follow weather forecasts and pack carefully. (13) During the summer months, temperatures inside the canyon can reach above one hundred degrees <u>Fahrenheit; during</u> winter months, the temperature can drop below zero degrees.

1

The writer's main purpose in this selection is to:

A.   describe the weather at the Grand Canyon.

B.   explain the geology of the Grand Canyon.

C.   introduce the reader to the Grand Canyon.

D.   discuss the tribes that live near the Grand Canyon.

2

Which underlined word or phrase should be replaced by a more appropriate word or phrase?

A.   sentence 1: who's

B.   sentence 2: which

C.   sentence 3: which

D.   sentence 6: that

3

Which organizational method does the writer use in the selection?

A.   comparison and contrast

B.   topical order

C.   chronological order

D.   cause and effect

4

Which underlined word or phrase should be replaced by a more appropriate word or phrase?

A.   sentence 4: Adjacent

B.   sentence 7: In fact

C.   sentence 10: Despite this

D.   sentence 11: however

5

Which change is needed in the selection?

A.   sentence 7: Replace the comma after *world* with a semicolon.

B.   sentence 5: Insert a comma after *achieved*.

C.   sentence 8: Remove the comma after *landmark*.

D.   sentence 2: Delete the comma after *canyon*.

6

Which change would best improve the development of ideas in the third paragraph?

A.   Reverse the order of sentences 12 and 13.

B.   Delete sentence 12.

C.   Reverse the order of sentences 11 and 13.

D.   Delete sentence 11.

7

Which change is needed in the selection?

A.   sentence 1: Insert a semicolon after *understood*.

B.   sentence 3: The first letters of the words *National Park* should be in lower case.

C.   sentence 2: Remove the comma after *wide*.

D.   sentence 13: The first letter of *Fahrenheit* should be in lower case.

8

Which change is needed in the selection?

A.   sentence 9: Delete the period after *autumn* and replace it with a comma and the conjunction *and* to connect it to the next sentence.

B.   sentence 9: Insert a comma after *camping*.

C.   sentence 6: Add a comma after *Service*.

D.   sentence 6: Replace the underlined word *that* (*the tribal nations that*) with *who*.

9

Which words or phrases, if inserted in the blank in sentence 6, are most appropriate, given the context?

A.   safe and free from harm.

B.   safe.

C.   safe and out of harm's way.

D.   safe and avoid injury.

10

To improve the structure of the selection, it would be most effective to begin a new paragraph starting with which sentence?

A.   sentence 3

B.   sentence 9

C.   sentence 4

D.   sentence 5

11

Which of the following alternatives to the underlined portion in sentence 13 would NOT be acceptable?

A.   Fahrenheit, and during

B.   Fahrenheit, during

C.   Fahrenheit, whereas during

D.   Fahrenheit, but during

12

Which change in word choice is needed to improve the effectiveness of the second paragraph?

A.   sentence 8: Change *generous* to *abundant*.

B.   sentence 8: Change *people* to *individuals*.

C.   sentence 10: Change *flyovers* to *tours*.

D.   sentence 10: Change *perspective* to *view*.

Selection Two

(1) Across the United States, a new trend in dining has taken hold. (2) Though the modern food truck phenomenon is still in it's prime, mobile dining is in no way a novel idea: precursors to the modern food truck can be traced back as far as the 1800s. (3) Cities like Austin, Portland, San Francisco, and Seattle are seeing a significant increase in one particular type of dining establishment—the Food Truck.

(4) The earliest predecessors to the modern food truck was actually not trucks; in fact, they were not motorized at all. (5) Push carts were some of the earliest vehicles for mobile food distribution and were popular in urban areas like New York City, where workers needed access to quick, cheap lunches. (6) Therefore, while these carts were mobile, they were not always available when they were most needed. (7) In the late 1800s, two new inventions marked important milestones in the development of the modern food truck. (8) In 1866, Charles Goodnight created the first chuck wagon a covered wagon that served as a mobile kitchen for cowmen who were herding cattle northward for sale. (9) The cooks, or "cookies," who traveled with the cowmen would wake early and prepare meals of beans, dried meats, and biscuits using the tools and ingredients on the chuck wagon. (10) Similarly, in 1872, a food vendor named Walter Scott conceived of the lunch wagon, from which he would serve sandwiches, coffee, and desserts to journalists outside a Providence, Rhode Island, newspaper office.

(11) In the 1900s, mobile dining took even more forms, as the invention of motorized transportation began to transform the industry. (12) Ice cream trucks followed in the 1950s, serving children and adults alike cold treats on hot summer afternoons. (13) In the 1960s, large food service trucks called roach coaches began to pop up near densely populated urban areas, often serving cheap meals from grungy kitchens.

(14) Therefore, the food truck industry has transformed the mobile dining experience from one of convenience to one of excitement. (15) Today, city dwellers and tourists will have flocked to food trucks not only for ease and affordability, but also for unique foods, new flavors, and fun experiences. (16) In some places, whole streets or even neighborhoods are devoted to hosting these food trucks, _____.

13

The writer's main purpose in this selection is to:

A.   tell the history of food trucks.

B.   describe the locations of food trucks.

C.   show why food trucks are popular.

D.   prove that food trucks are hygienic.

14

Which organizational method does the writer use in the selection?

A.   comparison and contrast

B.   topical order

C.   chronological order

D.   cause and effect

15

Which change is needed in the selection?

A.   sentence 2: Change *it's* to *its*.

B.   sentence 4: Replace the semicolon after *trucks* with a comma.

C.   sentence 5: Insert a comma after *distribution*.

D.   sentence 6: Insert a semicolon after *mobile*.

16

Which sentence contains an error in subject-verb agreement?

A.   sentence 2

B.   sentence 4

C.   sentence 7

D.   sentence 8

17

Which underlined word or phrase should be replaced by a more appropriate word or phrase?

A.   sentence 4: in fact

B.   sentence 6: Therefore

C.   sentence 10: Similarly

D.   sentence 15: Today

18

Which change is needed in the selection?

A.   sentence 9: Replace *who* with *which*.

B.   sentence 1: Delete the comma after *States*.

C.   sentence 8: Insert a comma after *chuck wagon*.

D.   sentence 10: Remove the comma after *Providence*.

19

Which underlined word in the selection should be replaced by a more appropriate word?

A.   sentence 1: Across

B.   sentence 7: milestones

C.   sentence 11: transform

D.   sentence 14: Therefore

20

Which underlined word or phrase in the selection contains an error in capitalization?

A.   sentence 3: Food Truck

B.   sentence 5: New York City

C.   sentence 8: northward

D.   sentence 10: Rhode Island

21

Which sentence contains an error in verb tense?

A.   sentence 12

B.   sentence 13

C.   sentence 14

D.   sentence 15

22

Which words or phrases, if inserted in order into the blank in sentence 16, would provide an ending most consistent with the statement made in the first sentence of the paragraph?

A.   so they are easier than ever to access.

B.   so you rarely run out of delicious options.

C.   but sometimes these areas can be busy.

D.   and people travel from all over the city, sometimes even farther, to try what they're offering.

23

To improve the structure of the selection, it would be most effective to begin a new paragraph starting with which sentence?

A.   sentence 7

B.   sentence 9

C.   sentence 10

D.   sentence 13, combining it with the next paragraph

24

Which change would best improve the development of ideas in the first paragraph?

A.   Delete sentence 1.

B.   Reverse the order of sentences 2 and 3.

C.   Reverse the order of sentences 1 and 3.

D.   Delete sentence 2

Selection Three

(1) Most people struggle to find what they want to do with <u>their</u> lives; but Neil deGrasse Tyson knew when he was nine years old. (2) He visited the Hayden Planetarium in New York City for the first time, Tyson discovered that he was fascinated by outer space. (3) From that moment on, he pursued his interest wholeheartedly and ultimately came to be one of the <u>more</u> famous and important astrophysicists of our day: his career has undoubtedly shaped the public's thinking about space and space exploration.

(4) Since the beginning of his professional career, Tyson has served on a number of important commissions and _____ have shaped the way the government and its agencies approach space exploration. (5) Two commissions to which he were appointed by President George W. Bush served to guide the future of American space research and travel by influencing policy and agenda formation, a third appointment, to NASA's <u>esteemed</u> Advisory Council, allowed Tyson to contribute to deliberations on NASA's financial planning. (6) In all, Tyson had a great deal of political clout when it came to discussions of America's future in space.

(7) Still, Tyson's political influence is often <u>outshined</u> by his popular influence. (8) On top of his professional accomplishments, he has found fame by making astronomy not only interesting _____ accessible to the average citizen. (9) In addition to writing a number of books for public consumption, Tyson has produced and hosted numerous popular documentaries and documentary series about space. (10) _____, Tyson's radio show, called *StarTalk Radio*, combine science, comedy, and celebrity guests to appeal to a diverse following. (11) Over the course of his career, Tyson has also earned a plethora of awards and acknowledgments for his unrelenting efforts at making space a bigger focus of public discourse. (12) NASA awarded him the highest honor it awards to citizens', the NASA Distinguished Public Service

Medal, and the International Astronomical Union named an asteroid, 13123 Tyson, in his honor. (13) Today, Neil deGrasse Tyson works as the Director of the Hayden Planetarium in New York City, the same planetarium _____ he first discovered his love of astronomy. (14) Through his work at the planetarium, he continue to pursue his mission of making astronomy and space exploration more accessible to the general public.

25

The writer's main purpose in the selection is to:

A.   detail Neil deGrasse Tyson's charismatic personality and popularity.

B.   argue the importance of the Hayden Planetarium for educating the public about outer space.

C.   describe Neil deGrasse Tyson's influence on popular culture.

D.   discuss Neil deGrasse Tyson's unique professional background and contributions.

26

Which organizational method does the writer use in the selection?

A.   chronological order

B.   topical order

C.   comparison and contrast

D.   cause and effect

27

To improve the structure of the selection, it would be most effective to begin a new paragraph starting with which sentence?

A.   sentence 3

B.   sentence 5

C.   sentence 9

D.   sentence 13

28

Which change is needed in the selection?

A.   sentence 4: Replace *his* with *their*.

B.   sentence 3: Replace the colon with a comma.

C.   sentence 2: Remove the comma after *time*.

D.   sentence 1: Replace the semicolon after *lives* with a comma.

29

Which change in word choice is needed to improve the effectiveness of the first paragraph?

A.   sentence 1: Change *most people* to *people*.

B.   sentence 1: Change *when he was nine years old* to *when he was a child*.

C.   sentence 2: Change *fascinated by* to *interested in*.

D.   sentence 2: Change *he visited* to *while visiting*.

30

Which underlined word in the selection should be replaced by a more appropriate word?

A.   sentence 1: their

B.   sentence 3: more

C.   sentence 5: esteemed

D.   sentence 7: outshined

31

Which words or phrases, if inserted in order into the blank in sentence 4, would correctly complete the sentence?

A.   councils, and

B.   councils; which

C.   councils, these

D.   councils, which

32

Which sentence contains an error in subject-verb agreement?

A.   sentence 5

B.   sentence 6

C.   sentence 7

D.   sentence 8

33

Which change is needed in the selection?

A.   sentence 5: Rewrite the word *President* so that the first letter, *p*, is lowercase.

B.   sentence 5: Replace the comma after *formation* with a period.

C.   sentence 5: Replace the comma after *appointment* with a dash.

D.   sentence 6: Delete the comma after the word *all*.

34

Which words or phrases, if inserted in order into the blank in sentence 8, would correctly complete the sentence?

A.   but nevertheless

B.   and still

C.   but also

D.   but still

35

Which words or phrases, if inserted in order into the blank in sentence 10, would correctly complete the sentence?

A.   Rather

B.   Furthermore

C.   Instead

D.   On the other hand

36

Which sentence contains an error in subject-verb agreement?

A.   sentence 9

B.   sentence 10

C.   sentence 11

D.   sentence 12

37

Which change is needed in the selection?

A.   sentence 12: Delete the apostrophe from *citizens'*.

B.   sentence 11: Replace the comma after *career* with a semicolon.

C.   sentence 7: Replace *by* with *for*.

D.   sentence 8: Replace the comma after *accomplishments* with a colon.

38

Which word, if inserted into the blank in sentence 13, would correctly complete the sentence?

A.   that

B.   which

C.   where

D.   when

39

Which sentence contains an error in subject-verb agreement?

A.   sentence 1

B.   sentence 2

C.   sentence 13

D.   sentence 14

Selection Four

(1) When I was a young child, my family moved <u>all the around the world</u> following my dad's job. (2) Usually, we would live in each new country for about a year, during which time I <u>had attended</u> an international school. (3) Like us, most of the <u>families whose students</u> attended these international schools were immigrants, people who had moved to the country from other countries. (4) At one of my first primary schools, <u>when I was eight years old</u>, my teacher taught a lesson about the word *immigration*. (5) She told us that it comes from the word *migrate*, which means to move to and settle in a new location, either temporarily or permanently. (6) As I got older, I learned that many animals migrate as well; and fish, birds, mammals, reptiles, amphibians, and even insects will move to new locations in search of more hospitable conditions. (7) Most animal migration is cyclical and occurs at predictable times each year in response to seasonal changes. (8) This type of migration occurs, for instance, when geese fly <u>south</u> to stay warm during the cold, inhospitable winter months and then return <u>North</u> during the summer when the weather is mild.

(9) This mass migration occurs over the course of a full year, when more than two million animals, including wildebeests, zebras, and gazelles, move around the outskirts of the park in search of food, water, and a safe place to bear their offspring. (10) One of the largest and most stunning examples of cyclical migration occurs in Africa's <u>Serengeti National Park</u>. (11) Thus, like almost all instances of cyclical migration, the mass migration of animals in Serengeti National Park occurs predictably in response to natural weather and water cycles.

(12) Consequently, sometimes animals must migrate for a specific reason in unique circumstances. (13) For example, overpopulation in a concentrated area could lead to <u>famine</u>, causing portions of the population to move elsewhere in search of alternative food sources. (14) Likewise, natural phenomena like wildfires or volcano eruptions might make an area uninhabitable and force out the animals that were living there.

(15) Human migration, like my family's trek around the world, most often occurs in this irregular form. (16) Some jobs or family situations might require regular, predictable movements between <u>locations, but, like us,</u> most people move with the knowledge that they will not be returning to the place they just left. (17) Instead, they know that they will soon be settling down to start a new life in a new home—even if it was just for a year.

40

The writer's main purpose in the selection is to:

A.   convince the reader that families with small children should not migrate.

B.   describe migration as a phenomenon affecting animals and humans alike.

C.   explain why human families migrate throughout the world.

D.   tell a childhood story about a unique family experience.

41

Which organizational method does the writer use in the selection?

A.   chronological order

B.   topical order

C.   comparison and contrast

D.   cause and effect

42

To improve the structure of the selection, it would be most effective to begin a new paragraph starting with which sentence?

A.   sentence 3

B.   sentence 4

C.   sentence 5

D.   sentence 6

43

Which underlined word or phrase should be replaced by a more appropriate word or phrase?

A.   sentence 1: all around the world

B.   sentence 2: had attended

C.   sentence 3: families whose students

D.   sentence 4: when I was eight years old

44

Which change in word choice is needed to improve the effectiveness of the first paragraph?

A.   sentence 2: Change *usually* to *sometimes*.

B.   sentence 3: Change *immigrants* to *refugees*.

C.   sentence 4: Change *primary* to *international*.

D.   sentence 5: Change *location* to *home*.

45

What change is needed in the selection?

A.   sentence 5: Change *or* to *and*.

B.   sentence 6: Replace the semicolon after *well* with a period, removing the word *and* and starting *fish* with a capital letter.

C.   sentence 7: Insert a comma after *cyclical*.

D.   sentence 8: Capitalize the words *north* and *south*.

46

Which change would best improve the development of ideas in the second paragraph?

A.   Reverse the order of sentences 9 and 10.

B.   Delete sentence 10.

C.   Reverse the order of sentences 10 and 11.

D.   Delete sentence 11.

47

Which change in word choice is needed to improve the effectiveness of the third paragraph?

A.   sentence 12: Change *Consequently* to *On the other hand*.

B.   sentence 13: Change *For example* to *However*.

C.   sentence 14: Change *Likewise* to *Nevertheless*.

D.   sentence 14: Change *force out* to *eliminate*.

48

Which sentence contains an error in verb tense?

A.   sentence 14

B.   sentence 15

C.   sentence 16

D.   sentence 17

49

Which underlined word or phrase in the selection contains an error in capitalization?

A. sentence 8: *south*

B. sentence 8: *North*

C. sentence 10: *Serengeti National Park*

D. sentence 13: *famine*

50

Which of the following alternatives to the underlined portion in sentence 16 would NOT be acceptable?

A. locations; like us, however,

B. locations. Like us, however,

C. locations; like us, though,

D. locations; but, like us,

ESSAY

Can we be too quick to judge the actions of another person? In an essay to be read by a general audience of educated adults, explain your ideas on this subject and include details to support your views.

Mathematics

The following questions test your familiarity with mathematics. For each question, choose the best answer.

1

Simplify: $10^2 - 7(3 - 4) - 25$

A.   −118
B.   −12
C.   2
D.   82

2

What is the domain of the piece-wise function shown in the graph?

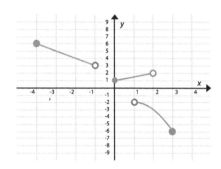

A. $D: (-4, -1) \boxtimes (0, 3)$
B. $D: (-4, 3)$
C. $D: (-4, 1) \boxtimes (0, 3)$
D. $D: (-4, -1) \boxtimes (0, 1) \boxtimes (1, 3)$

3

If $\triangle ABD \sim \triangle DEF$ and the similarity ratio is 3:4, what is the measure of DE if $AB = 12$?

A.   6
B.   9
C.   12
D.   16

4

The pie graph below shows how a state's government plans to spend its annual budget of $3 billion. How much more money does the state plan to spend on infrastructure than education?

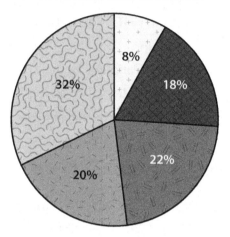

- ⊕ Employees
- ● Education
- ● Healthcare
- ◯ Pension
- ● Infrastructure

A. $60,000,000
B. $120,000,000
C. $300,000,000
D. $540,000,000

5

40% of what number is equal to 17?

A.   2.35
B.   6.8
C.   42.5
D.   235

6

Simplify: $\frac{7}{8} - \frac{1}{10} - \frac{2}{3}$

A. $\frac{1}{30}$

B. $\frac{4}{120}$

C. $\frac{13}{120}$

D. $\frac{4}{21}$

7

Which of the following is equivalent to $54z^4 + 18z^3 + 3z + 3$?

A. $18z^4 + 6z^3 + z + 1$

B. $3z(18z^3 + 6z^2 + 1)$

C. $3(18z^4 + 6z^3 + z + 1)$

D. $72z^7 + 3z$

8

If a student answers 42 out of 48 questions correctly on a quiz, what percentage of questions did she answer correctly?

A. 82.5%

B. 85%

C. 86%

D. 87.5%

$48\overline{)42.00}$

9

If the surface area of a cylinder with radius of 4 feet is 48π square feet, what is its volume?

A. 1π ft.³

B. 16π ft.³

C. 32π ft.³

D. 48π ft.³

$SA = 2\pi rh + 2\pi r^2$

$48 = 2\pi 4h + 2\pi 4^2$

$\frac{48}{8}\ 8\pi + 8\pi^2$

$4\pi\ 16\ h = 2$

10

Which of the following is a solution of the given equation?

$4(m + 4)^2 - 4m^2 + 20 = 276$

A. 3

B. 4

C. 6

D. 12

$4(3+4)^2 - 4(3)^2\ 20\ 20$

$4(9+16)$

$\frac{100 - 36}{20}$

16

11

Which of the following is the y-intercept of the given equation?

$7y - 42x + 7 = 0$

A. $(0, \frac{1}{6})$

B. $(6, 0)$

C. $(0, -1)$

D. $(-1, 0)$

12

The line $f(x)$ is shown on the graph below. If $g(x) = f(x - 2) + 3$, which of the following points lies on $g(x)$?

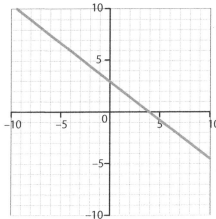

A. $(1, 2)$

B. $(2, 3)$

C. $(4, 0)$

D. $(6, 3)$

$1 - 2$

$-1 + 3 = -2$

$2 - 2$

$0 + 3 = 3$

$3 - 2$

$1 + 3 = 4$

$4 - 6$

$2 + 3 = 5$

13

If an employee who makes $37,500 per year receives a 5.5% raise, what is the employee's new salary?

A. $35,437.50

B. $35,625.00

C. $39,375.00

D. $39,562.50

14

Which of the following is listed in order from least to greatest?

A. $-0.95, 0, \frac{2}{5}, 0.35, \frac{3}{4}$

B. $-1, -\frac{1}{10}, -0.11, \frac{5}{6}, 0.75$

C. $-\frac{3}{4}, -0.2, 0, \frac{2}{3}, 0.55$

D. $-1.1, -\frac{4}{5}, -0.13, 0.7, \frac{9}{11}$

15

Which inequality is represented by the following graph?

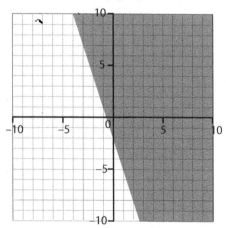

A. $y \geq -3x - 2$

B. $y \geq 3x - 2$

C. $y > -3x - 2$

D. $y \leq -3x - 2$

16

Fifteen DVDs are to be arranged on a shelf. 4 of the DVDs are horror films, 6 are comedies, and 5 are science fiction. In how many ways can the DVDs be arranged if DVDs of the same genre must be placed together?

A. 1,800

B. 2,073,600

C. 6,220,800

D. 12,441,600

17

50 shares of a financial stock and 10 shares of an auto stock are valued at $1,300. If 10 shares of the financial stock and 10 shares of the auto stock are valued at $500, what is the value of 50 shares of the auto stock?

A. $30

B. $20

C. $1,300

D. $1,500

18

In a high school with 1,200 students, 200 students are in the band and 150 are in the math club. If 20 students are in both the band and the math club, how many students are in neither the band nor the math club?

A. 330 students

B. 350 students

C. 450 students

D. 870 students

19

Points *B* and *C* are on a circle. Point *A* is located such that the line segments $\overline{AB}$ and $\overline{AC}$ are congruent. Which of the following could be true?

- I. *A* is the center of the circle. ☒
- II. *A* is on arc *BC*.
- III. *A* is outside of the circle.

- A. I
- B. I and II
- C. I and III
- D. I, II, and III

20

Michael is making cupcakes. He plans to give $\frac{1}{2}$ of the cupcakes to a friend and $\frac{1}{3}$ of the cupcakes to his coworkers. If he makes 48 cupcakes, how many will he have left over?

- A. 8
- B. 10
- C. 12
- D. 16

21

Juan plans to spend 25% of his workday writing a report. If he is at work for 9 hours, how many hours will he spend writing the report?

- A. 2.25
- B. 2.50
- C. 2.75
- D. 3.25

22

How many unique ways can the letters in the word *FOGGIER* be arranged?

- A. 42
- B. 210
- C. 1050
- D. 2520

23

Which of the following is a solution to the inequality $2x + y \leq -10$?

- A. $(0, 0)$
- B. $(10, 2)$
- C. $(10, 10)$
- D. $(-10, -10)$

24

If the length of a rectangle is increased by 40% and its width is decreased by 40%, what is the effect on the rectangle's area?

- A. The area is the same.
- B. It increases by 16%.
- C. It increases by 20%.
- D. It decreases by 16%.

25

Solve for *x*.

$x = 6(3^0)$

- A. 0
- B. 1
- C. 6
- D. 18

26

An ice chest contains 24 sodas, some regular and some diet. The ratio of diet soda to regular soda is 1:3. How many regular sodas are there in the ice chest?

A.   1
B.   4
C.   6
D.   18

27

The inequality $6 > x^2 - x$ is true for which of the following values of x?

I. $x < -2$
II. $-2 < x < -3$
III. $x > 3$

A.   I only
B.   II only
C.   III only
D.   I and III only

28

A cube is inscribed in a sphere such that each vertex on the cube touches the sphere. If the volume of the sphere is 972π cm³, what is the approximate volume of the cube in cubic centimeters?

A.   9
B.   104
C.   927
D.   1125

29

A bag contains 6 blue, 8 silver, and 4 green marbles. Two marbles are drawn from the bag. What is the probability that the second marble drawn will be green if replacement is not allowed?

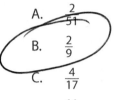

A. $\frac{2}{51}$
B. $\frac{2}{9}$
C. $\frac{4}{17}$
D. $\frac{11}{17}$

30

An equilateral triangle is drawn next to a trapezoid as shown in the figure below. What is the approximate area of the new figure?

A.   128.0 mm²
B.   137.7 mm²
C.   140.5 mm²
D.   142.1 mm²

31

What is $\frac{5}{8}$ as a percent?

A.   1.6%

B.   16%

C.   0.625%

D.   62.5%   *(circled)*

32

In the fall, 425 students pass the math benchmark. In the spring, 680 students pass the same benchmark. What is the percentage increase in passing scores from fall to spring?

A.   37.5%

B.   55%

C.   60%   *(circled)*

D.   62.5%

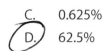

$$\frac{255}{425}$$

33

In the xy-plane, the line given by which of the following equations is parallel to the line $3x + 2y = 10$?

A. $y = -3x + 2$

B. $y = -\frac{3}{2}x - 10$

C. $y = \frac{1}{3}x + 5$

D. $y = \frac{2}{3}x - 10$

34

Which number has the least value?

A.   0.305

B.   0.035   *(circled)*

C.   0.35

D.   0.3

$$\frac{035}{1000}$$

35

Using the table, which equation demonstrates the linear relationship between x and y?

x	y
3	−18
7	−34
10	−46

A. $y = -6x - 6$

B. $y = -5x - 6$

C. $y = -4x - 6$

D. $y = -3x - 6$

36

Robbie has a bag of treats that contains 5 pieces of gum, 7 pieces of taffy, and 8 pieces of chocolate. If Robbie reaches into the bag and randomly pulls out a treat, what is the probability that Robbie will get a piece of taffy?

A. $\frac{1}{13}$

B. $\frac{1}{7}$

C. $\frac{7}{20}$ *(circled)*

D. $\frac{7}{13}$

37

In which quadrant is the point $(-3, -4)$ located?

A.   I $(+, +)$

B.   II $(-, +)$

C.   III $(-, -)$ *(circled)*

D.   IV $(+, -)$

38

Aprille has $50 to buy the items on her shopping list. Assuming there is no sales tax, about how much change will Aprille receive after buying all the items on her list?

Aprille's List	
Item	**Price**
Hammer	$13.24
Screwdriver	$11.99
Nails	$4.27
Wrench	$5.60

A. $12
B. $13
C. $14
D. $15

39

If angles *a* and *b* are congruent, what is the measurement of angle *c*?

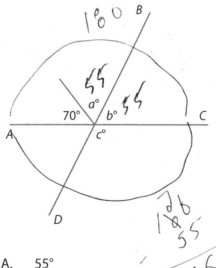

A. 55°
B. 70°
C. 110°
D. 125°

40

Out of 1560 students at Ward Middle School, 15% want to take French. Which expression represents how many students want to take French?

A. 1560 ÷ 15
B. 1560 × 15
C. 1560 × 0.15
D. 1560 ÷ 0.15

41

Justin has a summer lawn care business and earns $40 for each lawn he mows. He also pays $35 per week in business expenses. Which of the following expressions represents Justin's profit after *x* weeks if he mows *m* number of lawns?

A. $40m - 35x$
B. $40m + 35x$
C. $35x(40 + m)$
D. $35(40m + x)$

42

Lynn has 4 test scores in science class. Each test is worth 100 points, and Lynn has an 85% average. If Lynn scored 100% on each of the first 3 tests, what did she score on her 4th test?

A. 40%
B. 55%
C. 60%
D. 85%

43

Erica is at work for $8\frac{1}{2}$ hours a day. If she takes one 30-minute lunch break and two 15-minute breaks during the day, how many hours does she work?

A.   6 hours, 30 minutes

B.   6 hours, 45 minutes

C.   7 hours, 15 minutes

D.   7 hours, 30 minutes

handwritten: 8, -30, 7.5

44

Using the function table, what is the value of $f(20)$?

x	f(x)
5	12
10	22
15	32
20	44
25	52

handwritten: 5+7 = 16, 10+12 = 22, 15+17 = 32, 20+22 = 42

A.   20

B.   25

C.   40

D.   42

45

If a car uses 8 gallons of gas to travel 650 miles, how many miles can it travel using 12 gallons of gas?

A.   870 miles

B.   895 miles

C.   915 miles

D.   975 miles

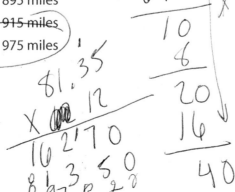

46

Two spheres are tangent to each other. One has a volume of 36π, and the other has a volume of 288π. What is the greatest distance between a point on one of the spheres and a point on the other sphere?

A.   6

B.   9

C.   18

D.   36

handwritten: 36)208, V=

47

A baby weighed 7.5 pounds at birth and gained weight at a rate of 6 ounces per month for the first six months. Which equation describes the baby's weight in ounces, y, after t months?

A. $y = 6t + 7.5$

B. $y = 6t + 120$

C. $y = 7.5t + 120$

D. $y = 6t + 7.5$

handwritten: y = 7.5 + 6t

48

A person earning a salary between $75,000 and $100,000 per year will pay $10,620 in taxes plus 20% of any amount over $75,000. What would a person earning $80,000 per year pay in taxes?

A. $10,620

B. $11,620

C. $12,120

D. $12,744

49

New York had the fewest months with less than 3 inches of rain in every year except:

Number of Months with 3 or Fewer Than 3 Inches of Rain

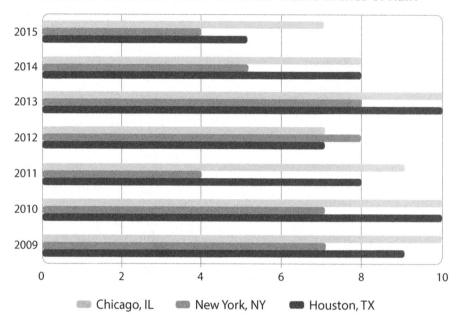

Chicago, IL　　New York, NY　　Houston, TX

A. 2011

B. 2012

C. 2013

D. 2014

E. 2015

50

Kim and Chris are writing a book together. Kim wrote twice as many pages as Chris, and together they wrote 240 pages. How many pages did Chris write?

A. 80

B. 100

C. 120

D. 160

51

What is the probability of selecting either a king of spades or a king of clubs from a deck of 52 cards?

A. $\frac{1}{104}$

B. $\frac{1}{52}$

C. $\frac{1}{26}$

D. $\frac{3}{52}$

52

Which graph shows the solution to $y = 2x + 1$?

A.

B.

C.

D.

E.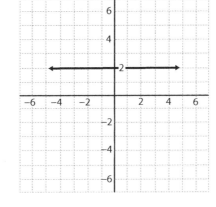

53

Which digit is in the hundredths place when 1.3208 is divided by 5.2?

A.   0

B.   4

C.   5

D.   8

54

Solve for x: $5x - 4 = 3(8 + 3x)$

A. -7

B. $-\frac{3}{4}$

C. $\frac{3}{4}$

D. 7

55

A grocery store sold 30% of its pears and had 455 pears remaining. How many pears did the grocery store start with?

A.   602

B.   650

C.   692

D.   700

56

Solve the system of equations for y: $5x + 4y = 20$; $x = 2y + 1$

A. $y = \frac{2}{5}$

B. $y = \frac{4}{5}$

C. $y = \frac{15}{14}$

D. $y = \frac{5}{4}$

57

Convert 55 meters to feet (round to the nearest tenth of a foot).

A.   16.8 feet

B.   21.7 feet

C.   139.7 feet

D.   180.4 feet

58

Which of the following defines y as a function of x?

I. $y^2 + x = 3$

II.

x	y
0	4
1	5
2	8
3	13
4	20

III. $y = \sin(\theta)$

A.   II only

B.   I and II only

C.   II and III only

D.   I, II, III only

59

What is the remainder when 397 is divided by 4?

A.   0

B.   1

C.   2

D.   4

60

In a theater, there are 4,500 lower-level seats and 2,000 upper-level seats. What is the ratio of lower-level seats to total seats?

A. $\frac{4}{9}$

B. $\frac{4}{13}$

C. $\frac{9}{13}$

D. $\frac{9}{4}$

Answer Key

READING

1)

A. Incorrect. The author points to the skills of the owner as the reason for The Hot Dog's long-term success, not the quality of the dining experience.

B. Correct. The passage states that restaurateurs must be "exact and ruthless with their budget and pricing." The success of The Hot Dog implies that its owners have done that.

C. Incorrect. The passage suggests that most new restaurants struggle but does not discuss how new restaurants affect the popularity of existing restaurants.

D. Incorrect. The passage implies that all restaurateurs must work with the low margin of return and simply suggests that the owners of The Hot Dog have made the most of it, not that they have any advantage in this respect.

2)

A. Incorrect. Wholesale Books does not have the lowest price: $100 + (80 \times 2) = 260$

B. Incorrect. The Book Barn does not have the lowest price: $98 \times 3 = 294$

C. Incorrect. Books and More has the highest price for seventy-five books: 299.25

D. Correct. Quarter Price Books has the lowest price: $(3.99 \times 25) + (2.99 \times 50) = 249.25$

3)

A. Incorrect. Wholesale Books does not offer the lowest price: $100 for the first twenty-five books.

B. Correct. The Book Barn would offer the lowest price: $98 for twenty-five books.

C. Incorrect. Books and More does not offer the lowest price: $99.75 for twenty-five books.

D. Incorrect. Quarter Price Books does not offer the lowest price: $99.75 for the first twenty-five books.

4)

A. Incorrect. The author identifies the ideals associated with idealism but does not offer an opinion on or advocate for them.

B. Correct. The purpose of the passage is to explain what an idealist believes in. The author does not offer any opinions or try to persuade readers about the importance of certain values.

C. Incorrect. The author states that social and political discourse are "permeated with idealism" but does not suggest that this is destructive or wrong.

D. Incorrect. The author provides the reader with information but does not seek to change the reader's opinions or behaviors.

5)

A. Incorrect. The author does not indicate that positive psychology does not necessitate psychotherapy or cognitive-behavioral treatment.

B. Incorrect. The author indicates that positive psychology is a relatively new field in the study of psychology ("In the early twenty-first century [...] a new perspective on psychology emerged [...]")

C. Correct. The author writes that positive psychology is "concerned with understanding the factors that contribute [...] to an individual's ability to live a happy, fulfilling, productive life" rather than with "helping individuals overcome or learn to manage mental illness and extreme emotional distress."

D. Incorrect. The author does not indicate that positive psychology would be focused on challenges.

6)

A. Incorrect. This answer choice does not fit in the context of the sentence.

B. Incorrect. This answer choice does not fit in the context of the sentence.

C. Correct. The author describes "positive emotions [...], engagement [...], and meaning" as being the three elements that we "pursue for their inherent value[.]" This implies that the value of these elements is intrinsic in them.

D. Incorrect. This answer choice does not fit in the context of the sentence. The value mentioned is described as intrinsic, not integral.

7)

A. Incorrect. The author does not indicate that the Declaration of Independence was used to evaluate the theory.

B. Incorrect. The author does not indicate that authentic happiness theory was inadequate in this way.

C. Incorrect. The author does not indicate that authentic happiness theory was inadequate in this way.

D. Correct. The author writes that "life satisfaction measures are too dependent on mood to be considered useful in evaluating an individual's overall welfare."

8)

A. **Correct.** The author writes, "Through his theory of authentic happiness, Seligman posited that human happiness could be understood in terms of three elements, all of which we pursue for their inherent value—positive emotions (like joy, amusement, and gratitude), engagement (the tendency to lose oneself in activity), and meaning (the extent to which one believes his or her life has purpose)."

B. Incorrect. Positive feelings were only one element of Seligman's theory.

C. Incorrect. Engagement was only one element of Seligman's theory.

D. Incorrect. Meaning was only one element of Seligman's theory.

9)

A. **Correct.** The author writes that well-being is determined by "a composition of elements" that includes subjective experiences and external factors. In other words, well-being is a combination of many factors.

B. Incorrect. The author does not imply that the elements of well-being are configured in any particular way.

C. Incorrect. The author does not imply that the elements of well-being are aligned, but that they work together to determine overall well-being.

D. Incorrect. This answer choice does not fit in the context of the sentence.

10)

A. Incorrect. The author writes, "Unlike authentic happiness theory, well-being theory addresses not only life satisfaction but also the extent to which one flourishes in his or her life[...]"

B. **Correct.** The author writes, "Unlike authentic happiness theory, well-being theory addresses not only life satisfaction but also the extent to which one flourishes in his or her life[...] According to this theory, an individual's well-being is determined by—in addition to subjective experiences like positive emotions, engagement, and meaning—external factors like constructive relationships and personal achievement."

C. Incorrect. The author writes, "According to this theory, an individual's well-being is determined by—in addition to subjective experiences like positive emotions, engagement, and meaning—external factors like constructive relationships and personal achievement." This implies that well-being theory does take into account positive emotions, engagement, and fulfillment in addition to other measures.

D. Incorrect. The author indicates that authentic happiness theory takes into account only elements that "could be evaluated through an individual's assessment of his or her life satisfaction[,]" not external measure of success or well-being.

11)

A. Incorrect. The author does not make an argument for or against therapy with respect to life challenges.

B. Incorrect. The author gives no indication that popular reception of the field of positive psychology has negatively affected its reception by professionals.

C. **Correct.** The author writes that positive psychology "has already begun to gain popular attention, proving that it is on its way to meeting the goal that Dr. Seligman initially set out to accomplish—to have a positive impact on the lives of everyday people who might otherwise have no motivation to seek therapy."

D.   Incorrect. The author does not indicate that the benefits of positive psychology are limited to those individuals who are not currently in therapy.

12)

A.   Incorrect. This is one of the supporting details of the passage, but it is not the central idea.

B.   Incorrect. One of the guidelines that psychology offers teachers is to arouse curiosity. Additional guidelines are explained; this option is a detail, not the central idea.

C.   Incorrect. Based on the passage, this statement is true, but it is not the central idea.

D.   Correct. The author explains, "A science only lays down lines within which the rules of the art must fall, laws which the follower of the art must not transgress; but what particular thing he shall positively do within those lines is left exclusively to his own genius." The passage offers three guidelines for teachers, but indicates that teachers are responsible for creating the lessons.

13)

A.   Incorrect. Teachers may need lesson objectives, but the passage does not mention them.

B.   Correct. The first guideline the author explains is, "engage the interest of students by determining what they need to know and being aware of what they already know and what they do not know." Teachers are to make lessons meaningful by considering what the students need to know. In addition, lessons should be targeted to what students do not know about a topic.

C.   Incorrect. Knowing the expected learning outcomes is important, but not one of the things mentioned in the passage.

D.   Incorrect. Student behavior is not considered in the passage.

14)

A.   Correct. The text says that teachers should present their lesson topic to the student "so impressively that he will remember the occasion to his dying day."

B.   Incorrect. Although some people do see education in this way, in terms of the passage, this is inaccurate. Psychology is a science, and teaching is an art.

C.   Incorrect. The passage begins by stating that the "function of thought is to guide action," but there is no mention of the thinking and organizational skills of students. The focus is on the thinking and planning of teachers in terms of their ability to generate curiosity and to make lessons relevant to student needs and abilities.

D.   Incorrect. The passage indicates that teachers are responsible for getting their students curious about a topic and therefore making their lessons so interesting that "every other object of attention is banished from his [the student's] mind." Teachers who follow this advice will have the attention of their students.

15)

A.   Incorrect. The passage implies that "the physical and biological consequences of nuclear war" have impacts that reach much further than the military.

B.   Incorrect. The second part of the second sentence suggests that the consequences of nuclear war—rather than the specific technology of nuclear weapons—are the focus of this student's paper.

C.   Incorrect. The author mentions the decision by world powers to cease testing nuclear weapons in the atmosphere; however, this is only one detail and is likely not the focus of the essay as a whole.

D.   Correct. The passage gives a short history of thermonuclear weapons and then introduces its main topic—the physical and biological consequences of nuclear war.

16)

A.   Correct. The passage states that "the best time to remove the roots, and take away the offsets, is in August."

B.   Incorrect. The passage states that the American Cowslip "flowers in the beginning of May."

C.   Incorrect. The passage suggests that "the seeds [of the American Cowslip] ripen in July."

D.   Incorrect. The author states that the time to remove the roots is in August "before the frost comes on."

17)

A.   Incorrect. The author indicates that the American Cowslip "is propagated by offsets[,]" which should be removed and replanted in order allow the species to reproduce.

B.   Correct. *Multiplied* best describes the passage's description of how the plant reproduces by producing offsets.

C.   Incorrect. The author indicates that the American Cowslip "is propagated by offsets[,]" which should be removed and replanted in order allow the species to reproduce.

D.   Incorrect. The author indicates that the American Cowslip "is propagated by offsets[,]" which should be removed and replanted in order allow the species to reproduce.

18)

A.   Incorrect. The passage is about babies' senses in general; therefore this answer choice is too specific.

B.   Incorrect. The passage is about babies' senses in general; therefore this answer choice is too specific.

C.   Correct. The passage states that babies' senses are much like those of their adult counterparts with the exception of their vision, which develops later.

D.   Incorrect. The passage indicates that a baby's vision "changes significantly in its first year of life[,]" but suggests that other senses are relatively well-developed at birth.

19)

A.   Incorrect. The passage states that "vision does not become the dominant sense until around the age of 12 months."

B.   Correct. The passage states that "infants rely primarily on hearing."

C.   Incorrect. The sense of touch in not mentioned in the passage.

D.   Incorrect. The sense of smell is not mentioned in the passage.

20)

   A.   **Correct.** The passage explains how a baby's senses develop and allow it to interact with the world.

   B.   Incorrect. The passage does not tell a story.

   C.   Incorrect. The passage is not intended to change the reader's opinions or behaviors.

   D.   Incorrect. The passage provides facts, not descriptions.

21)

   A.   Incorrect. The passage states that 402 students went on to attend college or university, and the chart shows that 11 percent of these students went on to attend small public colleges or universities. Four students would only represent about one percent of the students who went on the college or university.

   B.   **Correct.** The passage states that 402 students went on to attend college or university, and 11 percent of 402 is approximately 44 students.

   C.   Incorrect. The passage states that 402 students went on to attend college or university; 440 would represent more than one hundred percent of these students.

   D.   Incorrect. East River High School's graduating class of 2016 had only 525 graduates.

22)

   A.   **Correct.** The passage is written in a neutral, professional tone. It does not include any informal, emotional, or first-person language.

   B.   Incorrect. The passage is written in a professional tone and includes no informal, emotional, or first-person language.

   C.   Incorrect. The passage is written in a neutral tone and indicates no concern on the part of the author.

   D.   Incorrect. The passage is written in a neutral tone and indicates no celebration or congratulations on the part of the author.

23)

   A.   Incorrect. The author does not follow a sequence of events from beginning to end.

   B.   Incorrect. The author does not show how one event or occurrence led to another.

   C.   Incorrect. The author does not describe a problem that needs to be solved.

   D.   **Correct.** The loyal dog is presented in contrast with humans, who are not always trustworthy or faithful.

24)

   A.   **Correct.** The author is describing the constancy of dogs as friends. He concludes by stating, "When all other friends desert, he [a dog] remains."

   B.   Incorrect. The author mentions some examples of misfortune, but they are not the main focus of the text.

   C.   Incorrect. The author describes examples of human treachery but does so in order to provide a contrast to the dog's loyalty.

   D.   Incorrect. The author explains how dogs sometimes make their owners feel safe, but the main focus of the text is on the dog's loyalty.

25)

A. Incorrect. Though the author names some examples of betrayal, he does not suggest that all close relationships will end in betrayal, only that they "may."

B. Incorrect. Though the author illustrates how friendships can be painful, he does not suggest that they are altogether pointless.

C. Correct. The passage emphasizes that people can be treacherous, but a dog will be a constant friend. The passage does not suggest that relationships with other people are pointless or useless.

D. Incorrect. Though the author argues that the dog is the most loyal companion, he does not suggest that they are the only ones who can help a person through tough times.

26)

A. Incorrect. The author uses emotional language to persuade, not to inform.

B. Incorrect. The author uses a contrast to prove a point about the loyalty of dogs, not to entertain readers.

C. Incorrect. The author describes some loyal dog behaviors, but description is not the main purpose of the passage.

D. Correct. The author is trying to persuade his audience that dogs are the most loyal friends.

27)

A. Incorrect. The author does not seek to pique the reader's curiosity about celestial bodies and events but rather to inform the reader of the widespread availability of hydrogen and oxygen in space.

B. Incorrect. The author indicates that hydrogen and oxygen are plentiful within our solar system.

C. Incorrect. The author does not address the size of the earth as compared to the rest of the solar system.

D. Correct. The author writes, "The chemical elements in water, hydrogen and oxygen, are some of the most abundant elements in the universe. Astronomers see the signature of water in giant molecular clouds between the stars, in disks of material that represent newborn planetary systems, and in the atmospheres of giant planets orbiting other stars."

28)

A. Correct. The author writes, "There are several worlds thought to possess liquid water beneath their surfaces, and many more that have water in the form of ice or vapor."

B. Incorrect. The author does not indicate that water is a precious resource in our solar system.

C. Incorrect. The author indicates that water is available in numerous places across our solar system.

D. Incorrect. The author does not indicate whether water is a renewable or nonrenewable resource.

29)

  A.   Incorrect. The author does not indicate that understanding water distribution would allow us to create an efficient recycling system.

  B.   **Correct.** The author writes, "Understanding the distribution of water in our solar system tells us a great deal about how the planets, moons, comets and other bodies formed 4.5 billion years ago from the disk of gas and dust that surrounded our sun."

  C.   Incorrect. The author does not indicate that water distribution proves anything about life outside the "frost line."

  D.   Incorrect. The author does not indicate that understanding water distribution provides opportunities for transporting the substance.

30)

  A.   **Correct.** The author writes that there are "three ingredients needed for life as we know it: liquid water, essential chemical elements for biological processes, and sources of energy that could be used by living things."

  B.   Incorrect. The author does not indicate that terrestrial forms of life require substantial amounts of hydrogen and oxygen.

  C.   Incorrect. The author does not indicate that terrestrial forms of life require sunlight specifically.

  D.   Incorrect. The author does not indicate that terrestrial forms of life require frozen water, only that they require water.

31)

  A.   Incorrect. The author does not specify that planets outside the frost line cannot sustain life.

  B.   Incorrect. The author does not specify that the frost line is the only location at which liquid and frozen water exist simultaneously.

  C.   Incorrect. The author does not indicate that celestial bodies form at the frost line.

  D.   **Correct.** The author writes that the "'frost line' [...] is the approximate distance from the sun at which the ice on most comets begins to melt and become 'active.'" This implies that, outside this line, water begins to freeze.

32)

  A.   Incorrect. This answer choice does not fit in the context of the sentence.

  B.   Incorrect. This answer choice does not fit in the context of the sentence.

  C.   Incorrect. This answer choice does not fit in the context of the sentence.

  D.   **Correct.** The author writes that the "brilliant spray [of water melting from the surface of comets] releases water ice, vapor, dust and other chemicals, which are thought to form the bedrock of most worlds of the frigid outer solar system."

33)

  A.   Incorrect. The author does not indicate that Earth's liquid water was recycled from other planets.

B. **Correct.** The author writes that because "it was too hot in the solar system's early days for water to condense into liquid or ice on the inner planets, [...] it had to be delivered—possibly by comets and water-bearing asteroids."

C. Incorrect. The author does not indicate that Earth's water came from Jupiter specifically.

D. Incorrect. The author does not indicate that Earth's water was in the form of vapor before it reached our atmosphere.

34)

A. Incorrect. The table indicates that both Enceladus and Titan, both 9.5 AUs from the sun, contain water in some form.

B. Incorrect. Neither the passage nor the graph indicate that Jupiter's distance from the sun prevents it from hosting liquid water.

C. **Correct.** The passage and the table both indicate that numerous bodies in our solar system, including the moons of Jupiter and Saturn, show evidence of water.

D. Incorrect. Both the passage and the table indicate that water can be found on numerous planetary and celestial bodies throughout our solar system.

35)

A. **Correct.** The suggested idea is how thorough and practical the writers were as they studied the principles of government and analyzed their experience with government of the Confederation.

B. Incorrect. This option is too general; it does not mention the specifics of the work of the writers (studying government in view of the government of the Confederation).

C. Incorrect. This option offers no indication of what they were thorough and practical about.

D. Incorrect. This is only partially accurate. It omits the writers' study of the principles of government and the focus of their work, a Constitution that would protect freedom.

36)

A. Incorrect. Although the passage states that psychology is a science, it does not explain the science. The primary concern is distinguishing the science of psychology from the art of teaching.

B. **Correct.** The text states that educational programs and plans cannot be deduced from the laws of the mind.

C. Incorrect. Although the text indicates that teaching is an art, the practices and plans of educational programs are not described.

D. Incorrect. The focus of the art of teaching and of the science of psychology is identified, but their values are not mentioned.

37)

A. Incorrect. This is irrelevant because the plant produces offsets, which allow it to spread.

B. Incorrect. Inactive roots suggest the plant would not multiply.

C. Incorrect. Although the passage indicates that the plant needs moist soil, the soil may or may not stay moist throughout the year, depending on the weather.

D. **Correct.** An offset is like a daughter plant that comes off the mother plant.

38

A.   Incorrect. This answer choice leaves out many important steps in the process of brewing coffee.

B.   Incorrect. The passage suggests grinding the coffee beans while the water heats, not before.

C.   Incorrect. The passage suggests grinding the coffee beans while the water heats, not before.

D.   Correct. This choice lists the steps for brewing coffee in the same order as the passage.

39)

A.   Correct. The author describes the steps for making coffee in chronological order.

B.   Incorrect. The does not structure the text by focusing on a cause-and-effect relationship.

C.   Incorrect. The author does not structure the text by introducing a problem and providing a solution.

D.   Incorrect. The author does not draw a contrast between two or more things.

40)

A.   Incorrect. This answer choice provides fact-based instructions, not an opinion.

B.   Correct. The writer uses the first person, showing his or her opinion, to recommend a French press as the best way to brew coffee.

C.   Incorrect. This answer choice provides fact-based information about the process of brewing coffee.

D.   Incorrect. This answer choice provides fact-based instructions, not an opinion.

41)

A.   Incorrect. The author states, "The brew shouldn't require more than 5 minutes, although those of you who like your coffee a bit harsher can leave it longer."

B.   Incorrect. The author states, "The number of beans is entirely dependent on your personal taste. Obviously, more beans will result in a more robust flavor, while fewer beans will give your coffee a more subtle taste."

C.   Incorrect. The author describes many steps in the process of making good coffee but does not suggest that the process is too complicated for most people.

D.   Correct. The passage mentions several times that decisions about things like water minerals, ground size, and steep time will depend on the preference of the coffee drinker.

42)

A.   Correct. The passage as a whole describes from start to finish how to make a cup of coffee the drinker will enjoy.

B.   Incorrect. The passage offers no opinion on coffee's value as a start-of-day beverage.

C.   Incorrect. The French press is only a minor part of the process described in this passage, and it is only a recommendation; the passage describes the general coffee-making process.

D.   Incorrect. The grinding of coffee beans is only one part of the process described in this passage.

43)

A. **Correct.** The author writes that "[t]here's another class of symbiosis that is controversial among scientists" and goes on to say that "many scientists claim the relationships currently described as commensal are just mutualistic or parasitic in ways that haven't been discovered yet." This implies that scientists debate about the topic of commensalism.

B. Incorrect. The author does not imply that scientists disapprove of or protest commensalism, only that they disagree about whether it truly exists.

C. Incorrect. The author does not imply that scientists are confused about commensalism, only that they disagree about whether it truly exists.

D. Incorrect. The author does not imply that scientists are upset about commensalism, only that they disagree about whether it truly exists.

44)

A. Incorrect. Though the author explores this idea in the final paragraph, it is not the main focus of the passage as a whole.

B. **Correct.** The author writes that "[a]s these communities have evolved, the species in them have developed complex, long-term interspecies interactions known as symbiotic relationships." She then goes on to describe the different types of symbiotic relationships that exist.

C. Incorrect. Though the author introduces the passage with this idea, it is not the main focus of the passage as a whole.

D. Incorrect. Though the author does provide examples of interspecies interaction, this is not the primary purpose of the passage; rather, the examples provide further detail about the main topic—symbiotic relationships.

45)

A. Incorrect. The author writes, "In mutualism, both individuals benefit, while in synnecrosis, both organisms are harmed."

B. Incorrect. The author writes, "In mutualism, both individuals benefit, while in synnecrosis, both organisms are harmed."

C. Incorrect. The author writes, "Pollination, for example, is mutualistic[:]pollinators get nutrients from the flower, and the plant is able to reproduce[.]"

D. **Correct.** The author writes, "Often, relationships described as commensal include one species that feeds on another species' leftovers; remoras, for instance, will attach themselves to sharks and eat the food particles they leave behind. It might seem like the shark gets nothing from the relationship, but a closer look will show that sharks in fact benefit from remoras, which clean the sharks' skin and remove parasites."

46)

A. Incorrect. The author writes, "In mutualism, both individuals benefit[.]"

B. Incorrect. The author writes, "As it's long been defined, commensalism is a relationship where one species benefits and the other is unaffected."

C. **Correct.** The author writes, "A relationship where one individual benefits and the other is harmed is known as parasitism."

D.   Incorrect. The author writes, "In mutualism, both individuals benefit, while in synnecrosis, both organisms are harmed."

47)

A.   Correct. The author writes, "But is it possible for two species to interact and for one to remain completely unaffected?..."In fact, many scientists claim that relationships currently described as commensal are just mutualistic or parasitic in ways that haven't been discovered yet."

B.   Incorrect. The author does not indicate that scientists disagree about the classification of relationships, only that they recognize that they do not fully understand all relationships yet and may, therefore, be classifying some of them based on incomplete information.

C.   Incorrect. The author does not indicate that the example of remoras and sharks is the reason for the controversy about commensalism, only that it illustrates this controversy well.

D.   Incorrect. The author does indicate that the controversy around commensalism is limited to discussions of animal species only.

48)

A.   Incorrect. The author does not indicate that scientists disagree about the classification of relationships, only that they recognize that they do not fully understand all relationships yet and may, therefore, be classifying some of them based on incomplete information.

B.   Incorrect. The author provides no support for this in the passage.

C.   Incorrect. The author provides no support for this in the passage.

D.   Correct. The author writes, "The bacteria, fungi, insects, plants, and animals that live together in a habitat have evolved to share a pool of limited resources...As these communities have evolved, the species in them have developed complex, long-term interspecies interactions known as symbiotic relationships."

49)

A.   Incorrect. The text states, "When you say that a book was meant to be read, you mean, for one thing, of course, that it was not meant to be studied." Readers do not need to study a book that is meant "to be read" because it stays with them.

B.   Incorrect. "We read, if we have the true reader's zest and plate, not to grow more knowing, but to be less pent up and bound within a little circle." Readers do read for knowledge, but not books "to be read," which are read as an experience.

C.   Incorrect. There is no mention of a book changing the reader, just of providing an adventurous or renewing experience, with interesting people or characters.

D.   Correct. The text states, "We wish companionship and renewal of spirit, enrichment of thought and the full adventure of the mind; and we desire fair company, and a larger world in which to find them." A larger world or a renewal of spirit can be considered a refreshed or broader look at life.

50)

A.   Incorrect. The author does describe the varied reasons for reading, but that is not the primary purpose. The author goes on to show how a book "to be read" is not read for any of the purposes listed.

B. **Correct.** The author points out that "It is painfully evident, upon experiment, that not many of the books which come teeming from our presses every year are meant to be read." Then, books to be read are shown to be different from books to study and ponder.

C. Incorrect. Although the author insists that books to be read are different from all other books, he does not suggest that readers have difficulties with books that offer information or amusement.

D. Incorrect. The author does not indicate readers are bored by most of the books published; he says only that they are not renewed in the same way they are by reading a book to be read.

51)

A. Incorrect. The text says that ordinary books may "instruct, or inform, or startle, or arouse, or reform, or provoke, or amuse us."

B. Incorrect. A practical book that offers information on self-improvement is not a book "meant to be read."

C. **Correct.** The author points out that a book "meant to be read" is read "as those who take their pleasure" and "as a means of seeing and enjoying the world of men and affairs. We wish companionship and renewal of spirit, enrichment of thought and the full adventure of the mind."

D. Incorrect. The author emphasizes that books meant to be read are read "not to grow more knowing."

52)

A. **Correct.** The author provides an overview of the various elements that affect credit scores and offers suggestions about how to improve credit scores.

B. Incorrect. The author does not address bankers but people who may not understand their credit scores or how they work.

C. Incorrect. Though the author suggests that those without a credit score start a line of credit, the author does not seek to persuade readers to take this specific action; rather, he or she encourages readers to examine their own credit histories to understand how their scores can be improved.

D. Incorrect. The author does not provide details about the process of taking out a loan.

53)

A. Incorrect. The final paragraph warns readers to "keep an eye on unpaid student loans, medical bills, and parking tickets" because credit scores "will take a major hit from any bill that's sent to a collection agency[.]"

B. Incorrect. The author writes, "With every payment, your credit report improves and banks will be more likely to loan you money. These new loans will in turn raise your score even further (as long as you keep making payments, of course)." Thus, it can be inferred that someone who is in the process of paying back a student loan may be on the way to building a high credit score but may not necessarily have a high score yet.

C. Incorrect. The author writes that "having no credit score can often be just as bad as having a low one. Lenders want to know that you have a history of borrowing money and paying it back on time. After all, if you've never taken out a loan, how can a bank know that you'll pay back its money?" Thus, it can be inferred that someone who is paying bills on time but has never borrowed money or opened any lines of credit may not have a high score yet; he or she is on the way to building one.

D.   **Correct.** The author writes that "[w]ith every payment, your credit report improves and banks will be more likely to loan you money. These new loans will in turn raise your score even further (as long as you keep making payments, of course)." Thus, it can be inferred that someone who has paid off a large amount of money and paid it back in time will have a high credit score.

54)

A.   Incorrect. While these details are both mentioned in the passage, they are too specific to provide an adequate summary of the passage overall.

B.   Incorrect. While the first part of this statement is mentioned in the passage, it is too specific to provide an adequate summary of the passage overall.

C.   **Correct.** This statement provides an adequate summary of the passage, as it explains what a credit score is and how individuals can raise their credit scores.

D.   Incorrect. While these details are mentioned in the passage, they are too specific to provide an adequate summary of the passage overall.

55)

A.   Incorrect. This is the definition of a credit score; it is a factual description.

B.   Incorrect. This is a factual detail about what organizations are sometimes willing to do.

C.   Incorrect. This is a rhetorical question, meant to help the reader understand the preceding statements.

D.   **Correct.** The word "scourge" is emotional and representative of the author's personal opinion about predatory lenders.

56)

A.   Incorrect. The author writes that "[w]hen it comes to credit, everyone begins with a clean slate." However, the author does not indicate that it is possible to return to a clean slate once a line of credit has been opened.

B.   Incorrect. The author writes that "[w]hen payments are past due, it not only has a negative impact on your score, but new creditors will be reluctant to lend while you are delinquent on other accounts."

C.   **Correct.** The author writes that "having nothing on your credit report can result in low credit limits and high interest rates." This implies that someone who has borrowed and paid back a loan on time will likely have higher limits and lower interest rates than someone who has no credit history.

D.   Incorrect. The author writes that "[w]hen it comes to credit, everyone begins with a clean slate. The first time you access any credit—be it a credit card, student loan, or rental agreement—information begins to accumulate in your credit report." Thus, a student who has no credit cards or debt likely has no credit score at all.

57)

A.   Incorrect. The author writes, "In general, you can take a number of basic steps to raise your credit score."

B. Incorrect. The author writes, "When it comes to credit, everyone begins with a clean slate. "

C. **Correct.** The author writes that "[e]ven your employer can access a modified version of your credit report (although it will not have your actual credit score on it)."

D. Incorrect. The author writes, "Predatory lenders are a scourge on the young as well as the old."

58)

A. **Correct.** In this context, *distilled* refers to the process of creditors taking the "massive amount of information [that] is summed up in a credit report "and converting it into a single value that represents the overall reliability of the potential borrower or renter.

B. Incorrect. This answer is the opposite of the contextual meaning of the word *distilled*; rather than explaining an individual's credit history at length, the credit score exists to summarize an individual's credit history in a single value.

C. Incorrect. This answer choice does not fit in the context of this sentence.

D. Incorrect. This answer choice does not fit in the context of this sentence.

59)

A. Incorrect. Though the author mentions some details of his personal life, most of his letter is concerned with work-related matters.

B. Incorrect. Though the author's letter is primarily concerned with work-related matters, he includes personal details and friendly language.

C. **Correct.** The author and Alan have a friendly relationship, as evidenced by the author's casual tone and his offer to bring Alan a gift from his vacation.

D. Incorrect. The author's tone is casual, and he includes details that suggest he is not concerned or stressed about how things will go in his absence.

60)

A. Incorrect. Though the author does ask Alan if he wants any special treats, this is not his main purpose, as evidenced by the fact that he mentions it only in the final sentences of the letter.

B. Incorrect. The author's tone is not boastful; he spends more time on professional matters and offers to bring Alan a gift, showing consideration.

C. **Correct.** The author is writing to tell Alan that he will be out of the office. The details about his trip and the meeting support this idea.

D. Incorrect. Though the author mentions the upcoming meeting, he does not intend to help Alan prepare for the meeting, only to inform him of the team's plans.

WRITING

SELECTED RESPONSE

1)

A. Incorrect. While the writer does describe the weather at Grand Canyon National Park, this is not the main point of the selection; the weather only appears at the end.

B. Incorrect. There is some discussion of erosion in the beginning of the selection, but the writer does not discuss geology in detail.

C. Correct. The selection touches on the formation of the Grand Canyon, its location, its role as a tourist attraction, and its weather. The reader receives a general overview of the canyon and the national park.

D. Incorrect. The writer describes which tribes live near the canyon but does not discuss them in detail.

2)

A. Correct. The contraction *who's* means "who is." The phrase *a landmark who is enormity* is ungrammatical and does not make good sense.

B. Incorrect. The relative pronoun *which* is correctly used here to refer to *the canyon*.

C. Incorrect. The relative pronoun *which* is correctly used here to refer to *Grand Canyon National Park*.

D. Incorrect. The relative pronoun *that* is correctly used here to refer to *the tribal nations*.

3)

A. Incorrect. The author does not compare or contrast Grand Canyon National Park to any other national parks or landmarks.

B. Correct. The author brings up and discusses various topics related to the Grand Canyon: its formation, local tribes, management, tourism, activities, and weather.

C. Incorrect. There is no chronology of events in this selection; the writer discusses a series of topics.

D. Incorrect. The writer does not discuss any event or issue triggered by another; the selection describes Grand Canyon National Park by reviewing relevant topics such as tourism, weather, etc.

4)

A. Incorrect. *Adjacent* correctly suggests that the reservations are found next to the park.

B. Incorrect. The phrase *in fact* is correctly used as a transitional phrase to develop the idea that the park is a popular tourist destination.

C. Correct. The transitional phrase *despite this* suggests a contrasting idea is about to be introduced. However, airplane and helicopter flyovers need not take place in contrast to the activities discussed in the previous sentence; they may occur in addition to them. Thus, *despite this* is not appropriate here.

D. Incorrect. The word *however* correctly contrasts the idea of outdoor activities at the park with the limitations of the extreme weather.

5)

A. **Correct.** A semicolon is necessary here to connect the two independent clauses.

B. Incorrect. No comma is necessary here because the phrase *through the cooperation of many different groups* is neither an independent nor a dependent clause.

C. Incorrect. This comma is required to connect two independent clauses with the coordinating conjunction *so*.

D. Incorrect. This comma introduces the dependent relative clause *which was formed by millions of years of erosion by the Colorado River*.

6)

A. **Correct.** Sentence 11 states that temperature varies by season, so it would make more sense for sentence 13, which discusses the seasonal variations in more detail, to immediately follow sentence 11. Sentence 12, which discusses daily variations in temperature, could easily follow to provide more information about climate in the area.

B. Incorrect. Sentence 12 has useful information about daily variations in climate at the Grand Canyon and provides helpful advice to visitors about what to pack. This information is relevant to the paragraph and to the selection; it is also likely of interest to the reader, who may be planning a visit to Grand Canyon National Park.

C. Incorrect. Sentence 11 introduces the main idea of the paragraph—the weather at the Grand Canyon. Furthermore, it is a good transitional sentence from the topic of activities, as the word *however* tells the reader to expect caveats to the breadth of activities available at the Grand Canyon. Therefore, it should start the paragraph.

D. Incorrect. Again, sentence 11 is essential to the paragraph as it acts not only as the topic sentence, but also as a transitional sentence. It should not be deleted.

7)

A. Incorrect. The phrase *until it is experienced*, which follows *understood*, is not an independent clause and therefore cannot be connected with a semicolon. Furthermore, no punctuation is required here given the length of the sentence.

B. Incorrect. The words *National Park* are part of the proper noun *Grand Canyon National Park*, the name of the park. Thus, their first letters must be capitalized.

C. **Correct.** Since the conjunction *and* is already used here, no comma is necessary.

D. Incorrect. *Fahrenheit* is always a proper noun.

8)

A. Incorrect. There is no need to connect these two sentences, which are already lengthy.

B. Incorrect. No comma is needed here.

C. **Correct.** Two commas are needed to correctly set off the appositive phrase *like the National Park Service*.

D. Incorrect. Though the nations are composed of people, they are not people themselves, so *that* is appropriate here.

9)

A. Incorrect. *Safe* and *free from harm* have similar meanings, so using both is redundant.

B. **Correct.** Since *safe* and *free from harm* have similar meanings, using just one of them is sufficient. Using both would be redundant.

C. Incorrect. *Safe* and *out of harm's way* have similar meanings, so using both is redundant.

D. Incorrect. The phrases *kept safe* and *avoid injury* have about the same meaning, so using both is redundant.

10)

A. Incorrect. Sentence 3 continues to build on the same ideas as sentence 2. It makes sense for them to be in the same paragraph.

B. Incorrect. Sentence 9 builds upon the idea introduced in sentence 8: that many activities are available to park visitors. It does not make sense to separate these sentences into different paragraphs.

C. Incorrect. While sentence 4 might seem to introduce a new idea—the local tribes—the next sentences discuss management of the park. Sentence 4 does not introduce that information and thus would not be a good introductory sentence for a new paragraph there. Moreover, sentence 4 would still be appropriate in the first paragraph as it continues to describe the spatial location of the park.

D. **Correct.** Sentences 5 and 6 describe management of the park in detail, while sentences 1 through 4 describe the park's location and surroundings. It makes sense for sentences 5 and 6 to become their own entity.

11)

A. Incorrect. This choice is an acceptable alternative to the original wording and punctuation.

B. **Correct.** This choice creates a comma splice.

C. Incorrect. This choice is an acceptable alternative to the original wording and punctuation.

D. Incorrect. This choice is an acceptable alternative to the original wording and punctuation.

12)

A. **Correct.** *Generous* is not the best choice in this context. The word *abundant* makes better sense as a predicate adjective for a nonhuman subject.

B. Incorrect. The word *people* is used correctly here. Furthermore, visitors may arrive in groups, not necessarily as lone individuals, so the word *individuals* could be misleading.

C. Incorrect. *Flyovers* implies that visitors may actually fly over the canyon and its landscape, affording them a good view of the terrain. Therefore, it is a good choice for this descriptive sentence.

D. Incorrect. The word *view* implies that there is only one way to see the canyon. Using the word *perspective* implies the viewer has the chance to look at something from more angles. Not only do they get a better look at the canyon, but they also get the opportunity to view the canyon from several different angles, depending on the flight path of the helicopter or airplane.

13)

    A.   **Correct.** The selection introduces the idea of the food truck; it then discusses the evolution of mobile food service in the United States from the nineteenth century to the present day.

    B.   Incorrect. The writer only briefly mentions specific cities where food trucks are popular.

    C.   Incorrect. The selection explains that food trucks are popular and mentions some reasons for their popularity, but that is not the main point of the reading.

    D.   Incorrect. The writer does not discuss food truck hygiene practices.

14)

    A.   Incorrect. The author does not compare or contrast food trucks and mobile food service with other forms of food service

    B.   Incorrect. The author describes food trucks from a historical, not a topical, perspective.

    C.   **Correct.** The author provides a chronology of the use of food trucks, outlining the history and evolution of mobile food service.

    D.   Incorrect. The writer does not discuss any event or issue triggered by another; the selection describes food trucks over the decades from the mid-nineteenth century to the present day.

15)

    A.   **Correct.** The contraction *it's* means "it is." The phrase *is still in it is prime* is ungrammatical and does not make good sense.

    B.   Incorrect. A semicolon is necessary here to connect two independent clauses.

    C.   Incorrect. No comma is needed here since the coordinating conjunction *and* is not followed by a noun or pronoun; the following structure is not an independent clause.

    D.   Incorrect. The structure *while these carts were mobile* is a dependent clause; it cannot connect to the rest of the sentence with a semicolon.

16)

    A.   Incorrect. There is no subject-verb error in sentence 2.

    B.   **Correct.** The singular verb *was* does not agree with the plural noun *predecessors*.

    C.   Incorrect. There is no subject-verb error in sentence 7.

    D.   Incorrect. There is no subject-verb error in sentence 8.

17)

    A.   Incorrect. The author uses *in fact* to develop the sentence and provide even more information about food trucks' predecessors.

    B.   **Correct.** The word *therefore* does not make good sense here. A better choice would be a transition word such as *however* that implies contrast, for the sentence discusses the negative traits of push carts, contrasting with their positive qualities just addressed in the preceding sentence.

    C.   Incorrect. The word *similarly* is correctly used here to indicate resemblance or similarity.

    D.   Incorrect. The author correctly uses *today* to clarify that the position of food trucks as urban tourist destinations is a recent phenomenon.

18)

A.   Incorrect. Since the relative pronoun refers to humans (*cooks*), the word *who* should remain.

B.   Incorrect. This comma correctly sets off an introductory phrase.

C.   Correct. This construction correctly conveys the idea that a chuck wagon was a covered wagon that served as a kitchen.

D.   Incorrect. A comma always separates a city and its state.

19)

A.   Incorrect. *Across* implies that food trucks are widespread throughout the United States.

B.   Incorrect. A milestone is a marker of an important stage in development. Here, the word *milestones* refers to the first chuck wagon and the lunch wagon, key features in the evolution of food trucks.

C.   Incorrect. *Transform* means "to change"; furthermore this word works well with the adverb *newer* found earlier in the sentence.

D.   Correct. The adverb *therefore* incorrectly implies a cause-effect relationship between the last two paragraphs.

20)

A.   Correct. Even though food trucks are the subject of the selection, the term *food truck* is not a proper noun and should not be capitalized.

B.   Incorrect. New York City is the name of a city; as such, it is a proper noun and should always be capitalized.

C.   Incorrect. Here, *northward* is simply an adverb modifying the verb phrase *were herding* and need not be capitalized.

D.   Incorrect. Rhode Island is the complete name of a state; it should always be capitalized.

21)

A.   Incorrect. There is no verb tense error in sentence 12.

B.   Incorrect. There is no verb tense error in sentence 13.

C.   Incorrect. There is no verb tense error in sentence 14.

D.   Correct. In sentence 15, the future-perfect verb tense in *will have flocked* does not make good sense. The author is describing the present, not the future.

22)

A.   Incorrect. The first sentence describes people's excitement about today's food trucks. Easy access might please people but would probably not excite them.

B.   Incorrect. This choice might describe a reason to feel excited by food trucks. However, choice D is a better option.

C.   Incorrect. The first sentence describes people's excitement about today's food trucks. Having to wait in line usually causes people to feel annoyed rather than excited.

D.   Correct. This description echoes the first sentence: both sentences convey people's excitement about the new food trucks.

23)

A. **Correct.** Sentence 7 introduces a new topic: the two new inventions breaking away from the description of push carts in New York City. The writer describes the chuck wagon and the lunch wagon in depth in the sentences following sentence 7, a departure from sentences 4, 5, and 6. Therefore, it makes sense to start a new paragraph here.

B. Incorrect. Sentence 9 describes chuck wagons in depth; it does not make sense to separate it from the introduction provided by sentence 8.

C. Incorrect. Sentence 10 introduces the lunch wagon; it alludes to the second of the *two* inventions mentioned in sentence 7, so it does not make sense to put it into a new paragraph.

D. Incorrect. This paragraph provides a chronological discussion of the evolution of food trucks in the twentieth century. It does not make sense to break it up.

24)

A. Incorrect. Sentence 1 is a good introduction to the paragraph and the selection, piquing the reader's interest: what is the new phenomenon?

B. **Correct.** Sentence 3 introduces the food truck, and sentence 2 provides a better transition to the beginning of the history of the food truck, which aligns better with the next paragraph. The order of these two sentences should be reversed.

C. Incorrect. Sentence 1 does not provide a good transition to the next paragraph. It does not make sense here. Sentence 2 would be better; B is the best answer.

D. Incorrect. Sentence 2 provides a good transition to the next paragraph and is an important part of the first paragraph.

25)

A. Incorrect. It is implied that Tyson has an interesting personality and is popular since he has an impact on popular culture, but this is not the main point of the selection. The selection discusses other elements of Tyson's life, too.

B. Incorrect. The selection only mentions the planetarium as Tyson's inspiration and as his current place of work.

C. Incorrect. While the selection does discuss Tyson's radio show, books, and awards, it also describes other aspects of Tyson's life.

D. **Correct.** The selection describes Tyson's professional accomplishments, his inspiration for his career, and his impact on popular culture, which is unlike that of most astrophysicists.

26)

A. **Correct.** The author provides a chronology of Tyson's life. The author discusses his childhood and provides a basic timeline of his career to the present day.

B. Incorrect. The selection discusses several topics in Tyson's career, but the author provides enough context about Tyson's life that the selection is organized more chronologically than topically.

C. Incorrect. The author describes Tyson's life and impact; the author does not compare Tyson to anyone else.

D. Incorrect. The writer does not discuss any event or issue triggered by another; the selection discusses Tyson's childhood and notable events in his career.

27)

A.   Incorrect. Sentence 3 begins with the phrase *From that moment on*, alluding to Tyson's first visit to the planetarium described in the earlier sentences. It does not make sense to separate those ideas into different paragraphs.

B.   Incorrect. Sentence 5 describes the commissions Tyson was nominated to. It does not make sense to separate this sentence from sentence 4, which introduces the commissions.

C.   Incorrect. Sentence 9 describes Tyson's popular books and documentaries about space. These details expand on ideas introduced in sentences 7 and 8; it does not make sense to separate sentence 9 from these earlier sentences.

D.   **Correct.** Sentence 13 introduces a new idea: Tyson's current work at the Hayden Planetarium. It is a good place to begin a new paragraph.

28)

A.   Incorrect. The pronoun *his* refers to Tyson; therefore the pronoun *there* is incorrect.

B.   Incorrect. The colon is necessary to connect two independent clauses; a comma would cause a comma splice. Even though this sentence is long, it is grammatically correct.

C.   Incorrect. This comma correctly sets off an introductory phrase.

D.   **Correct.** In a compound sentence connected by a conjunction (in this case, the conjunction is *but*), a comma should precede the conjunction.

29)

A.   Incorrect. The selection does not imply that all people are unsure about what career to pursue.

B.   Incorrect. The additional detail in the original description is of interest to the reader; it shows just how long Tyson has been interested in space and space exploration.

C.   Incorrect. The term *fascinated by* has a stronger impact on the reader than *interested in*; it shows that Tyson was particularly taken by studying outer space and so affected by his trip to the planetarium that it changed his life.

D.   **Correct.** Using the phrase *while visiting* resolves the comma splice.

30)

A.   Incorrect. The pronoun *there* agrees with its antecedent, *people*.

B.   **Correct.** *More* should be used to compare two people, as in "He is more famous than she is." Here, *more* should be replaced by *most*. *Most* is correctly used to compare more than two people or things.

C.   Incorrect. If something is *esteemed*, it is respected or well regarded. This word makes good sense here to describe NASA's Advisory Council.

D.   Incorrect. The author is making the point that Tyson's influence on popular culture often makes a bigger impression than his other professional accomplishments. *Outshines* is a good choice to clarify this to the reader.

31)

A.   Incorrect. The conjunction *and* should be replaced with the relative pronoun *which*. The singular noun *Tyson* does not agree with the plural verb *have shaped*.

B.   Incorrect. The semicolon should be changed to a comma.

C.   Incorrect. Using the demonstrative pronoun *these* changes the sentence into a comma splice.

D.   Correct. It is correct to place a comma before the relative pronoun *which*. Using *which* here correctly indicates that the plural subject *commissions and councils* goes with the plural predicate *have shaped*.

32)

A.   Correct. The verb *were* should be replaced by *was*, as *he*, a singular third-person pronoun, is the subject of this verb.

B.   Incorrect. There is no subject-verb error in sentence 6.

C.   Incorrect. There is no subject-verb error in sentence 7.

D.   Incorrect. There is no subject-verb error in sentence 8.

33)

A.   Incorrect. When *president* is used as someone's title, the first letter should be a capital letter. Here, the word is a person's title (*President George W. Bush*).

B.   Correct. Breaking the lengthy sentence into two shorter ones is a good decision on the writer's part for clarity.

C.   Incorrect. This change would only be correct if the comma after *Council* was also changed to a dash. The appositive phrase *to NASA's esteemed Advisory Council* must be contained by two commas or two dashes, not a mix of the punctuation marks.

D.   Incorrect. This comma correctly sets off an introductory phrase.

34)

A.   Incorrect. The word *nevertheless* means "in spite of that." The phrase *not only interesting but in spite of that accessible* does not make sense.

B.   Incorrect. The phrase *not only interesting and still accessible* does not make sense; it is also ungrammatical.

C.   Correct. The phrase *not only interesting but also accessible* makes sense in this sentence.

D.   Incorrect. The phrase *not only interesting but still accessible* does not make sense; it is also ungrammatical.

35)

A.   Incorrect. The word *rather* implies contradiction.

B.   Correct. A transitional word implying addition is required here to introduce the example of Tyson's radio show, which enhances the description of his media endeavors. The word *furthermore* accomplishes this.

C.   Incorrect. The word *instead* implies contradiction.

D.   Incorrect. The phrase *on the other hand* implies contradiction.

36)

A.   Incorrect. There is no subject-verb error in sentence 9.

B. **Correct.** The verb *combine* should be *combines* as it has a singular subject, the *StarTalk* radio show.

C. Incorrect. There is no subject-verb error in sentence 10.

D. Incorrect. There is no subject-verb error in sentence 12.

37)

A. **Correct.** The phrase *awards to citizens* should have no apostrophes. None of the words is a contraction or a possessive noun.

B. Incorrect. The introductory phrase *Over the course of his career* is not an independent clause, so it cannot be followed by a semicolon here.

C. Incorrect. The preposition *by* indicates who or what is doing the activity. In this case, Tyson's popular influence is more noteworthy, and overwhelming his political influence.

D. Incorrect. A colon is ungrammatical here because the phrase *On top of his professional accomplishments* is not an independent clause. Furthermore, a colon does not make good sense because when not introducing a list, it often implies cause and effect, which is not entirely applicable here.

38)

A. Incorrect. The sentence requires a relative pronoun that refers to location; the word *that* is incorrect.

B. Incorrect. The sentence requires a relative pronoun that refers to location; the pronoun *which* refers to objects and is not a good choice here.

C. **Correct.** The relative pronoun *where* refers to a location—in this case, the Hayden Planetarium.

D. Incorrect. The sentence requires a relative pronoun that refers to location; the word *when* refers to time.

39)

A. Incorrect. There is no subject-verb error in sentence 1.

B. Incorrect. There is no subject-verb error in sentence 2.

C. Incorrect. There is no subject-verb error in sentence 13.

D. **Correct.** The verb *continue* should be *continues* as it has a singular subject, *he*.

40)

A. Incorrect. The writer does not express an opinion on whether families with small children should migrate.

B. **Correct.** The writer provides examples of animal and human migration and the reasons for it.

C. Incorrect. The writer provides some examples of human migration and the reasoning behind it, but this is not the primary purpose of the selection.

D. Incorrect. Only a small part of the selection is devoted to the writer's personal experience.

41)

A.   Incorrect. The author addresses different time periods in the selection, but the piece is not organized chronologically.

B.   Incorrect. The selection revolves around only one topic—migration—and includes examples and explanations. The writer begins by talking about humans, discusses animals, and returns to discussing humans.

C.   Correct. The topic of the selection is migration; the author compares human and animal migration.

D.   Incorrect. While the writer does discuss some reasons for migration and some of its effects, the selection is not organized around this premise.

42)

A.   Incorrect. Sentence 3 discusses students in international schools. Since the author introduces international schools in sentence 2, it does not make sense to start a new paragraph here.

B.   Incorrect. Sentence 4 introduces the term *immigrant*; sentence 5 expands on the concept of immigration. It would not make sense in this context to divide the text into two different paragraphs here.

C.   Incorrect. Sentence 5 explains the meaning of the word *migrate*; this explanation is rooted in sentence 4. Consequently, it does not make sense to split the text into two different paragraphs here.

D.   Correct. Sentence 6 introduces text discussing animal migration, a new topic and a departure from the material discussed in the first five sentences.

43)

A.   Incorrect. The adverbial phrase *all around the world* correctly modifies the verb *moved*, showing that the author's family moved worldwide.

B.   Correct. The past perfect verb tense in *had attended* does not agree with the conditional tense in *would live*.

C.   Incorrect. This phrase correctly consists of a plural noun, a relative pronoun, and a second plural noun.

D.   Incorrect. The writer is emphasizing his or her youth at the time of learning about migration and immigration. Not only is there no grammatical error here, but this reference also gives the author credibility.

44)

A.   Incorrect. The word *usually* effectively communicates the idea that the family moving and the author changing schools was a common occurrence. Using *sometimes* would imply that this did not happen frequently, which is untrue.

B.   Incorrect. This change would completely change the meaning of the paragraph and the selection. *Refugees* flee dire threats in their countries of origin; *immigrants* move to other countries for a variety of reasons. Furthermore, the author explains immigration in the next sentence, building on the discussion in sentence 3.

C.   Correct. In the context of the selection, it makes sense to clarify that the author is discussing childhood experiences in international schools. Furthermore, since the author has mentioned his or her age at the time of schooling, it is redundant to include the word *primary*. Finally, the phrase *international school* is mentioned in sentence 2, so it makes sense to reference the phrase again later in the selection here in sentence 4.

D.   Incorrect. The word *location* is a safer choice because the author emphasizes that migration may not be permanent. While a temporary location may still be considered by some residents to be a *home*, and while the author alludes to this at the end of the selection, the word implies a sense of permanence that is not necessarily correct here and could be contested. It is best avoided in a definition.

45)

A.   Incorrect. The construction *either…or* cannot use the conjunction *and*.

B.   Correct. This choice simply and correctly breaks one long sentence into two shorter ones.

C.   Incorrect. Using a comma after the word *cyclical* is inappropriate because *and* is not behaving as a coordinating conjunction; it is not followed by an independent clause. Therefore, no comma is needed.

D.   Incorrect. In sentence 8, the words *north* and *south* are not behaving as proper nouns, so they need not be capitalized.

46)

A.   Correct. Sentence 9 offers more details on the migration in Serengeti National Park. Sentence 10 introduces the idea of the migration in the park. The order of these sentences should be reversed.

B.   Incorrect. Sentence 10 is necessary for the paragraph to make sense, as it introduces Serengeti National Park. It simply must be moved.

C.   Incorrect. Sentence 11 draws a conclusion about the details of the migration in Serengeti National Park. While it must indeed follow sentence 9, sentence 10 should actually come before both of these sentences for the paragraph to make any sense at all; it cannot follow sentence 11.

D.   Incorrect. Sentence 11 draws an important conclusion about the migration in Serengeti National Park. It is an essential part of the paragraph and should not be deleted.

47)

A.   Correct. The adverb *consequently* creates an incorrect cause-effect relationship between the information in paragraphs 2 and 3. The phrase *on the other hand* makes good sense here. It correctly indicates that the two kinds of migration are different from each other.

B.   Incorrect. Sentence 13 explains why animals migrate by providing one example. *For example* is a good choice here.

C.   Incorrect. *Nevertheless* means "in spite of that." This word incorrectly indicates that the second kind of migration happens in spite of the fact that the first kind happens.

D.   Incorrect. The verb *eliminate* could imply that the animals are killed; however, the selection implies that the animals are forced to migrate, so it would be incorrect to suggest they are killed.

48)

A.   Incorrect. There is no verb tense error in sentence 14.

B.   Incorrect. There is no verb tense error in sentence 15.

C.   Incorrect. There is no verb tense error in sentence 16.

D.   Correct. The word *was* in the dependent clause *even if it was just for a year* should be in the present tense (*is*) in order to agree with the present tense context of the sentence.

49)

A.   Incorrect. Here, *south* is acting as an adjective, not a location, and therefore it need not be capitalized.

B.   Correct. Here, *North* is used as an adjective indicating direction; it is not a proper noun or part of the name of a location. As such, it should not be capitalized.

C.   Incorrect. *Serengeti National Park* is a proper noun—the name of the park—and must be capitalized.

D.   Incorrect. *Famine* is not a proper noun and thus need not be capitalized.

50)

A.   Incorrect. A semicolon may combine the two independent clauses "Some jobs or family situations might require regular, predictable movements between locations" and "like us, most people move with the knowledge that they will not be returning to the place they just left." Adding *however* retains the sense of opposition the coordinating conjunction *but* brought to the original sentence.

B.   Incorrect. Inserting a period and beginning a new sentence at the beginning of the second independent clause is grammatically correct.

C.   Incorrect. A semicolon may be used to connect two independent clauses, provided there is no coordinating conjunction.

D.   Correct. A semicolon cannot be used with a coordinating conjunction like *but*, which is combining two independent clauses here.

ESSAY

All people make mistakes, and it is easy to judge them from the outside. However, sometimes people behave in harmful ways as a result of unseen hardships. People should refrain from judgment until they have the full story. Still, an unusual challenge does not absolve someone from all responsibilities. Even those at a disadvantage are accountable for their responsibilities, but they may be forgiven for certain harms as long as they take steps to rectify them.

For instance, my parents do not get along with their neighbor because he has a messy yard, which brings down their property value. He also has a dog which he lets wander on the streets. My parents' dog, on the other hand, must stay in the house and is only allowed to run freely behind the fence in the yard or at a dog park. However, everyone in the area has approximately the same income. Furthermore, the neighbor is seemingly in good physical health and works normal hours. There seems to be no reason that he cannot spend a little time each week on yard work and keep his dogs in his yard like everyone else. However, he does have one unique characteristic: allergies.

The neighbor's health situation presents a dilemma. While he is responsible for cleaning his yard, he struggles with yardwork because his allergies prevent him from spending too much time among shrubs, bushes, and trees. In addition, it is hard for him to keep his dog in his house for long periods of time, as pet dander makes his allergies worse, but the more time the dog spends in the yard, the messier the yard gets. And on top of all that, he lives alone, with no one to help with chores. Meanwhile, both of my parents enjoy outdoor activity, have no allergies, and can tackle yardwork together quite easily. They are able to keep their dog inside without any health concerns and can take turns walking him. Taking these differences into account, it becomes clearer why the neighbor's yard is in disarray and why his dog is often out. These issues may be less about his character than his circumstances.

Still, the neighbor has a responsibility to those around him. First, he should not have a dog if he cannot properly care for it or keep it in his home. Not only is a dog roaming the streets a nuisance to other neighbors, but it is unsafe for the dog, which could be hit by a car or injured in some other way. Next, he should find a way to properly care for his yard. Perhaps he could pursue medical treatment for his allergies, hire workers to assist periodically, or even ask a friend, family member, or neighbor for assistance if his budget is tight. Even if he is struggling to care for his yard, as a homeowner he is responsible for it.

In this case, the neighbor could be forgiven if he took steps to fix the situation, because he is clearly at a disadvantage when it comes to yardwork and pet care due to his allergies, which are not his fault. However, if he does not take responsibility and make amends, his disadvantages do not matter, and he should not be forgiven. At that point, he could be judged as a poor neighbor or as a person of poor character because he has chosen to remain a nuisance in the neighborhood despite other options.

MATHEMATICS

1)

D. Simplify using PEMDAS.

$10^2 - 7(3 - 4) - 25$

$= 10^2 - 7(-1) - 25$

$= 100 + 7 - 25$

$= 107 - 25 = \mathbf{82}$

2)

A. The domain is the possible values of x from left to right. Here, the domain starts at -4, inclusive, and stops at -1, exclusive. It starts again at 0, inclusive, and goes to 3, inclusive. The two line segments from 0 to 3 cross over each other, so the domain includes this whole interval. Note that closed circles represent inclusion (square bracket), and open circles represent exclusions (round bracket).

3)

D. Set up a proportion and solve.

$\frac{AB}{DE} = \frac{3}{4}$

$\frac{12}{DE} = \frac{3}{4}$

$3(DE) = 48$

$\mathbf{DE = 16}$

4)

A. Find the amount the state will spend on infrastructure and education, and then find the difference.

$infrastructure = 0.2(3,000,000,000) =$ 600,000,000

$education = 0.18(3,000,000,000) =$ 540,000,000

$600,000,000 - 540,000,000 =$ **$60,000,000**

5)

C. Use the equation for percentages.

$whole = \frac{part}{percentage} = \frac{17}{0.4} = \mathbf{42.5}$

6)

C. Convert each fraction to the LCD and subtract the numerators.

$\frac{7}{8} - \frac{1}{10} - \frac{2}{3}$

$= \frac{7}{8}\frac{15}{(15)} - \frac{1}{10}\frac{12}{(12)} - \frac{2}{3}\frac{40}{(40)}$

$= \frac{105}{120} - \frac{12}{120} - \frac{80}{120} = \mathbf{\frac{13}{120}}$

7)

C. Factor the expression using the greatest common factor of 3.

$54z^4 + 18z^3 + 3z + 3 =$

$\mathbf{3(18z^4 + 6z^3 + z + 1)}$

8)

D. Use the formula for percentages.

$percent = \frac{part}{whole}$

$= \frac{42}{48}$

$= 0.875 = \mathbf{87.5\%}$

9)

C. Find the height of the cylinder using the equation for surface area.

$SA = 2\pi rh + 2\pi r^2$

$48\pi = 2\pi(4)h + 2\pi(4)^2$

$h = 2$

Find the volume using the volume equation.

$V = \pi r^2 h$

$V = \pi(4)^2(2) = \mathbf{32\pi \ ft.^3}$

10)

C. Plug each value into the equation.

$4(3 + 4)^2 - 4(3)^2 + 20 = 180 \neq 276$

$4(4 + 4)^2 - 4(3)^2 + 20 = 240 \neq 276$

$4(6 + 4)^2 - 4(6)^2 + 20 = \mathbf{276}$

$4(12 + 4)^2 - 4(12)^2 + 20 = 468 \neq 276$

$4(24 + 4)^2 - 4(24)^2 + 20 = 852 \neq 276$

11)

C.   Plug 0 in for x and solve for y.

$7y - 42x + 7 = 0$

$7y - 42(0) + 7 = 0$

$y = -1$

The y-intercept is at **(0, −1)**.

12)

C.   The function $g(x) = f(x - 2) + 3$ is a translation of ⟨2, 3⟩ from $f(x)$. Test each possible point by undoing the transformation and checking if the point lies on $f(x)$.

$(1, 2) \rightarrow (-1, -1)$: This point is not on $f(x)$.

$(2, 3) \rightarrow (0, 0)$: This point is not on $f(x)$.

$(4, 0) \rightarrow (2, -3)$: This point is not on $f(x)$.

$(6, 3) \rightarrow (4, 0)$: **This point is on $f(x)$.**

$(7, 2) \rightarrow (5, -1)$: This point is not on $f(x)$.

13)

D.   Find the amount of change and add to the original amount.

amount of change = original amount × percent change

$= 37{,}500 \times 0.055 = 2{,}062.50$

$37{,}500 + 2{,}062.50 = $ **$39,562.50**

14)

D.   Write each value in decimal form and compare.

$-0.95 < 0 < 0.4 < 0.35 < 0.75$
FALSE

$-1 < -0.1 < -0.11 < 0.8\overline{3} < 0.75$
FALSE

$-0.75 < -0.2 < 0 < 0.\overline{66} < 0.55$
FALSE

$-1.1 < -0.8 < -0.13 < 0.7 < 0.\overline{81}$
TRUE

$-0.0001 < -0.\overline{83} < 0 < 0.\overline{66} < 0.8$
FALSE

15)

Eliminate answer choices that don't match the graph.

A.   Correct.

B.   The graph has a negative slope while this inequality has a positive slope.

C.   The line on the graph is solid, so the inequality should include the "or equal to" symbol.

D.   The shading is above the line, meaning the inequality should be "y is greater than."

16)

D.   Use the fundamental counting principle to determine how many ways the DVDs can be arranged within each category and how many ways the 3 categories can be arranged.

ways to arrange horror $= 4! = 24$

ways to arrange comedies $= 6! = 720$

ways to arrange science fiction $= 5! = 120$

ways to arrange categories $= 3! = 6$

$(24)(720)(120)(6) = $ **12,441,600**

17)

D.   Set up a system of equations and solve using elimination.

$f =$ the cost of a financial stock

$a =$ the cost of an auto stock

$50f + 10a = 1300$

$10f + 10a = 500$

$$50f + 10a = 1300$$
$$+\ {-50f - 50a = -2500}$$
$$-40a = -1{,}200$$
$$a = 30$$

$50(30) = $ **1,500**

18)

D. Let *B* equal the set of students in the band and *C* equal the set of students in the math club. Use set theory to find the number of students in either the band or the math club, then subtract this number from the total number of students in the school.

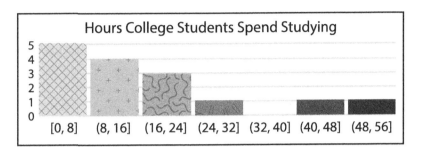

$B \cup C = B + C - B \cap C = 200 + 150 - 20 = 330$

$1,200 - 330 = \textbf{870}$

19)

D. As shown in the figure, A can be placed inside, on, or outside the circle.

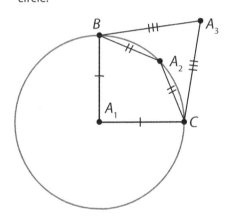

20)

A. Add the number of cupcakes he will give to his friend and to his coworkers, then subtract that value from 48.

# of cupcakes for his friend:
$\frac{1}{2} \times 48 = 24$

# of cupcakes for his coworkers:
$\frac{1}{3} \times 48 = 16$

$48 - (24 + 16) = \textbf{8}$

21)

A. Use the equation for percentages.

$part = whole \times percentage =$
$9 \times 0.25 = \textbf{2.25}$

22)

D. Use the fundamental counting principle to find the number of ways the letters can be arranged. Because the two G's are indistinguishable, divide by the number of ways those 2 letters can be arranged.

$\frac{7!}{2!} = (7)(6)(5)(4)(3) = \textbf{2520}$

23)

D. Plug in each set of values and determine if the inequality is true.

$2(0) + 0 \leq -10$ FALSE

$2(10) + 2 \leq -10$ FALSE

$2(10) + 10 \leq -10$ FALSE

$2(-10) + (-10) \leq -10$ TRUE

$2(0) + 10 \leq -10$ FALSE

24)

D. Use the formula for the area of a rectangle to find the increase in its size.

$A = lw$

$A = (1.4l)(0.6w)$

$A = 0.84lw$

The new area will be 84% of the original area, a decrease of **16%**.

25)

C. $6(3^0) = 6(1) = \mathbf{6}$

26)

C.   One way to find the answer is to draw a picture.

Put 24 cans into groups of 4. One out of every 4 cans is diet (light gray) so there is 1 light gray can for every 3 dark gray cans. That leaves 18 dark gray cans (regular soda).

Alternatively, solve the problem using ratios.

$$\frac{Regular}{Total} = \frac{3}{4} = \frac{x}{24}$$
$$4x = 72$$
$$x = 18$$

27)

B.   Move the terms to the same side and factor. Use the zeros to find the intervals where the inequality is true.

$$6 > x^2 - x$$
$$0 > x^2 - x - 6$$
$$0 > (x + 2)(x - 3)$$

For $x < -2$:
$$0 \boxtimes (x + 2)(x - 3)$$

For $-2 < x < -3$:
$$0 > (x + 2)(x - 3)$$

For $x > 3$:
$$\mathbf{0 \boxtimes (x + 2)(x - 3)}$$

28)

D.   Use the formula for the volume of a sphere to find its radius.

$$V = \frac{4}{3}\pi r^3$$
$$972\pi = \frac{4}{3}\pi r^3$$
$$r = 9$$

Use the super Pythagorean theorem to find the side of the cube.

$$d^2 = a^2 + b^2 + c^2$$
$$18^2 = 3s^2$$
$$s \approx 10.4$$

Use the length of the side to find the volume of the cube.

$$V = s^3$$
$$V \approx (10.4)^3$$
$$V \approx \mathbf{1125}$$

29)

B.   Find the probability that the second marble will be green if the first marble is blue, silver, or green, and then add these probabilities together.

P(first blue and second green) $=$
P(blue) $\times P$(green|first blue) $= \frac{6}{18}$
$\times \frac{4}{17} = \frac{4}{51}$

P(first silver and second green) $=$
P(silver) $\times P$(green|first silver) $= \frac{8}{18}$
$\times \frac{4}{17} = \frac{16}{153}$

P(first green and second green) $=$
P(green) $\times P$(green|first green) $= \frac{4}{18}$
$\times \frac{3}{17} = \frac{2}{51}$

P(second green) $= \frac{4}{51} + \frac{16}{153} + \frac{2}{51}$
$= \mathbf{\frac{2}{9}}$

30)

B.   Add the area of the trapezoid and the area of the triangle.

trapezoid: $A = \frac{h(b_1 + b_2)}{2} = \frac{10(14 + 8)}{2} =$ 110 mm^2

triangle: $A = \frac{1}{2}bh = \frac{1}{2}(8)(4\sqrt{3}) =$ $16\sqrt{3}$ mm^2

$110 + 16\sqrt{3} \approx \mathbf{137.7 \ mm^2}$

31)

D. $5 \div 8 = 0.625$

$0.625 \times 100 = 62.5\%$

32)

C. Use the formula for percent change.

$percent\ change = \dfrac{amount\ of\ change}{original\ amount}$

$= (680 - 425) / 425$

$= 255/425 = 0.60 = \mathbf{60\%}$

33)

B. Find the slope of the given line. Any parallel lines will have the same slope.

$3x + 2y = 10$

$2y = -3x + 10$

$\mathbf{y = -\dfrac{3}{2}x + 5}$

34)

B. Write each decimal as a fraction and compare the numerators.

A. $0.305 = \dfrac{305}{1000}$

B. $0.035 = \dfrac{\mathbf{35}}{\mathbf{1000}}$

C. $0.35 = \dfrac{350}{1000}$

D. $0.3 = \dfrac{300}{1000}$

E. $3.5 = \dfrac{3500}{1000}$

35)

C. Substitute one (x, y) pair into each anser choice to find the correct equation.

A. $y = -6x - 6;\ (3, -18)$

$y = -6(3) - 6$

$y = -18 - 6$

$y = -24 \neq -18$

B. $y = -5x - 6;\ (3, -18)$

$y = -5(3) - 6$

$y = -15 - 6$

$y = -24 \neq -18$

C. $y = -4x - 6;\ (3, -18)$

$y = -4(3) - 6$

$y = -12 - 6$

$\mathbf{y = -18}$

D. $y = -3x - 6;\ (3, -18)$

$y = -3(3) - 6$

$y = -9 - 6$

$y = -15 \neq -18$

36)

C. Use the equation for probability.

$probability = \dfrac{possible\ favorable\ outcomes}{all\ possible\ outcomes}$

$= \dfrac{7}{(5 + 7 + 8)} = 20$

$= \dfrac{\mathbf{7}}{\mathbf{20}}$

37)

C. Correct.

A. Points in quadrant I have a positive x and a positive y coordinate.

B. Points in quadrant II have a negative x and a positive y coordinate.

C. Points in quadrant III have a negative x and a negative y coordinate.

D. Points in quadrant IV have a positive x and a negative y coordinate.

38)

D. To estimate the amount of the change, round the price of each item to the nearest dollar amount and subtract from the total.

$\$50 - (\$13 + \$12 + \$4 + \$6)$

$= \$50 - \$35 = \mathbf{\$15}$

39)

D. Use the two sets of linear angles to find b and then c.

$a = b$

$a + b + 70 = 180$

$2a + 70 = 180$

$a = b = 55°$

$b + c = 180°$

$55 + c = 180$

$c = \mathbf{125°}$

$$4\overline{)300} = 75$$
$$\frac{28}{20}$$

$$\frac{300 \div 4}{4} = 85$$

$$300$$

40)

C. Use the formula for finding percentages. Express the percentage as a decimal.

part = *whole* × *percentage* = **1560 × 0.15**

41)

A. His profit will be his income minus his expensions. He will earn $40 for each lawn, or 40*m*. He pays $35 is expenses each week, or 35*w*.

profit = 40m − 35x

42)

A. To calculate the average, add all of the scores and divide by the total number of scores. Use the variable *x* in place of the missing score.

$$\frac{(100 + 100 + 100 + x)}{4} = 85$$

$$\frac{(300 + x)}{4} = 85$$

$$(300 + x) = 340$$

x = 40%

43)

D. Find the time that Erica spends on break and subtract this from her total time at work.

$$30 + 2(15) = 1 \text{ hour}$$

$$8\frac{1}{2} - 1 = 7\frac{1}{2} = \textbf{7 hours, 30 minutes}$$

44)

D. $f(x) = 2x + 2$

$f(20) = 2(20) + 2 = \textbf{42}$

45)

D. Set up a proportion and solve.

$$\frac{8}{650} = \frac{12}{x}$$

$$12(650) = 8x$$

x = 975 miles

46)

C. The greatest distance will be between two points at opposite ends of each sphere's diameters. Find the diameter of each sphere and add them.

$$36\pi = \frac{4}{3}\pi r_1^3$$

$$r_1 = 3$$

$$d_1 = 2(3) = 6$$

$$288\pi = \frac{4}{3}\pi r_2^3$$

$$r_2 = 6$$

$$d_2 = 2(6) = 12$$

$$d_1 + d_1 = 6 + 12 = \textbf{18}$$

47)

B. There are 16 ounces in a pound, so the baby's starting weight is 120 ounces. He gained 6 ounces per month, or 6*t*. So, the baby's weight will be his initial weight plus the amount gained for each month:
y = 6t + 120.

48)

B. Add the base amount and the tax on the extra percentage of the person's income.

$10,620 + 0.2(80,000 − 75,000) = **$11,620**

49)

B. In 2012, New York had more months with less than 3 inches of rain than either Chicago or Houston.

50)

A. *p* = number of pages written by Chris

2*p* = number of pages written by Kim

$p + 2p = 240$

p = 80

51)

C. Use the formula for probability.

$$probability = \frac{desired\ outcomes}{possible\ outcomes} =$$
$$\frac{2\ cards}{52\ cards} = \frac{1}{26}$$

52)

A. The line $y = 2x + 1$ will have a slope of 2 and y-intercept of 1. The lines shown in graphs C and D have negative slopes. The line in graph B has a y-intercept of -2.

Alternatively, use a table to find some coordinates, and identify the graph that contains those coordinates.

x	y
0	1
1	3
2	5

53)

C. Divide 1.3208 by 5.2.

```
       .254
  52 ) 13.208
        104
        280
        260
        208
        208
          0
```

There is a **5** in the hundredths place.

54)

A. Isolate the variable x on one side of the equation.

$$5x - 4 = 3(8 + 3x)$$
$$5x - 4 = 24 + 9x$$
$$-4 - 24 = 9x - 5x$$
$$-28 = 4x$$
$$\frac{-28}{4} = \frac{4x}{4}$$
$$x = -7$$

55)

B. Set up an equation. If p is the original number of pears, the store has sold $0.30p$ pears. The original number minus the number sold will equal 455.

$$p - 0.30p = 455$$
$$p = \frac{455}{0.7} = \mathbf{650\ pears}$$

56)

C. Solve the system of equations using substitution:

$$5x + 4y = 20;\ x = 2y + 1$$
$$5(2y + 1) + 4y = 20$$
$$y = \frac{15}{14}$$

57)

D. Multiply by the converstion factor to get from meters to feet.

$$55\ m\ \left(\frac{3.28\ ft.}{1\ m}\right) = \mathbf{180.4\ feet}$$

58)

B. Only I and II define y as a function of x.

I. This is not a function: the equation represents a horizontal parabola, which fails the vertical line test.

II. This is a function: each x-value corresponds to only one y-value.

III. This is a function: the graph passes the vertical line test.

59)

B. Find the highest possible multiple of 4 that is less than or equal to 397, and then subtract to find the remainder.

$$99 \times 4 = 396$$
$$397 - 396 = \mathbf{1}$$

60)

C.

$$total\ seats = 4,500 + 2,000$$
$$\frac{lower\ seats}{all\ seats} = \frac{4,500}{6,500} = \frac{9}{13}$$

Go to **http://www.cirrustestprep.com/westb-reading-writing-and-mathematics** to access your second WEST–B Core Academic Skills practice test and other online study resources.

Sources

Anthony, Susan B., "On Women's Right to Vote," 1873.

Curtis, William. *Curtis's Botanical Magazine*, 1790.

Cusack, Mary Frances. *An Illustrated History of Ireland from AD 400 to 1800*, 1868.

Dalton Frank Eugen. "Swimming Scientifically Taught," 1912.

James, William. *Talks to Teachers on Psychology*, 1899.

Meynell, Alice. *The Rhythm of Life*, 1905.

Shelley, Mary Wollstonecraft. *Frankenstein*, 1818.

de Tocqueville Alexis. *Democracy in America*, 1835.

Truman, Harry. Statement to Congress (Truman Doctrine), March 12, 1947.

United States Arms Control and Disarmament Agency. *Worldwide Effects of Nuclear War: Some Perspectives*, 1996.

Vest, George Graham. "Tribute to the Dog," c. 1855.

Washington, George. Farewell Address to Congress, December 19, 1796

Wheeler, Candace. *Principles of Home Decoration, With Practical Examples*, 1903.

Wilson, Woodrow. *On Being Human*, 1897.

Made in the USA
Monee, IL
11 August 2022